If you want to love, suffer.
If you want to suffer, love.
What really matters
Is how well you love
In the time allotted to you.

THIS IS A FICTIONAL STORY.
Names of persons and places
are used only to give realism;
and people's names do not
represent actual persons.

THE CAT OF VILLA DE LEYVA

A Spellbinding Love Story

HENRI SYDNEY ALBRECHT

Copyright 2018 by the author

Other writings by the same author:
Black Cappuccino:
A Theater Drama @2012
Stories of Very Strange Dogs @2013
Bohemian Paradise @ 2014
Crossroads of Destiny @ 2016

Copyright 2018 by the author.
All rights reserved.
Laurens Publishers @2018
ISBN 13 9781726876766
Printed in the United States of America

To Yvonne,
 Jacqueline,
 Michèle
 Laura.

*Without whose inspiration
this book could not
have been written.*

The Cat of Villa de Leyva

Chapter 1

The Arrival.

Evidently Dr. Osborne had dozed off. In his mind he saw a sudden flash of light, a turning skirt slit above the knee revealing a smooth lightly tanned thigh, and then just as quickly, a blank background in his mental picture. Next he felt a gentle tug on the shoulder: "Dr. Osborne?"

He was momentarily startled. Looking up he saw a friendly smiling flight attendant saying: "Sir, you dropped your book. But we'll be landing very shortly, kindly straighten your back and move the little cage under your seat. Thank you, sir." She smiled again and moved away. He quickly concluded that flight attendants generally treat their passengers in business and first class more correctly than in tourist class, the democratic chicken coop behind, as their livelihood depends on their performance. They're not glorified waitresses any more, as people perceived them at one time before the airline industry was fully developed. Now more than ever they are responsible for many lives in case of an emergency. Including the special cat in the cage under his seat.

Doctor John Osborne Mounier was a well-known and distinguished Professor of Extra Sensory Magnetism and Spatial Electronic Wave Physiometry at the *Zurich Politechnikum und Universität* in Switzerland. For the last few years he had dedicated his research to what he labeled *PCSS*, or Predictive Cognitive Sensory System. He was a Swiss citizen of British extraction, a world renowned brain scientist, expert in neuron intelligence networks and a polished polyglot. He was a handsome looking man in good physical shape for his 35 years, with a pleasant bearing and a friendly attitude toward people, and by nature extremely respectful and appreciative of women, their instincts and sense of prioritized behavior patterns.

Dr. Osborne straightened his large comfortable business seat, checked the unique small leather cage stored under him between his legs and prepared for landing at the airport of El Dorado in Bogotá, Colombia. After fifteen long hours traveling with Lufthansa, which had given him the best connection from Zurich to Bogotá via Frankfurt since there were no direct flights to his destination, he would be glad to finally set foot on solid ground.

He turned to the flight attendant, and motioned to her as he thought: 'They don't call them stewardesses anymore; if you do, you'll never see them again and they'll never talk to you on your next flight'. They are important flight attendants now; they can even be over twenty-five and married. Don't you dare to touch them with your finger when you want their attention; it would be akin to rape and molestation. Always use the overhead call button. Dr. Osborne beckoned his attendant and asked her for a last free farewell glass of Moët-Chandon, which she promptly brought over, and said: "You don't have much time before we land Dr. Osborne, but quickly enjoy it." He answered: *"Dankeschön, Fraulein"* - thank you very much, miss. He appreciated her professional behavior, noticed her cheerful disposition and then proceeded to get ready for landing.

The large late-model Super 747-400 airplane flying like an imposing metal condor in the mournful dusk skies over the mountainous landscape of the northernmost country in South America descended slowly and gracefully over the extensive valley called the *Sabana de Bogotá,* a long and wide fertile plain high in the Andes mountains in the central area of Colombia, where millions of flowers and roses exported worldwide are grown in the special high altitude cool climate. Gentle cows are bred and raised in green pasture lands to produce milk for a variety of local soft cheeses.

While savoring his delightful and refined last glass of champagne in an elegant Waterford flute goblet, Dr. Osborne reflected on how this was still a rare free treat on airlines in the class conscious section designed for the privileged passengers who ironically could surely afford it.

He knew from his extensive travel experience that the immense city of Bogotá was originally called *Santa Fé de Bogotá* - Holy Faith of Bogotá - to reflect the Spanish religious influence of its Hispanic benefactors - or its bloody conquerors, as many other people perceive them. With its present population of nine million inhabitants, of mixed rich and poor people including a growing and established middle class, the colonial capital is surrounded by the Andes Mountains which do not seem overwhelmingly high like the French Alps because they stand on a high plateau. The Sabana makes the mountain ranges appear lower than they really are because you don't see them in their full glory from sea level.

The city is located at an altitude of 2,640 meters or 8,600 feet. It is one of the highest capitals in the world. In daylight one can see the vast plain sheltered by green forested mountains, like nature's own monument to its old Muisca and Chibcha Indian cultures; or what was left of them after their annihilation by Spain during several centuries of a lingering colonial past.

As the plane touched ground, it shook momentarily and continued to proceed carefully on the long landing runway to the arrival terminal. Dr. Osborne suddenly remembered an article he had read in the *Economist* or similar English publication that Bogotá has the most beautiful Gold Museum in the world; but it contains only one-percent of all the gold and valuable precious stones left behind by the Spanish *conquistadores* and colonial viceroys.

Ironically, he thought for a moment of the words of a popular Spanish song of the 1980s: "¡Viva España!" Was it only coincidental? Dr. Osborne thought - at that precise moment, - that Spain, the

Crown, the Spaniards, *los Españoles*, look at the Latin American continent as if Spain were still *the Madre Patria* – the Country's National Mother. The heterogeneous *'Hispanic' population'* – which includes Portuguese, Chinese, Japanese, Arabs, left-over Indians of all kinds, descendants of black African slaves and their mixed progeny, mulattos, mestizos, criollos and other people of assorted ethnicities and racial origins - , is perceived to be the so-called *Hispanic ascendancy* and encompasses all of its historical stepchildren. "Viva España!" he thought again with a wry and somewhat melancholy smile, as the plane coasted to a stop in the long runway, so needed for take-offs by large planes in the thin altitude air.

The large and modern El Dorado Airport is a beautiful and important air travel hub with a perfect symbolic name of the City of Gold which was sought by the Spanish and Portuguese explorers all over the continent, including Central and North America but never discovered, except in bits here and there, like the *Huisca Laguna de Guatavita*, the sacred Huisca lake not far from old *Bacatá*. A famous symbol is in Bogotá's Gold Museum: a precious raft in pure gold with a Cacique chieftain and his native retinue.

Then the usual announcement came over the speakers: "Please remain seated until the captain has turned off the engines at the gate," followed by the standard "Thank you for flying with us; we hope to see you on your return flight." Just then Dr. Osborne caught a glimpse of the attractive flight attendant, smiled gently at her, and said to himself "Thank you, Lord, for another safe flight." He waited another five minutes before getting off. He got up and put on his jacket. He knew Bogota could be cool, especially if there was a drizzle.

He then put on his sleek white hat – not precisely adequate for the conservative dress code of the capital - which he had purchased two years before in the Quindío Department, when he had made a visit to the Coffee Zone while giving a scientific Conference on Spatial Magnetism in Medellín. Besides, he had thought this white hat made it easier to be recognized in the crowd by his expectant driver.

He gathered all his belongings and his carry-on bag which held his valuable computer and scientific documents. He then very carefully brought out the black leather small cage from under his seat. He cautiously checked on Infinity, his priceless black cat which was his special traveling companion. The noble animal had never uttered a meow during the entire trip. She was superbly trained by Dr. John Osborne Mounier.

Finally, he gladly walked off the plane after greeting the attendants and the pilots by the door. They all respectfully and sincerely wished him a happy stay in Bogotá and again repeated with a smile the company litany: "Thank you for flying with us, Dr. Osborne. We hope to see you on your flight back." He couldn't help but question automatically and instantaneously: 'How do they know or what makes them think I will be going back or even flying with their airline?' Nevertheless he smiled and gave an acknowledging bow to the pilots and crew and especially to the friendly flight attendant who had been so helpful during their flight from Frankfurt. He tipped his white hat in her direction as she had been genuinely concerned about his and Infinity's comfort during the trip.

As he slowly walked toward Passport Control before the baggage collection area, John Osborne carefully checked his security pouch under his jacket for his Swiss passport, a special international veterinarian certificate and a formal letter from the Colombian Ambassador in Bern authorizing him to enter and travel anywhere in Colombia with his research cat, named Infinity von Braun. It instructed all government agents and other official personnel to extend every possible courtesy to Dr. Osborne, and to keep his presence low-key and discreet so as to respect his privacy.

This time he was traveling primarily on vacation, as a Swiss tourist and not in any official capacity or as a representative of the select educational facilities of the *Zurich Politechnikum und Universität* in Switzerland where he carried out most of his scientific research.

Sadly and unexpectedly, Dr. Osborne had lost his young wife Madeleine de Monleon three years before during a tragic incident while she was in Africa for a United Nations Peace Mission. The Swiss Red Cross had brought her body back to Geneva, where a somber and distraught husband had received her remains.

The international incident had been publicized extensively in the international press, all over Europe and within the Swiss Confederation. Only recently had John started to recover from the trauma and shock. Since the tragic event he had plunged headlong into his scientific world and dedicated himself to research and applications in his area of remote communications, wireless technology, software development, telepathy, magnetic field technology and other cognitive applications.

His cat, named Infinity von Braun in reference to the Universe and the famous German scientist, was his assistant, his proudest and most meaningful accomplishment, only upended by an artificial black cat code-named Infini-Two which he was carrying in the carry-on bag, and whose value was incalculable as it was a comprehensive mechanical consolidation of his sensitive research.

When Dr. Osborne reached the passport control window the official inspector checked his identification and other documentation. He quickly straightened up and wished him a respectful welcome greeting: "Bienvenido a Colombia, Dr. Osborne." After checking and stamping his passport, he sent him with a courteous wave to another area reserved for diplomats, crew and evidently VIPs.

After presenting his Swiss passport and other pertinent attached documents, he was again welcomed with another "Bienvenido a Colombia, Dr. Osborne." He was greeted by an important inspector,

/apparently of higher rank, who was waiting for him with his assistant.

He was obviously expecting his arrival. "I am Coronel Roberto Jaramillo, Dr. Osborne. This is my assistant, Capitán Virginia Cosmos. It's an honor to welcome you to my country. Did you have a good trip?" "Yes, sir, I did, thank you. I am very glad to be here, Coronel Jaramillo."

The Coronel smiled and said: "By the way, allow me to compliment you on your fine-looking hat. It is somewhat unusual in our conservative city. If I am not mistaken, you are wearing a great symbol from our Department of Quindío, the land where we grow the world's best coffee. I know because my parents live in the Zona Cafetera near Armenia." "Muchas gracias, Coronel Jaramillo," Dr. Osborne answered. "Thank you so much. Indeed I bought it in the Coffee Zone near Armenia two years ago. I am very fond of it."

Dr. Osborne was then taken into a well furnished private office where the Coronel carefully checked his passport again, the Veterinarian Certificate and the Colombian Ambassador's letter. "If you don't mind, Doctor, now please let me look at your cat. It is a mandatory inspection." John proceeded to comply. "What is its name?" said the coronel, smiling. "Her name is Infinity von Braun, sir," answered Dr. Osborne.

The traveler then reached into the cage and gently pulled out a beautiful black cat, sleepy and somewhat upset at being disturbed. Infinity sat on the table. She stretched out to her heart's content and politely greeted the official inspector with a friendly meow and a seductive purr. "Dr. Osborne, said Coronel Jaramillo, that *gato* is indeed a beautiful animal. Take good care of it during your visit. Welcome to Bogotá."

John answered: "Many thanks, muchas gracias, Coronel Jaramillo. Infinity von Braun is indeed a very valuable companion, well trained and very smart. She is my research assistant." Infinity was wearing her plain travelling collar, a simple leather collar that her master used for transporting her. It was actually used for pragmatic and discreet reasons. The other prized collar used for scientific research was in the carry-on bag. It was not very conspicuous, on purpose, and was mixed with toilet articles, soap, a shaving cream container and toothpaste.

Inspector Jaramillo said: "I presume your cat has an identity chip in case it should get lost." Dr. Osborne answered affirmatively; and added to prevent further questioning: "She actually has two chips, Coronel, one for identification in English, and another in French and German for use in my research at the *Politechnikum* in Zurich." He offered no further details.

The inspector then asked the usual question: 'What is the official purpose of your trip?' That question is always asked as a first control of illegal immigration. Dr. Osborne answered: "Tourism, I am on vacation. Except for tomorrow when I have to give a brief conference at the Botero Museum in Bogotá. Afterward I am going to take a personal two-week vacation at Villa de Leyva in Boyacá." Captain Cosmos interjected: "What a wonderful plan, you'll love our colonial gem. Where are you staying?" He said: "I'll probably stay at the Hotel Plaza Mayor, overlooking the main town plaza. I understand that plaza has remained unchanged for several centuries."

Coronel Jaramillo said: "Ah, good, *Doctór Osborne*, muy bien, that's a wise choice. The Plaza Mayor is a very colorful, attractive and secure hotel. That's a very good plan; you should enjoy it very much." He gave the passport to his assistant Captain Virginia.

While all these formalities were going on, Captain Virginia Cosmos had been studying Dr. Osborne's demeanor. She looked at his posture and thought he was quite handsome and pleasant. His appearance exuded intelligence and good breeding. She didn't dwell long in her analysis as she suddenly felt an involuntary *frisson* of interest in the foreigner. She perused the passport, and quickly noticed the doctor's height was 178 cm, he had green-blue eyes, was a widower and his home residence was in Rapperswill, near Zurich. Captain Cosmos spoke French, English and some German, in addition to her native *castellano* - the Castilian Spanish spoken by Colombians - which made it very expedient for her professional security operations. She handed the passport back to the Colonel, and noticed Dr. Osborne rapidly looking at her over the coronel's shoulders.

Coronel Jaramillo took the passport from Captain Virginia and pointed to the cat. He stated firmly but courteously: "Doctor Osborne, you may now put Infinity von Braun back in her cage. Please take all her documents and your passport, everything is in order." He smiled slightly and stated: "You know we have to check everything for the record." Then he reached into his shirt pocket and gave Dr. Osborne a business card. "Here is my official card. If you have any problem, please do not hesitate to contact me or my assistant. You can also contact Customs or the Police headquarters anytime. *Bienvenido y mucha suerte.*"

In response to the good luck and welcome wishes by both inspectors, Dr. John Osborne replied without hesitating: "Thank you, Coronel Jaramillo and Captain Cosmos." After a brief moment he promptly added: "By the way, I would like to invite you to my conference tomorrow at the Botero Museum." Inspector Jaramillo paused for a second and said: "*Doctór* Osborne, thank you very much, but I'm afraid I will not be able to accept your invitation, as I have a previous appointment at our Security Headquarters. Besides, it might not seem completely appropriate for me to be there with you. People love to spread rumors about professional favors." He waited a few seconds and said: "However, I will instruct my assistant Capitán Virginia Cosmos to attend on my behalf if she is free. I'm sure she will find it a most interesting affair."

After wishing *Doctór Osborne* and his *gato Infinity von Braun* another *'Bienvenidos'* to Colombia, Inspector Coronel Jaramillo finally stamped his illustrious visitor's passport: *'Visa valid for 90 days. Renewable.'* Dr. Osborne shook hands with the officer, saying *'muchas gracias, Coronel Jaramillo, hasta la vista'* – thank you very much, until next time.

He then bade farewell to Capitán Cosmos, saying: "I hope to see you tomorrow, Capitán Virginia. If you can make it, it would make me very happy to at least know one person in the crowd." The captain shook hands and smiled. Dr. Osborne suddenly realized Captain Cosmos was actually a very attractive and sophisticated military officer, imposing in her sharp uniform, with her hair neatly wrapped under her officer's cap, a minimum touch of lipstick to lightly emphasize her gentle yet sensuous lips and perfectly aligned white teeth. He caught a quick glimpse of her deep penetrating eyes as she commented: "*Doctór Profesor* Osborne, I will follow the Coronel's orders and I will be very glad to attend your conference. I know it should be interesting, especially if you bring Infinity von Braun. They never have cats in the Botero Museum, except the ones Botero may have sculpted himself."

Dr Osborne smiled and retorted gently: "But Infinity von Braun is not just any cat. She is my able assistant, like you are the Coronel's. I'm really looking forward to seeing you tomorrow." He looked rapidly at her. She quickly replied: "Me too, Doctor Osborne."

Dr. Osborne left the office and continued walking toward the baggage area, noticing the presence of many trained police dogs, specialists in crime and drug detection searches – while Infinity in her small cage couldn't care less nor did she contribute any feline purrs for the occasion. Several times the police dogs, mostly imposing German shepherds, sat next to or on top of carrying bags or suitcases and waited until their masters came over to inspect the selected item.

After checking the baggage carousel, Dr. Osborne picked up his bag. Walking among dogs and passengers, he finally arrived out to where his driver was waiting with a simple sign: 'Señor Juan Osborne.' Dr. Osborne recognized him from his previous visit two years before.

He had specifically requested to Andes Tours to use him again if he were available. He went over to him and said "I am Dr. John Osborne. I believe you are Pedro Perdomo from Andes Tours." "Yes, hello, Dr. Osborne, I am Pedro Perdomo Sanchez. Welcome back. Did you have a good trip?" "Yes, Pedro, I did. It was long and I'm happy it's over. I'm glad to see you again."

Dr. Osborne remembered that Pedro spoke English quite well. He said: "Yes Doctor. I'm here as requested by Andes Tours. I will be your driver again during your travels in Bogotá and to Villa de Leyva." "That's great, Pedro, I'm happy to hear that Andes Tours has confirmed it." Dr. Osborne asked Pedro: "Where do you have the car?" "In the parking lot, Doctor. They don't let me bring the car here into this area for security reasons. Please let me take your bag."

They walked toward the parking lot. Dr. Osborne looked around and commented how modern and beautiful the airport buildings were and how much the airport had grown in two years since his last visit. He said to Pedro: "Before we get into the car I have to let Infinity out for a minute to have a taste of *tierra colombiana*, good Colombian soil for cat relief." "Sí señor Osborne, con mucho gusto. We don't want to keep *señorita* Infinity waiting any longer after such a long trip." He smiled and added a colloquial saying he had acquired from his English tutor: "Ladies first." They both smiled.

The original instructions from Andes Tours were to take the illustrious visitor to the elegant Four Seasons *'Hotel Casa Medina'* on 69th Street, but the plan was subsequently changed to *'Casa Dann'* on 93rd street as it seemed more practical for a short stay. Casa Dann was also the operating base for Pedro the driver.

Dr. Osborne had already thought about having dinner the next evening at the luxurious *'Castanyoles Raciones y Tapas Restaurant'* of Casa Medina with a senior representative from the University Museum of Science called *Museo de la Ciencia y el Juego* of the *Universidad Nacional de Colomb*ia. Though now, much more to the point, he was actively visualizing a considerably more pleasant evening: he would instead invite Capitán Virginia Cosmos; if dinner was not possible, then at least lunch. Would he dare to ask her tomorrow when she went to the Botero conference? From what he perceived in her formal and somewhat stiff uniform, she was a very beautiful woman with an attractive figure, undoubtedly a charismatic and educated person, and certainly better looking than a representative from the Science Museum who would probably be greatly relieved from not having to attend an obligatory social commitment.

Moreover, Dr. Osborne was supposed to be on a long anticipated and often postponed vacation. He now was a free bachelor, a young widower, wasn't he? It sounded very tempting. The appointment with the Science Museum delegate could be easily cancelled. Science could wait, pleasant social occasions should not be overlooked.

Once Infinity von Braun had a chance to contribute to her needs on Colombian soil, discreetly by a darkened tree area, Dr. Osborne, his special feline assistant Infinity and Pedro the chauffeur got in the car and finally left for Casa Dann. It was already evening when they reached the hotel. Dr. Osborne and Infinity were quite tired, so they were glad to get to their destination, check their accommodations and relax for the evening.

Dr. Osborne was pleased with the facilities at Casa Dann. It was a luxurious hotel in El Norte, the best area of Bogotá. Soon after his arrival he went down to one of the restaurants for a quiet snack. Once he was back in his room he ordered from 24-hour Room Service a chicken sandwich, two servings of yellow rice and three portions of lentils for Infinity. Surely they must have been somewhat puzzled about the unusual tastes of this foreign visitor, but he was used to it. It was for Infinity, not for him. And it wasn't all for eating; but his request was no more unusual than those of some Arab guests who like to sit in the middle of expensive carpeted floors in a hotel room with a portable grill to eat their special diet.

Dr. Osborne was used to traveling with his assistant Infinity, so he always brought an inflatable portable container for her necessities which he emptied into a plastic bag every day before leaving the hotel. Even though he had official permission to lodge with his special assistant, he was careful to give a minimum amount of additional work to the room service attendants. Actually, the yellow rice and lentils from room service were a most practical replacement for the usual cat litter, as they were readily available everywhere. Cat litter was actually a luxury in some countries. And a generous tip to the room attendants always made them happy.

It had been a very long and tiring day. As Dr. Osborne was turning off the lights in his comfortable bedroom and putting his head on the soft inviting pillows, he suddenly saw again a flash of brightness in his mind, projecting the image of a turning white skirt which quickly revealed a smooth and sleek soft warm thigh; but then, just as swiftly, there was a sudden blank screen in the background. He couldn't quite make out the reason for such an image. So he just let it go back into the recesses of his mind. He was too tired to give it any further importance.

He felt a gentle purr on his shoulder. Infinity had jumped on the bed to wish him good night. As he slowly drifted into the arms of Morpheus he petted Infinity's neck. It felt strangely reassuring. Besides, he needed to get used to the 8,600 meter altitude of Bogotá, as tomorrow was going to be another special day. But what about Captain Virginia? Would she show up at the Botero Museum?

He was ready to go to sleep promptly, without even looking at the news on the large television screen hanging from the wall. It wouldn't take long for him and Infinity von Braun to be dead to the world in the large comfortable bed. He knew Pedro would pick him up on time as planned after breakfast downstairs.

****

 *Chapter 2*

Meandering in Colonial Downtown

At the crack of dawn, Dr. Osborne was ready for the activities of the new day. After he had carefully shaven, he had splashed on his face his favorite Cedrat from L'Occitane after-shave cologne and dressed up in an elegant yet casual suit that should please the small and select crowd he expected at his lecture at the Botero Museum. It was a *by-invitation-only* affair that had been arranged for a selected group of professionals and intellectuals through the cultural offices of the Colombian Embassy in Bern and the Zurich Politechnikum in Zurich.

Dr. Osborne had gone for breakfast at one of the hotel restaurants which had wooden beams on the ceiling and other colonial-inspired architecture for its mainly international clientele. He had thoroughly enjoyed his first cup of Colombian coffee. It had been served in an old fashioned porcelain pot decorated with Simón Bolivar's colorful coat of arms on one side and what resembled three modern marching figures on the other side. He couldn't figure out if there was a symbolic reason for the three stylized figures, which in his mind could have represented some kind of modern bakers in a royal palace tea room or ephemeral dancers, but he quickly thought that they more likely symbolized Chibcha or Muisca deities at an Indian celebration.

He gave that idea only a cursory thought. Instead, he reflected that, if as claimed, Colombia exported all its best coffee beans and only kept the rest for national consumption, why did his particular cup of coffee taste so good? He had read comparative information in one of the Lufthansa magazines on his flight. As he sipped his coffee, he concluded that maybe his Casa Dann five star hotel had preferential access to the best quality Colombian beans like *Supremo Peaberry-Volcanica* or *caracolillo*. Remembering complicated descriptive names, even in Spanish, was a sign of Dr. Osborne's extraordinary memory.

The article said that coffee could only be compared to very select and expensive brands from the Blue Hills of Jamaica or volcanic Hawaiian Kona plantations. He may have been an acclaimed scientist in brain cognition, but as far as coffee beans were concerned, he was only a demanding consumer who enjoyed superior java brews.

Dr. Osborne had something more serious in mind. He kept thinking about the presentation he would be making at the Botero Museum later that morning. But although that conference had priority in his mind, he was really more intrigued by the tempting idea of asking Capitán Virginia Cosmos to lunch or dinner. Would he be able to ask her discreetly? Would she be offended or pleased? What about if she were married? He didn't recall seeing any wedding ring on her finger, although that is not always a definitive indication – but perhaps much more in conservative cultures like South America. His eyes had only caught a vision of an obvious military pistol in a black holster by her side. As a captain in the Special National Security Police, would she be permitted to accept an invitation from an unfamiliar foreigner she had just met, even though he was a well-known and respectable research scientist? Then he remembered it was her commander Coronel Jaramillo who had insisted she attend his lecture. That was the opening he needed to be successful in his unplanned quest.

These meddlesome thoughts kept going through his mind as he ate his breakfast. He was enjoying the local *huevos pericos,* a local culinary creation he fondly remembered from his previous trip two years before. He recalled this was a most appetizing preparation of fresh scrambled eggs that had to be cooked on a solid *black iron skillet,* with a touch of diced onions and tomato tidbits. He had been looking forward to enjoying this specialty again during his present stay in Bogotá.

He had insisted on the iron skillet at the restaurant and would not accept anything else. The staff had to search for one in the kitchen. For practical purposes (less work, less time, more profit) all egg preparations were served to the general public only in standard Hotel Casa Dann porcelain.

Pedro was already waiting in the lobby when Dr. Osborne came out of the restaurant and walked to meet him. After greeting him, Dr. Osborne excused himself for a few minutes while he went to his room to get his assistant. He came down the elevator carrying the special black cage with Infinity von Braun. The cage looked like a large portable laptop which was very unobtrusive to the unobservant eye.

When he again met Pedro, the latter was accompanied by a young guide, who said to Dr. Osborne:

"Dr. Osborne, my name is Javier Gutierrez Urrutia. I am a graduate student at the Universidad de los Andes and work as a guide as part of my civic studies." They smiled and shook hands.

"Doctor, I will be your guide today and tomorrow."

"Very well, Javier. I'll follow your instructions; but I must be at the Botero Museum by 10:45 in time for my conference at 11:00."

Javier continued: "Today we will visit the center of Bogotá. We'll walk around Plaza Bolívar, stop by the National Cathedral, admire the President's house *Casa de Nariño* from the outside, and walk to the Museum of Santa Clara, which is no longer a consecrated church. Now it is an outstanding art museum converted from an earlier convent."

"Javier, you seem very proud of this colonial museum."

"Indeed, we all are. It is a unique historical monument."

"However don't forget, Javier, I have to be at the Botero Museum by 11."

"Yes, sir. After you finish your visit at the Santa Clara Museum, we'll go directly to the Botero Museum in time for your lecture. At noontime, after your conference, we will drop you at the colonial Casa Vieja Restaurant for lunch."

"Javier and Pedro, I see you are planning to keep me very busy," said Dr. Osborne smiling.

"They assented and added: We received a call from the manager at Andes Tours advising us they had been requested by the Special Security Office at the airport to take very good care of you and your gato – I mean Infinity. Obviously you must be a very well-known scientist."

Dr. Osborne caught the clear reference to the Security Office but did not make any comment.

Pedro added: "As you know, on Wednesday I will drive you and Infinity to Villa de Leyva. You may recall it's a beautiful three to four hour trip on very good roads, which is not always the case in our country. We'll make a short detour before getting to Villa de Leyva and your hotel, to visit the famous *Puente de Boyacá*. That's the bridge where our Liberator Simón Bolívar, heavily outnumbered and leading a mixed group of soldiers, peasants and unprofessional fighters, defeated the Spaniards in 1819 and gained our Independence. Actually, it's a very small bridge."

"In about ten days or two weeks, after your visit to Villa de Leyva, I will pick you up again to bring you back to your hotel in Bogotá so you can catch your return flight to Zurich the next morning - unless you need my services at any other time while you are in that colonial town. Just contact me directly or through Andes Tours. Here is my business card and phone number."

Just then Dr. Osborne really noticed Pedro's right hand – *his driving hand* – was deformed and bent inwards. Yet he drove a gear stick shift and maneuvered without any hesitation. Dr. Osborne had already noticed this deformity the first time Pedro drove him but somehow had forgotten about it. He had meant to ask Pedro if he had been injured by the FARC or FNL guerrilla groups, one of the paramilitary gangs or in an accident; but he felt the question was out of place. It was a very private matter; though he might ask Pedro at some time in the future when they would be alone during this stay.

Dr. Osborne thanked both men for their explanations. He asked them to join him for lunch at the Casa Vieja. Javier accepted, but Pedro stated he preferred to stay with the van for safety reasons, as it was difficult to park in that section of the old colonial area of La Calendaria, and sometimes there were robberies. He would stay with Infinity von Braun while Dr. Osborne and Javier were having lunch. Besides, Javier might decide not to join Dr. Osborne if he were accompanied by people from the Botero Museum.

Dr. Osborne had surmised earlier that it would be preferable to invite Capitan Virginia alone for dinner rather than lunch. She probably had to get back to her security endeavors in the afternoon. And more important, the thought of a pleasant unrushed dinner seemed so much more stimulating than a simple business-like lunch. He was hoping they would have more time to get to know each other. He now realized he was really intrigued by her. He liked her. And to be frank with himself, he didn't really mind it. No, not at all. He had missed the companionship and warmth of an intelligent woman for many years since the terrible tragedy of his beloved wife in Africa.

He would ask Pedro to invite his contact from the Museo de la Ciencia for lunch – even on short notice - so that at least he wouldn't fail to fulfill his scheduled official get-together —or *the get-it-over-*

with – as he considered the often tiring bits of socializing at rather inopportune times, even though it was essential in his profession. This instance he was on vacation! Perhaps that person could join him and other people from the Botero Museum who might go for lunch with him. And that way Dr. Osborne would be free from all his professional and social obligations.

He quickly asked himself if he was doing this to be alone or to have more private time with Captain Virginia. Even her name seemed sensuous and mysterious. Time would tell how precious it would be.

Those touring arrangements that Javier and Pedro were explaining were similar to those Dr. Osborne had planned two years before through Andes Tours, the same reliable and efficient travel agency he had used then to visit Bogotá's main sights. That tour had included the magnificent Monserrate Church that he would be visiting again the next day.

He clearly recalled the splendid panoramic site on top of the Monserrate Mountain where you have an extraordinary view of the Sabana Valley and the sprawling capital city of nine million people. He had gone up in a funicular designed by Swiss engineers almost one hundred years before - in the 1930s; but he came down in the modern aerial Alpine bubble built more recently, maybe less than fifty years earlier, suspended from a double cable like those in a skiing resort.

At that time Dr. Osborne had also scheduled a personal four-day visit to friends in a magnificent country estate, Finca Agricola of Los Grisones, which was owned by a four-generation family of Swiss origin, located about one and a half hours away and three thousand feet below Bogotá.

He had as well paid a short side visit to the small town of Sasaima about 10 km below that remarkable *finca* property. It was a typical Colombian pueblo which kept its peaceful and pastoral feeling with a few stores and simple restaurants around the main town square and the ever omnipresent church. Trucks and cars were mixed with horses, burros, mules and even chickens and dogs around the town's central plaza.

His visit to that subtropical temperate area had been followed by a trip to see the spectacular Zona Cafetera, the coffee plantations zone in the Pereira-Armenia region. He had flown to Armenia in a vintage prop-jet. One expected to see Humphrey Bogart or Ingrid Bergman come down the aisle. That had been quite an experience; it was a very bumpy flight. A couple of elderly women were so scared they were screaming and praying at the same time. It took only one-hour by plane while it would have taken ten hours of heavy dangerous curvy driving through the mountains.

He had flown to Armenia for a visit of several days to the Coffee Zone in the Department of Quindío. That's where he had purchased the elegant *típico* white hat which he had brought back from Switzerland for the present trip and that Coronel

Jaramillo had pointed out at the airport Security office. Nevertheless it was a beautiful and special hat.

He had finally flown back to Bogotá to continue his trip by car with Pedro, the same reliable driver, to the peaceful colonial city of Villa de Leyva in Boyacá, about four hours from the cosmopolitan capital.

The entire trip two years before had been a revelation to Dr. Osborne: the beauty of the striking valleys and mountains, the variety of local food, exotic flowers and different cultural experiences, the kindness of the populace, the apparent contentment of a growing middle class, and the overwhelming politeness, education and civility of all the people. Not to leave out the smiles and beauty of the Colombian women, even the old grandmothers in the humble towns.

Dr. John Osborne had read several times that the capital city of Bogotá was originally called Bacatá by the Muisca Indians, an advanced pre-Columbian ancient civilization that dwelled in numerous small villages. When the civilized and religious Spanish gold and silver seekers arrived on the natives' lands, they forcefully subverted and annihilated them – *for the Indians' own good, of course*. Natives were simply going to reach Heaven faster while overcoming slavery working for the invaders.

All the while the Spaniards kept applying their efforts as Indian revilers and native exploiters in their new role as conquistadors and explorers for the greater eternal glory of the King and Queen of Castile - Castilla - and Spain. Nevertheless they did manage to have unrepentant and unabashed sexual relations with innocent half-naked Indian women to satisfy their egos and hormones while procreating Spanish culture. Now he understood where the oligarchy culture came from: aggressive Spanish men and subjugated innocent Indian women or enslaved young boys.

At the same time they did not forget, through the presence of a few well-meaning friars and Christ's representatives on earth, to justify the Existence above them in the Heavens of a fair, kind, peaceful and judgmental God.

Churches and cathedrals were constructed everywhere. The conquerors had arrived for their devastating conquest with hundreds of horses, steel swords, armored suits and intimidating crosses. The powerful and metal covered soldiers were led by one glorious warrior, Gonzalo Jiménez de Quesada, who according to royal records in the mother country's archives founded the colonial city of Santa Fé de Bogotá in 1538.

The Muiscas and Chibchas were very adept and proficient at mining, collecting gold and silver, and working a very diverse range of decorative pieces and adornments. They excelled at weaving beautiful tapestries and creating exquisite pottery and gold jewelry. As far as the Spaniards were concerned, because of their talent the natives must have been inspired by the Devil. Otherwise how else could these advanced expressions of art be produced by a backward, heathen, non-European culture? That seemed somehow to be an unwanted and unacceptable affront toward the superior Spanish royal family and European religious establishment. So in jealousy and greed the Spanish conquistadors razed the Muisca's sacred sites, and instead built their Catholic colonial churches on the natives' hallowed grounds.

Oh yes! thought Dr. Osborne, there are beautiful and impressive monuments to faith and glory, but the indigenous communities were plundered for their gold and the population of more than half a million natives was ultimately destroyed - all for the glory of the King and Queen of Spain and their Castilian paradise.

Various resources were exerted, like using native women, men and children as slaves, controlling their culture through forced labor, transmitting cholera, syphilis and other creative European sicknesses to the poor innocent natives, and applying assorted applications of cruelty and sanguinary behavior. Evidently it was quite a tiring exertion and an accomplishment with consequences lasting to this day. Not that the Indians did not also exercise their own kind of savagery and cultural oppression.

All of this was made more obvious the last time Dr. Osborne returned to the heavily severe and unbending protestant surroundings of Swiss-Germanic Zurich. He already had thought then that he would be glad to get back to Villa de Leyva; and now, two years later, he was going to be able to do just that. In the next few days he had planned to do some important quiet research with Infinity von Braun, while at the same time enjoying a calm vacation; no complicated plans, no pre-arranged activities, no tourist traps or celestial celebrations. Just himself and his Gato Infinity.

He stopped and breathed deeply for a couple of minutes. Now something new had appeared in the horizon. What about Virginia? The sharp Captain Virginia Cosmos, with a captivating and sensuous smile? Deep crystalline eyes and sensually hypnotizing lips? That was an unexpected new moon among the stars of the universe which he had not counted on.

****

 *Chapter 3*

The Old Convent

As carefully planned by his travel agency, before Dr. Osborne made his presentation later that morning at the Botero Museum, the driver Pedro, Infinity von Braun and the tour guide Javier took him downtown so he could make a couple of special visits.

First they went toward the main central colonial square of Plaza Bolivar. Since the area was a pedestrian only district, Pedro stopped the car to drop the Doctor and Javier off. Pedro kept Infinity in the car in her singular travel cage that attached circumspectly to the laptop bag.

Dr. Osborne took the laptop shoulder bag without his assistant's discreet external cage accessory and went into the *Catedral Primada*, the colonial cathedral of Colombia - which Javier pointed out had been started in 1807 - to have a private moment of recollection and contemplation among the rather austere white walls of the monumental structure. He asked the Lord for confidence and inspiration during the forthcoming conference, and for a fruitful rest with Infinity during their Villa de Leyva vacation. He then quickly wondered if Captain Virginia Cosmos was a religious person at all.

After Dr. Osborne had visited the cathedral, he stepped out into the gigantic colonial plaza. There were many old street vendors, mostly older women, selling paper bags of seeds to feed the pigeons fluttering on the stone pavement – in a scene reminiscent of the main San Marco square in Venice, Italy where hundreds of pigeons congregate on tourists hands, shoulders and even heads while they are observing the impressive buildings of the Renaissance. The tourists seem unflustered by the pigeons' excremental contributions all over the place – but the birds are forgiven, just as in Plaza Bolivar, because of the momentous historical glory and joy.

Dr. Osborne had seen old pictures of the unique plaza Bolívar taken in the nineteen forties, when the government of the time had modified the vast majestic square. It had built four very large round fountains around an impressive statue of Simón Bolivar on his horse, created in 1846 by Italian sculptor Pietro Tenerani. The fountains were added to 'improve' the beauty of the old colonial plaza by creating – or so they thought - a monumental architectural collection of royal grandeur like you would find in Madrid, Paris, London, Vienna or Rome.

But eventually that cultural experiment had been reversed and the entire plaza was left an open space as in colonial times, thus highlighting the beautiful capitol and other period buildings. Javier explained that at the southern end of the plaza the elegant Capitol houses the Colombian Parliament. It was started in 1826, designed by Thomas Reed, an English architect. Originally it was supposed to have had an impressive dome on top but to save time and money it was finally deleted from the final design.

Javier then elucidated that at the other end of the plaza the Government had originally erected the country's Judicial Court in 1921; but it had been set on fire and destroyed on April 9, 1948 during a terrible incendiary revolution called *El Bogotazo*.

After that terrible destruction by the mob, the *Palacio de Justicia* was completely rebuilt. But it was destroyed again in 1985 when it was occupied by a rebel guerrilla group called M-19. A criminal attack and kidnapping venture by that seditious group killed many people and destroyed innumerable valuable documents during a fight with the Army. The structure was left in ruins for a period of four years before it was finally demolished and a new building budgeted and constructed to replace it.

In the middle of the twentieth century there still was a romantic tramway going from the convent area in the center of town – el Centro - to the 'faraway' North Section of Bogotá, 'all the way' to Avenida de Chile. Now it is an integral part of the city, but at that time it was considered the end of town, 'way out in the country.' El Norte had fancy private schools, embassies, mansions and the Country Club established for select social members of the wealthy class. There were still some very elegant mansions in that area as Dr Osborne would fortuitously find out later.

Dr. Osborne crossed the large imposing colonial square on his way to visit the Museum Convent of Santa Clara, located in the previous Church of the same name, which had been built between 1629 and 1674. With the Iglesia of San Francisco it was the oldest colonial Church in the city. The Museo de Santa Clara was no longer used for Mass or other religious ceremonies. After it had been determined that it was too expensive or impractical to be used for sacred services, it had been unconsecrated by the Roman Catholic Church and sold to the government who converted it into a national Art Museum.

Dr. Osborne entered the historic building with a certain sense of awe and respect. He quietly admired the long impressive single-nave built without supporting columns, the high ceiling vault decorated with carved flowery motifs and the ornate sculptured altars. He carefully gazed at the walls which were entirely covered from top to bottom with paintings and sculptures of religious figures and colonial personages and other imposing scenes of historical events from past centuries.

After checking his watch for the available amount of time before his conference, he slowly walked around the whole structure carefully taking in the overall atmosphere of old artistic representations. He turned around and looked at the other end of the gallery to see the area where in the past the cloistered nuns' choir was separated and protected from the general church attendants by a wooden grilled partition.

Perhaps because it was mid-morning on a school and work day, there were no visitors in the exhibit area. As he slowly walked back looking at the wall's overwhelming collection of medieval art, he suddenly felt an unexpected dizziness which he attributed to Bogotá's high altitude. This was something not unusual, having been warned about it, but the swooning felt uncomfortable. In the middle of the long wall he noticed two openings like door spaces.

Quickly he entered the first one as he saw a chair inside on which he could rest. It was a very confined space, but large enough for a person to sit down. He thought that at one time there could have been a curtain or door for greater privacy. He then gradually noticed an opening like a small window to the right of the chair where he was sitting, through which he could see a long austere narrow passageway. For a moment he closed his eyes, trying to recover his full balance. His mind went gray.

Perhaps he may have dozed off for a couple of minutes. In his momentary stupor, without being fully aware of it, he saw a beautiful but an indefinite face appear through the opening. A woman gently said: *'Excuse me Father, for I have sinned. I went to confession a week ago with all my other Sisters.'* She paused. *'I had a deeply disturbing vision yesterday when I saw a naked man in my dreams.'* She hesitated for a moment. *'I had a sudden reaction that made my body tremble. I'm so sorry, father. I have sinned. Please forgive me.'*

Dr. Osborne was startled, even mystified. In the imperfect light of the uncomfortable room he saw a nebulous face which somehow looked vaguely familiar. It took him several seconds to realize that the imprecise apparition looked like Capitán Virginia Cosmos wearing the habit of a young virginal nun or humble novice rather than the sharp official uniform of a governmental security officer.

At that same moment, still only half-conscious, he heard a knock on the wall. He was surprised to see a museum's female security guard asking him politely if he felt unwell, as he was not allowed to sit in that area. He shook his head and suddenly realized that by mistake he had sat in the small space originally reserved for a priest when listening to confession by the sheltered nuns. He quickly came to his senses and explained to the young guard that he had felt a little dizzy, probably because of the altitude. She was most understanding as she politely escorted him out of the confessional area. Fortunately, there was nobody around to cast curious looks at the two people.

Dr. Osborne, on the other hand, remained puzzled by the image he had seen, obviously a cognitive dream. He was still mystified. He checked his watch and realized he should hurry to get back to the driver for his conference at the Botero Museum.

He joined his guide Javier who, after not seeing Dr. Osborne inside, had decided to wait for him in front of the old church. Dr. Osborne asked him to quickly cross the large plaza and go alert Pedro that he was ready. He also wanted to see Infinity the cat. He was concerned about her, as it seemed to him that he had been gone for a long while. Yet the time on his watch put him at ease. He could wait a few more minutes by the door to get completely refreshed from the momentary discomfort.

Dr. Osborne instructed Javier to retrieve Infinity. He told him that, once he could see Dr. Osborne from the other side of the plaza, he should signal him and the Doctor would raise his right hand. Then Pedro should let Infinity out of her case, if possible making sure she was looking toward her master. Javier could walk back toward Dr. Osborne, if he wanted to, after Infinity had started walking in his direction. He assured him she would not pay any attention to the few passersby or birds, or to Javier. Dr. Osborne had taken out his special laptop. Unbeknownst to Pedro and Javier, he would be sending wireless signals to Infinity's collar, instructing the cat through coded pulses to proceed directly to where he was waiting for her. The children feeding the pigeons and the few dogs playing around would not distract Infinity in the least. She was a trained professional.

The secret transmitter, receiver, memory chip, controlling software, microprocessor and super-minuscule camera were so cleverly disguised within the collar that they were difficult if not impossible to locate even after a detailed search by proficient investigators, let alone amateurs. Thus the immigration agent at the airport and even the experienced security officer Coronel Jaramillo had not noticed anything unusual. Of course, at that time Infinity was wearing a simple elegant red traveling collar and not the special customized black collar which during the trip was mixed casually among the toiletries. In any case, Dr. Osborne had documents permitting him to travel with the tools necessary to carry out his scientific research with his assistant.

Dr. Osborne wanted to test if his instruments were still in perfect working order. He wanted to make sure before the demonstration at the Botero Museum. He wondered what Capitán Virginia would think about the whole confidential set-up? Would she accept it or be upset? Since she was an Intelligence Officer, should he reveal some of his secret research to her now or only at a later date?

It was an unusually cool, clear and sunny morning. Dr. Osborne was still wondering about the peculiar incident in the confessional box. Actually he found it almost amusing. He, the famous researcher in cognitive reactions had been listening to confession by an innocent novice or a virginal young nun; or was it just a vision?

In the meantime, Javier had crossed Bolívar square and waved at Dr .Osborne. The latter had signaled Javier as agreed and now Infinity was prancing undisturbed on the colonial stones in the direction of her master. In a few short minutes she reached him, let an audible meow out to alert him and sat down.

He bent down to strike her silky fur, looked into her intelligent eyes and gently picked her up. "Well done, Infinity," he said smiling, "you are such an extraordinary animal! I wouldn't want any other assistant!"

He slid her into the laptop bag, which in addition to the detachable cage-like pouch that Pedro had kept in the car, also had a small compartment designed for her next to the computer. He commented to himself: "That was a good test. You are really an astonishing creature, Infinity von Braun."

As he finished, he suddenly heard two weapons cocked next to him against his back. He recoiled in shock and saw two young soldiers pointing their rifles at him, saying: "STOP! Don't move! *No se mueva!*" They moved their rifles toward his head and said with a menacing unfriendly scowl: "Señor, please show us your ID documents right now! *Su* p*asaporte, enseguida!* Your passport right away! What are you hiding in that case? You are not allowed to carry any weapons or animals in this high security area!"

Dr. Osborne complied and reached into his pocket to produce the copy of his Swiss passport. As he gave it to them, he said to the young security guards: "Excuse me, officers - *perdón, señores agentes* - I have a special permit."

One of the young guards retorted in an unfriendly manner: "That's what you oligarchs always say. You foreigners are all imperialists. You rich people think you own our country." The other guard scornfully added: *"En Colombia, todos somos iguales.* Yes sir! Here in Colombia we are all equal! *El pueblo es el dueño.* The people run the show. We the soldiers give the orders, not you!"

They looked at the color copy of his impressive Swiss passport. In sheer ignorance they said, after seeing the red document cover with a small white cross no bigger than a square centimeter: "Ah, la Cruz Roja, the Red Cross! You're not allowed here!" They snickered in an indecorous way. They thought it was from the Red Cross, so little did they know of the world's geography. Red cross on white background: The Red Cross. White cross on red background: The Swiss Emblem.

Then at that very same moment the situation changed abruptly. In two seconds they suddenly straightened up, grabbed their rifles, wiped their insipid smiles off their faces and stood at attention, promptly saluting a military officer who had appeared next to them. Dr Osborne had not noticed the person in uniform who had arrived behind the soldiers as he was busy handling his documentation.

The military officer was saying to the two young recruits: "I heard you making derogatory comments about this foreign gentleman, and talking in a disparaging way about our country. I have noted your names on your breastplate and I will be reporting you to your headquarters. Now please get your asses out of here, get going and leave immediately!" They were silent, discomfited and fear-struck. They saluted the commanding officer, who returned their salute, and promptly walked away, briskly and not looking back.

The officer turned around and looked at Infinity and Dr. Osborne. The latter was momentarily stunned as he slowly recognized the officer. He was completely silent. He couldn't believe it. Standing in front of him was Captain Virginia Angelica Cosmos, flashing a friendly smile. Obviously, she was enjoying the rather amusing situation. Looking into his eyes she said: "Good morning, Dr. Osborne. What a surprise to see you here! I was down at the end of the plaza at the Justice Palace doing an errand for Coronel Jaramillo. As I came out on my way to your conference, I saw the street disturbance. I wondered what was going on with these two young recruits. At first I didn't recognize you until I saw Infinity's head."

"Captain Virginia, am I ever grateful for your help! I thought I was getting into deep trouble and wouldn't make it to the Botero Museum on time. You saved my day, as they commonly say. Would you like to walk together toward the Museum? I have my car and driver down the street."

"I'm sorry Dr. Osborne, but I have to get my official car from the parking lot at the Justice Building. I'll join you at the Museum in a short while."

Dr. Osborne replied: "Very well, then. I'll see you soon." And before he realized it, he blurted out: "Captain Virginia, perhaps you would honor me by having lunch together if allowed?" He wondered what her reaction would be. Had he been too forward?

She quickly answered: "I'm sorry, Dr. Osborne, but I cannot join you for lunch today as I must get back to our Security airport office after your conference. Confidentially, we've busted a large drug operation at daybreak." He was momentarily silent.

She paused briefly; and then continued, sure of herself and looking directly into Dr. Osborne's eyes, with her own enticing glowing look: *"But I would be delighted to accept an invitation for dinner tonight."* He was almost taken aback, like the sudden rush of a mountain river, but he quickly controlled his surprise. He replied forthwith: "I would be greatly honored, Captain Virginia. I would be truly delighted." He emphasized once more: *"Absolutely, it will be my great pleasure."*

She added: "I'll give you my private home address when we are at the Museum. You can pick me up tonight at seven thirty. We won't be alone: You'll have a chance to meet my grand-mother Carmen. It's her house." As they parted, he softly said: "May I call you Virginia in private?" She hesitated, but for only a second and said: "Sí, Dr. Osborne, but only in private." They went their different ways.

Dr. Osborne walked rapidly through the plaza toward Pedro the driver who had been watching the entire scene from the other end of the plaza. The guide Javier was walking with Dr. Osborne. They climbed in the car as Infinity uttered an assenting meow.

After a short ride through old colorful colonial streets of the Candelaria area, Pedro stopped the car at 10:45 sharp, in front of the thick front door of the residential building housing the *Museo de Botero*.

Javier explained: "Doctor, this house functioned as the Archbishopric of Colombia until 1955. It is now the famous Botero Museum. The wealthy artist Fernando Botero Angulo donated part of his large private collection of paintings and sculptures to the Bank of the Republic in the year 2000. The Bank subsequently acquired the property from the Catholic Church to turn it officially into the Botero Museum. As of November 1, 2000 it is open to the public free of charge, which was one of the main conditions by Botero to donate his works.

From the quiet sidewalk one could see inside through the main entrance a large Botero sculpture of an open Michelangelo-style hand. It was a symbolic creation that seemed to say: Welcome.

Since the car was stopped in front of the Museum, Pedro opened the door with a little extra flair and proceeded to prepare the way for *Doctór John Osborne*, the distinguished guest speaker at the *Botero* Museum. He was carrying Infinity's unobtrusive small black cage which looked like a simple laptop leather case except for an inconspicuous grilled opening from where Infinity could be seen peeking out. The accompanying guide Javier walked next to Dr. Osborne.

As Dr. Osborne prepared to enter the Museo Botero, he again perceived suddenly in his mind a flash of light; he saw a turning white skirt that quickly revealed a smooth warm thigh and then, just as quickly, the screen went blank. Then, disconnected, a grey imprecise image replaced it: a young woman kneeling in a confessional and then disappearing. He couldn't quite understand the reason at this time for such images in the niche of his mind. He might think about them later.

He could not give them any further thought now as he was concentrating on Infinity, Sensory Perception, and Mental Parameters; and a complex cognitive discourse he had to give to a select audience.

******

 *Chapter 4*

A Sensory Botero Interlude

Dr. Osborne said farewell to Pedro by the front door, and told him to remain with the car until the meeting was over. Anyway, Pedro had told him it was difficult to find a safe parking spot in the Candelaria area, where there were occasional car break-ins, so he would park down the street.

The guards at the main door greeted Dr. Osborne and Javier, and welcomed them to the Museum. They had been told to expect Dr. Osborne and were alerted to receive this very important guest with all the necessary courtesies. He was to be speaker at today's Conference. The guards were not too sure what the talk subject of Cognition meant, but that was not their problem; and many people didn't know either. The guards' job was door security and general protection. Forget psychology, and use a gun instead.

Dr. Osborne was carrying his laptop case with Infinity. There was a clear sign on the door indicating that all handbags, purses and such articles would be thoroughly inspected at the museum entrance for security reasons. The uniformed guards inquired what was inside the case and Dr. Osborne said: My *Gato Infinidad*, my assistant Cat Infinity.

The guards looked incredulous and gave him an almost dim-witted smile. Their job was to search for pistols, grenades or other dangerous weapons, and now they were faced with securing a black gentle cat. Animals were not allowed in the Museum, unless the master Botero himself brought them for his artistic creations.

He loved to sculpt felines, females and corpulent people, including presidents, generals and plain people; but they were either on canvases or marble blocks. They were unmoving and dead, and represented no menace or danger.

Dr. Osborne was prepared for this kind of situation at the entrance . To prevent any problem or needless confrontation with security personnel, he immediately showed the guards his Swiss passport and the document from the Colombian Ambassador in Bern, all the while politely saying: *"Tengo un permiso oficial.* Here is my official permission from the Colombian Ambassador - *Embajador de Colombia* - in Switzerland. You may check the handbag if you want, but perhaps it is not necessary. I know it's your job; but my cat is really called Infinity von Braun and she's really my assistant at the conference today." He showed them her documents and a picture of Infinity among laboratory paraphernalia. She looked so peaceful and intelligent, he sensed the guard smiled.

As he said that, one of the Museum's managers, Señor Guillermo Olivera, came rushing out the door. He approached the illustrious visitor and cheerfully said: "Good morning, Dr. Osborne, *muy buenos días!* Welcome to our Museum. I am Guillermo Olivera Oviedo, Manager of Cultural Affairs. We are so glad you are able to honor us with your presence here today."

He thanked the guard and told him it was all right to let Dr. Osborne in with the handbag containing Infinity. Javier followed amused at the whole episode.

Dr. Osborne gave him the handbag to carry, saying: "Javier, please hang on to Infinity for me, and treat her with your life." He smiled. They were immediately joined by a couple of museum staff members – named Maria and Juanita - who immediately offered Dr. Osborne the customary *tinto*, which pleased him to no end. That flavorful small cup of coffee – the size of an espresso but not with Italian density - hit the spot after the morning unusual excursion to Plaza Bolivar and its surrounding monuments.

While in the entrance lobby, Dr. Osborne inquired about the enormous Left Hand sculpture not far from the museum's main door. "Señoritas, can you tell me what is the meaning of this unusual hand?" It was a powerful sculpture, depicting an open hand with open fingers reaching upward, as if trying to contact a heavenly creature.

Maria, one of the young ladies in attendance explained the symbolism of the stretched hand. She said: "This famous sculpture was done in 1975, a year after Fernando Botero had suffered a disastrous car accident in Spain. His car had collided with a truck while driving between Seville and Madrid with his family."

"At first, it was thought they all had died in that terrible crash. They did not; but unfortunately and truly heart rendering, his younger son Peter who was only four years old at the time was killed as a result of the terrible collision. Botero himself suffered serious injuries to his creative right hand."

Dr. Osborne exclaimed: "My God, what a tragedy! What a terrible disaster! Such unexpected sorrow for Botero; but then, nobody escapes life's fate. Sooner or later Destiny touches your shoulder and then it's your turn."

There was a short but painful signal in his brain. He briefly saw the African countryside scene where his wife had been massacred three years before while on a U.N. mission.

Maria the guide continued. "Sometime after the accident Botero made a series of paintings in which he paid tribute to his late son. Who knows, except for the Master himself, if this sculpture is meant to be a fitting artistic tribute to his son's hands or a compensation for the damage to his own right hand?" For an instant Dr. Osborne thought about his wife's murder in Africa, and he reasoned: "One never knows when and what destiny has in storage for all of us. God said it through His Son in the Sacred Scriptures: You never know the time or the place."

Maria continued to escort Dr. Osborne past some other sculptures and paintings. As they walked toward the conference hall, Dr. Osborne noticed from the corner of his eye that Capitan Virginia Cosmos was coming into the room. She gently smiled and waved at him; and signaled not to interrupt. She walked closer and stopped behind the museum guides.

Dr. Osborne couldn't help thinking: 'She looks so striking even in her uniform. I really like this woman.' It had been a long time since thoughts of that kind had entered his mind, let alone a tremor infiltrate his heart.

He momentarily turned around and quickly smiled at her, greeting her by saying: "It's so good to see you, Captain Cosmos." And for the benefit of people standing around wondering about this chance encounter, he added: "I presume Coronel Jaramillo was unable to join you?" She answered affirmatively and very casually: "Yes, as a matter of fact, you're right Dr. Osborne. He is very sorry he cannot attend your lecture. The Coronel was kept away by an unexpected investigation; but he sends his kind regards and wishes he could have been here. He sent you his business card."

Dr. Osborne grasped the card she had handed him, on which he saw a hand-written address on the back. He quickly looked at her, in a very formal way, controlling his real pleasure at seeing her, and said: "Thank you Captain Cosmos. Please tell the Coronel that I appreciate his interest. He has made my day by remembering me today." He knew she would understand the double meaning. "We'll be starting my talk very shortly. I hope you'll find a good seat." Virginia waved, turned around and left for the conference hall.

Maria escorted Dr. Osborne past a sculpture of a naked woman lying down and a man holding a child while standing on her. It was a typical Botero creation, oversized, overweight and yet realistic.

For a minute the Doctor visualized the French painter Paul Gauguin's Tahitians masterpieces with exotic large women, oversized like Botero's. From his knowledge of art he knew that Gauguin, at age 35, father of five children with his Danish-born wife, had given up his business career as a stock broker in 1883 to devote his life to painting; and Peter Paul Rubens in the 17th century and Michelangelo in the 16th century were precursors of large robust women and plump muscular men. Dr. Osborne mulled that some people think they are symbolic homosexual images, but that seemed rather odd and exaggerated.

Not far from this nude and serene family scene, as they continued to walk, Dr. Osborne saw the sculpture of a crouching cat, twice the size of a normal feline creature. At that moment the other guide Juanita interrupted the artistic saunter. "*Perdón*, Dr. Osborne. We still have a couple of minutes before your conference. Allow me to distract your trend of thought with a short history about this sculpture, called *El Raval Cat*."

"As you can surmise, Señor Botero loves cats; but this is not the original El Raval Cat sculpture, which is enormous. The original one is displayed in Cataluña, on a street sidewalk in the Raval section of Barcelona.' As he thought about Infinity, Dr. Osborne commented: "That is most interesting, please go on, Juanita." She said: "The original Botero bronze statue is 7 meters or 23 feet long, 2.3 meters high and 2.3 meters wide. As you can tell, it's a very large sculpture."

"It was purchased by the Barcelona City Council in 1987; but then they didn't know what to do with it. For 16 years it was a homeless cat! It went to different places in the large cosmopolitan city in search of a permanent site: *Parc de la Ciutadella*, near its fellow animals at the real Barcelona Zoo. Afterwards, it was taken to a site by the new Olympic Stadium."

"A few years later, Botero's Cat was put up in a little square area behind Barcelona' medieval shipyards. There it was really misplaced, used by transients and homeless for sleeping, urinating and unsavory ends. Finally, in 2003 the Botero Cat was moved to a permanent location at the end of a newly created street called Rambla del Raval, where everybody loves it, especially the school children on their way home. Because of its location, Botero's Cat name was changed to *El Gato del Raval*."

Dr. Osborne said: "Señorita Juanita, thank you so much for that detailed information. It's a fascinating story." He quickly looked at his watch. "But now I'm afraid we have no more time, we have to get to the conference room."

When they reached the conference area Dr. Osborne saw the room was full. Was he really that famous and well-known? He thought of himself as only a modest scientist in spite of his renowned eminence. He thanked Maria and Juanita for their courteous assistance. He saw Javier standing near the podium with his laptop bag. He thought of Infinity, which was so delicate, refined, black and priceless. But he was satisfied: now he knew Infinity had famous marble friends: Botero's cats.

The exhibit room where the Conference would take place was already crowded with guests, anxiously waiting for the presence of Dr. Osborne. He saw Señor Guillermo Olivera shaking hands with various spectators. Then he noticed in the second row, by one of the aisle seats, what he was unconsciously looking for: Virginia, his special guest. She had come as promised; somehow he felt a sense of contentment and comfort. Even under her military cap she was seductive and alert. She discreetly smiled at him. She was sitting comfortably, talking to a few people. Evidently she was not entirely unknown.

Señor Olivera saw Dr. Osborne and immediately went to the desk and stood by the podium at the head of the room. He asked the public to 'please be seated.' After a couple of minutes he proceeded to introduce Dr. John Osborne, summarizing his background and specificity of scientific research. He emphasized how honored they all were having him at the Museum and thanked him profusely for having accepted to talk to them on the difficult subject of mind and cognition.

Dr. Osborne was always very comfortable in these situations and made the public feel at ease. As he stood at the podium and greeted the crowd, he looked around to get the feeling of the auspicious spectator presence – was it a friendly and receptive audience or a gathering of old fashioned and non-understanding square heads? In any case, they had been invited because of their general interest in processes of the mind and the subject matter of neuroscience.

*****

 *Chapter 5*

Cognition Conference

After the usual clapping and acknowledgement by the public, Dr. Osborne stood at the podium, not far from a hand-carved Spanish desk where Javier had carefully placed the precious case with Infinity. Dr. Osborne knew people think scientists and mathematicians are peculiar anyway, so the mysterious case was appropriate and fit the part. He could sense the guests were wondering what was in that leather bag, especially after he got close to it, talked into it and said to his assistant: 'Relax, Infinity, we are set again.' Not a meow. She was ready for another conference, something she didn't find particularly amusing; she preferred working at the laboratory learning challenges. But after all, it was her master's job.

Dr. Osborne started his presentation without any further ado. "Ladies and gentlemen, Señor Olivera, friends of the Botero Museum: Thank you for your presence here today. It is indeed an honor and great pleasure to be able to address you on this beautiful morning at this extraordinary Museum, on the rather complex and perhaps pedantic topic of

Cognitive Science. I am sure that title, by itself, creates waves of confusion and misunderstanding."

"As Mr. Olivera has just pointed out, my name is Dr. John Osborne. I am a scientist specializing in cognitive science, with many years of experience in that field. After I graduated from Oxford University, I earned my Master of Science in Psychology at Heidelberg University in Germany. Afterwards I obtained my Doctorate in Neuroscience at the Zurich Politechnikum a few years ago, where I continue to do my Applied Research at the Center for Cognitive Science and Publications on Neurological Studies. Last year, I was honored with a Doctorate in Philosophy from Oxford University. Later in the fall I lectured for one term as Doctor *Honoris Causa* in the Psychology Department at Princeton University in New Jersey."

I have brought my assistant Infinity von Braun with me. You'll have an opportunity to meet her a little later." He paused, while the public looked around for Infinity, but obviously they didn't see anyone.

He continued: "Most encyclopedic publications and online descriptions describe Cognitive Science as the *interdisciplinary* study of minds. That automatically put this discipline in a category by itself. It is distinguishable from other sciences theoretically and methodologically. Perhaps we can understand better if we use a simple description from a popular source of information, like Wikipedia. Theoretically, cognitive science differs from some other fields that study minds since it tends to focus on a *particular level of analysis* – that of *information processing*. Methodologically, the *tools* for investigation will differ, yet the *aim* of our research is similar: *information processing*."

"A short overview of what I'll talk about today is simply to understand that there is an association between the *creative* process in the brain and the actual system in the *transmission* of such knowledge. There is a common misconception that cognitive scientists like me only view minds as *computers*. Perhaps this was the case early on, but today *'computer program'* is a better and more correct metaphor. Cognitive science looks for explanations that are encoded at the computer program level of detail. Oftentimes this science generates its own distinctive linguistic application which negates interest and perception by non professionals in the field."

He continued speaking for awhile on the subject of cognition and other related scientific subjects. At one time he commented: "I have even heard that some US Military forces maintain their high performance on their battlefield performance through the use of certain set of smart drugs that enhance cognitive brain function and neural connectivity, while strengthening the prefrontal cortex and boosting memory and recall. This allows brains to be sharper than ever, more clear and focused. I cannot confirm this information, but cognition is an ever important field of study."

Dr. Osborne realized that the whole topic of

cognition was very complex and perhaps could be too didactical or pedantic or even boring for non-professional visitors, so he slowly took his discourse to a distinct and pertinent area: *Animal Cognition*.

"To avoid getting too didactical or pedantic, let me now touch on a related topic which is one of my principal research applications: Animal Cognition. Everybody with few exceptions loves animals. This field of action describes the mental capacities of animals and their study."

"The study of animal cognition involves assigning a cause and a branch of knowledge dealing with human character, behavioral ecology and evolutionary psychology. Many behaviors associated with the term animal intelligence are also absorbed into animal cognition."

"Many different studies separate this field into *perception* and *attention*. They indicate that some major areas of research are influenced by perception like processing information from eyes, ears and other sensory organs to perceive the environment. Attention refers to mental processes that select relevant information, reduce irrelevant information and switch among these as needed by a situation. This research invariably leads to *Selective Learning*: animals are trained to discriminate between two stimuli. Divided attention is developed between two or more stimuli. All these concepts enable humans and animals to *organize* their world into *functional* groups."

At this point, before continuing his presentation, Dr. Osborne decided that the moment had come to distract the audience from the rather pedantic and even tiring subject of cognition in its various forms. Since he was describing animal applications, he told the audience that for the benefit of those present he wanted to make a practical demonstration of the training and intelligent behavior of his assistant.

He carefully studied his public, resting his eyes for an extra second on Virginia, and said: "Allow me to introduce you to my Assistant Infinity from Braun. I only ask you to please refrain from making any sudden or startling noises. By the way, I have a special permit from Bogotá's Central Security Authorities to have Infinity here, as animals are not allowed in the museum."

He slowly bent down toward his laptop case and called Infinity, asking her to come out of her cage, where she had been patiently waiting for that command. Gradually, she emerged and greeted Dr. Osborne. She acknowledged him with a perceptibly meow. She sat on the desk, looking at everybody, as if to question the audience: '*What did you expect, a lion? I am Infinity von Braun, an important research creature. I work for Dr. John Osborne.*' The spectators had already expressed their surprise by exclaiming a long 'OOOHHH, it's a *gato negro*, a black cat!' not quite sure what to think, while respectfully waiting for further explanations from Dr. Osborne.

He smiled and continued: "Ladies and gentlemen, please meet my assistant, Infinity von Braun who supports me in developing theories of scientific animal cognitive applications at our research facilities in the Technikum Center in Zurich and other places. She is very conscious of people's presence. If you clap, she will be happy to acknowledge your recognition." He looked at the public, including Virginia. As the audience clapped, the black cat rose to its full height, as if acknowledging their presence, made a complete turn on the desk top and then squatted down near Dr. Osborne, looking at him for additional instructions.

He said: "I will make a demonstration of Infinity's *intelligence* – not to be confused with just animal *instinct* – and afterwards I will take a few questions to bring this conference session to a close. Besides, it's getting close to noontime and I am sure you need to get back to your activities."

Dr. Osborne took his special laptop out of the case and opened it very casually. He had prepared the demonstration the previous evening at the hotel. He had programmed it in advance: he had entered all the software coordinates and proper key wireless signal connections that he would send to the control collar. Nobody knew about these proprietary electronic applications, fruit of years of ultra secret research, trials and tribulation. It had crossed his mind that perhaps he might tell Virginia, at a later date, if their friendship and intimacy developed.

He faced the audience and said: "I will instruct Infinity von Braun to get off the desk and go back to the end of the room; come back here to report to me; and then repeat her tour once more. After her second stop, I will put this small card envelope on her collar and ask her to proceed to Mr. Botero's special sculpture of the Left Hand which we have all seen by the entrance to the museum. After she gets there, Infinity is to gracefully jump on it without disturbing anything and sit on the palm of the hand until someone picks up the envelope."

"I will now ask someone in the audience, perhaps Señor Guillermo Olivera - if you allow me, sir, - to follow and check my assistant Infinity until she sits on the Left Hand, to make sure you can pick up the envelope which contains a card. After you have the envelope, she will jump down again and come back here to her place on the desk. At that time Señor Olivera will do me the great favor of reading the card to the audience. Is that okay with you, *Don Guillermo*?"

As soon as Dr. Osborne had finished saying that, Señor Olivera waved and got up from his seat. He came forward to where Dr. Osborne was standing, looked at the audience, smiled and said: "Dr. Osborne, if it doesn't hurt, I will be happy to cooperate! I've never worked with a cat before; and the only other ones around this museum don't move or do anything." The audience laughed and applauded.

Dr. Osborne instructed Señor Olivera to stand with him by the podium while he directed Infinity to do her job, saying into the laptop: "Infinity, please go around the room, come back, go around one more time, come here to get an envelope and go on to the Left Hand sculpture, climb on it, and wait to give the card to Señor Olivera. Finally, please return back here." He took the laptop and unobtrusively pressed a key. Infinity looked at him and immediately followed his verbal instructions, reacting to the sensory orders he was giving her from the computer via a wireless micro transmitter through her black collar.

What Dr. Osborne would not tell or let the audience see were the control keys he was pressing on the laptop which guided Infinity through ultra-sound signals which she received through her special black collar: her trip across the room, back to the desk and around the room a second time, coming back afterwards to the ornate desk where Dr. Osborne put a thin gold-colored string around her neck with a small envelope containing a card; and then continuing on to the famous sculpture of the Left Hand.

All the while, in a small corner of the screen, through an infinitesimal micro camera secretly installed on Infinity's black collar, Dr. Osborne could follow his assistant moving forward without hesitation through her various turns and motions. He had programmed the complex and unique software to issue the sensory signals at the appropriate times so that Infinity, through her training and own perception, could carry out her various tasks.

The Botero Museum Manager of Cultural Affairs, *don Guillermo Olivera*, a conservative gentleman normally not involved in unusual scientific or artistic games of this sort, followed Infinity into the room where the Left Hand sculpture was located and watched her approach the sculpture and stop in front;

following instructions from Dr. Osborne through his wireless device in the collar, which sent her vibrating signals, she deftly jumped into the palm of the Left Hand and waited on the black solid surface for Señor Olivera to retrieve the card. At this time, Señor Olivera leaned forward and as requested by Dr. Osborne, picked up the envelope and card held by Infinity and returned to the podium. Shortly thereafter, Infinity jumped down and followed him. Back in the conference room she jumped unto the ornate desk and waited for her master's further instructions.

The audience had followed the entire activity as if hypnotized. They actually were mesmerized. The demonstration had been an incredible performance by Infinity – with the help of Señor Olivera who was beaming like a Cheshire cat, something Juanita and Maria had never seen him do. He was usually a very serious executive.

Dr. Osborne said to Mr. Olivera: "Señor Olivera, thank you for your help, you have been a superb assistant with Infinity. Would you be kind enough to read the card?" Señor Olivera answered : "*Sí, doctor Osborne*, with great pleasure." He took the card out of the small envelope and read aloud: "*Muchas gracias a todos*. Thank you to the Botero Museum, its amiable and gracious staff, and the wonderful audience for participating today. Thank you for the honor and opportunity to be your guest here. Remember me. El Gato Infinity." Señor Olivera smiled as the audience clapped. He went back to sit at his place. While he did so Dr. Osborne carefully and unobtrusively put down his laptop. He gently put Infinity and the laptop back in their case. The audience heard a 'meow,' as if to say, 'thank goodness that's over.'

Dr. Osborne continued his presentation. Realizing the complexity of the scientific language which he used in his own professional experience at presentations of this nature, usually to smart though probably untrained individuals, he said: "Before I take a few questions, since its getting close to twelve o'clock, let me give you a couple more concrete examples of cognition applications."

"We need to examine how lab researchers examine bilingual and multilingual children juggling languages. While lecturing at Princeton University, I discussed communications with Case Lew-Williams, an assistant professor of psychology. He thought communications is a central part, if not *the* central element of what it means to be human. Probably many of you are bilingual. Therefore, this should be of interest to you."

"Ask yourselves: Should you hesitate to teach very young children two languages at once? When you speak two or more languages in your home, should parents avoid mixing languages and different words in the same sentence? What do we know about young children overcoming the complexities of learning two or more languages at the same time? From recent research it appears toddlers and babies are better equipped than we realize to detect differences in languages."

"Young children learning two or more languages at home must sort through an overwhelming number of sounds and body gestures and apply them to whatever objects they want to use in order to make an understandable meaning. Bilingualism must avoid developmental delays and disorders, as it doubles the challenge of requiring children – all children – to switch between two languages or two objectives, sometimes within the same conversation or sentence."

Dr. Osborne wanted to avoid overwhelming his audience. He continued for a short time, explaining how tests are carried out by observing subtle changes in behavior and physiology, such as pupil dilation to study alterations to various stimuli.

He then added some conclusions by the Princeton teacher Lew-Williams: "Even at a young age, children have learned the probability of certain words going together, and they can prioritize the language they are hearing."

Dr. Osborne reached the end of his presentation. Before concluding, he invited the audience to ask a few questions. Several people raised their hand. He answered a few of them, dwelling a bit longer on those he thought were most appropriate. One of the most intriguing inquiries happened to be made by Capitán Cosmos: "How do you control the performance of your subject Infinity? Can you give us a clue, if it is not confidential in your ongoing research?"

The question from her was not surprising, since she worked in secret intelligence services. Dr. Osborne elucidated: "I'll tell you in general terms what is my basic procedure. However, as you surmised, some of the details are confidential in nature and I cannot talk about them. When we select a candidate, like in this particular case Infinity von Braun, I first make sure with our associate veterinarians she is in perfect health, especially her vision and her eyes, her hearing which is essential to our project success, and her mouth and teeth. Since training the chosen animal is a very costly operation, we have to start with as perfect a creature as possible. I then determine with my colleagues if the selected subject has a high degree of ingrained intelligence, which can be judged from evaluating the animal's performance in different tests prior to applying our training procedures."

"Let me say that once we have completed the above steps, the next phase is the application of certain specific training methods. Perhaps the one of most interest to you is the one that establishes that success of our training is a combination of cognitive responses based primarily on the feline *instinctive reactions* and its *intelligent choices* of action."

"This is determined by experimenting with a multitude of tasks, such as finding a play target like a stuffed toy behind an obstacle, or climbing a partition to reach the intended goal. Our aim is to be able to control those actions so that the test creature will *respond* to our signals on *order* and according to our plan. To achieve this cognitive preparation, we rely on modern day technology by adapting special software, micro speakers and such highly developed sound transmitters that I control from a computerized center like a large server, desk computer or even laptop. I am also thinking of adapting our technological applications to mobile smart devices like i-phones; but this is only a possible future development."

"To refer specifically to the question posed by the Captain, let me say that in the case of my assistant Infinity, she's been trained to receive a series of sounds through a special collar, and *interpret* her responses to them, like the sound of one bell means go right or two bells go left. There is obviously a long list of transmittable signals that instruct Infinity to go forward, stop, turn around, jump up unto a table or other object like the Left Hand sculpture this morning, and so forth. I think this gives you a basic overview of how my associates and I accomplish our difficult task of teaching our feline participants the interpretation of sound signals and even verbal instructions."

"This morning you've seen a demonstration which is intended to exhibit the feasibility of our research and its applied technology."

"With this explanation, I will ask your permission to end my presentation. I thank you profoundly for your participation and interest in my lecture about theoretical and implemented cognitive practices. I know it can be a heavy and pedantic subject for some of you. So I leave you with a simple question: is that how scientists hide the secret of their virtues; or is it instead how they show the virtue of their secrets?"

At the end of Dr. Osborne's conference, the enlightened audience clapped in appreciation for his clear and informative lecture on a most difficult subject. When that expression of recognition was completed, Señor Olivera came up to the podium and thanked Dr. Osborne and the public – and even said thank you to Infinity.

As they were going on their way out, many people came forward to personally thank Dr. Osborne. While this was going on, Dr. Osborne had quickly looked again at the back of the card from Coronel Jaramillo, so that when Virginia came to say good bye, all he had to say was: "Please give my regards to Coronel Jaramillo. 7:30 is perfect. Thank you so much for coming." She smiled and said: "Dr. Osborne, thank you for your lecture. It was very informative. Maybe someday we can discuss this complex subject again. *Hasta mas tarde* - until later." This was almost like a coded message.

Javier too had approached Dr. Osborne, who gave him the laptop case with Infinity and told him to take it to Pedro who was waiting outside. Before turning around, Javier told Dr. Osborne that Pedro had been able to change that evening's appointment with Professor Alfonso Santamaría Santos of the Science and Games Museum - *Museo de la Ciencia y el Juego de la Universidad Nacional.* They would instead meet at Casa Vieja for lunch.

That pleased the doctor immensely, since now he was free to enjoy a personal evening with Virginia while still fulfilling his formal obligations. He also invited Señor Olivera to join them for lunch. He accepted very gladly as he knew Alfonso Santamaría quite well since university days and as the result of joint museum activities on many occasions.

Dr. Osborne was greatly relieved. He had other plans for later. He had already thought about having dinner that evening at the luxurious *'Castanyoles Restaurant'* of Casa Medina with Virginia instead of the senior representative from the University Museum of Science and Technical Audio-Visual Games. Of course he could change restaurants if Virginia preferred another establishment, but the evening plans now seemed to be falling into place.

*****

Chapter 6

A Didactic Luncheon at Casa Vieja

When the conference was over and people had left the Botero Museum, Dr. Osborne said his last farewells to the staff and walked toward his car. At the entrance of the museum Dr. Osborne met his driver Pedro and his guide Javier. When he climbed into the waiting car, he checked and made sure that Infinity was in the front seat, safe and comfortable. As if understanding his concern, she meowed a gentle greeting.

The most valuable items he was carrying on his trip, besides his Swiss passport, were his Cognition Assistant Infinity with her special collar, and his priceless laptop with its customized and inaccessible software programs. His original passport was secure in the safe of his hotel room; he was carrying only a copy, as Coronel Jaramillo had recommended when he arrived at El Dorado Airport. When Infinity was not with him, Pedro and Javier were carefully guarding her. He felt well protected, as he had heard many rumors about pick pocketing and street thieving, especially in that central area of the city, which comprised the lively and well maintained colonial district of La Calendaria.

He knew the old colonial section of town was now a popular area with tourists, local Bogotanos and university students. Street crime had been reduced considerably in the last few years. While driving to Plaza Bolivar in the morning Dr. Osborne had admired the narrow colonial streets, the picturesque architecture, the Spanish hanging balconies, the cheerful wall colors and the myriad fresh flowers.

It was like stepping back into centuries-old Spain, in typical surrounding of Seville and Granada, or in the unique classical town of Ronda, high in the mountains of Málaga in Andalusia. For a minute he thought how names sounded so much more romantic in the original Spanish language: *Andalucía! Ronda! Sevilla! Granada!* He loved Spain! He had planned to visit all those cities with his late wife Madeleine so many years ago - it really seemed so long ago! - before she had died tragically. Destiny had cut down unexpectedly that romantic dream. He would never see with Madeleine the Royal Palace of Aranjuez – *Palacio Real de Aranjuez* – located fifty kilometers south of Madrid! That would only be possible if in the future he ever found a new and lovable companion with whom he might be able to go there.

Meanwhile, Pedro had been able to confirm that *Profesor* Guillermo Santamaría Santos from the Museum of Science and Games would be meeting him at the Restaurante Casa Vieja. The *Profesor* had agreed with Pedro to change the schedule from dinner to lunch as actually this would be better for him, just as Dr. Osborne had foreseen. For no obvious reason the latter was vaguely amused how the Spanish word *'profesor'* was so similar to 'professor' with double 's' in English - except for the emphasis on the last syllable. He observed how thoughts like these come quickly into our mind for no reason at all and disappear like a breath of fresh air.

They would also be joined by s*eñor don* Guillermo Olivera from the Botero Museum who had gladly accepted the invitation which Dr. Osborne's had made during the conference. Señor Olivera had said he would join them shortly at Casa Vieja. He had to give a few last minute instructions to his staff in his office.

Dr. Osborne stepped out of his car after Pedro had stopped in front of La Casa Vieja. He saw Señor Olivera being dropped behind them. His guest had come out of the museum only a few minutes after Dr. Osborne had departed. They had left almost at the same time for the short ride to the restaurant. When they got out of their cars, they saw Professor Guillermo Santamaría waiting for them by the entrance.

Dr. Osborne asked Pedro and Javier if they wanted to join him, but they both declined; the first one because he had to stay with the car to safeguard it and protect Infinity; Javier, because he thought it might not be quite appropriate to join those three important personages.

After Dr. Osborne had left, Julian smiled and said to Pedro: "That way they can freely discuss whatever important people converse while having lunch in a sixty year old typical Colombian restaurant. I'll go to have something to eat at a nearby *tienda* and bring you back an empanada or something appetizing from that small eatery." Pedro added: "And, of course, Julian, don't forget to bring some rice with ground meat for Infinity. After all, she was this morning's star."

The three gentlemen greeted each other standing in the restaurant's courtyard. They were approximately of the same age, dressed elegantly, wearing subdued ties, and projected a picture of modern Bogotano businessmen. The small entrance yard was surrounded by flowering bushes of red carnations and orchids hanging on clay pots on the banister of an old fashioned wooden staircase that went to a second floor. The smell of wood burning stoves opened their appetite. The place was already very busy with the noontime clientele.

Mr. Olivera introduced Dr. Osborne to his colleague from the Museo de Ciencia. Dr. Osborne said: "*Mucho gusto, profesor* Santamaría, I am delighted to meet you." He answered: "Likewise, Dr. Osborne." *Profesor* Santamaría smiled. "It's a real pleasure and an honor to get together with you and my associate Guillermo. We've heard so much about you. Actually, our conservative society is changing a lot and the newer generation is quite curious about cognition and its complementary fields."

Mr. Olivera added: "That's correct, Dr. Osborne. I know Alfonso well because of our professional relationship." He added: "Now let's go have a good lunch. I am actually quite famished. As you probably know, Casa Vieja is a very pleasant and well-known restaurant, about fifty or sixty years old, serving typical Colombian food."

Dr. Osborne replied: "Yes, I know, that's perfect. I think we're all hungry after our busy morning."

They were greeted by a charming hostess wearing a colorful and cheerful native dress. She smiled at them, with the usual bright Colombian exuberance and showed them to their reserved table in the main dining room downstairs. It was already quite crowded, with local people and a few European – mainly German - and American tourists. Guillermo explained that the restaurant is popular with local Bogotanos and other Colombians because of the quality of its traditional dishes; and with a foreign clientele which seeks a legitimate place for genuine good native dishes. The location in the center of the capital, in the Candelaria district, makes it convenient to find. It's a traditional place that makes you feel comfortable and relaxed.

After they had sat down, they studied the special menu and ordered their appetizers and *platos fuertes* – entrées - and something to drink. They chatted for awhile about the weather, Colombia, the Magdalena River, Bogotá, the FARC guerrillas and what have you. After their refreshing local beer was served, they toasted each other with the usual *Salud señores* –'to your health.' While enjoying their drink, Alfonso explained he had been unable to attend the Conference that morning as there was an event at his museum which he couldn't miss: A group of young students had been anxiously waiting for him to give them a demonstration of some of the unique scientific interactive displays.

Guillermo remarked: "I understand Alfonso; although that's too bad. The Doctor's conference was very unusual and interesting. The subject of cognition, intuition and such things is not well known generally and can be quite complicated. But I'm glad to say Doctor Osborne handled this complex subject in a most comprehensible manner that made it easier for the public to understand – at least most of it." He smiled and continued. "In addition, the doctor had a most distinguished and spectacular assistant; she was not the usual two-legged kind but a feline creature: a gentle black cat bordering on genius intelligence. Her name is Infinity von Braun"

Alfonso breathed deeply and repeated half-incredulously: "Guillermo, did I hear correctly? A live cat at a conference in the Botero Museum? That's not possible! The only animals I have ever seen there are already sculpted by Botero, immovable in marble or fixed in a frame!"

Dr. Osborne cut in and explained about Infinity: "Alfonso, I've been training Infinity for several years. Her special preparation involves applying cognition stimuli and experience."

Guillermo emphasized: "She demonstrated her unique education and intelligence at the conference, and carried out tasks that left the spectators almost stupefied."

Dr. Osborne remarked, smiling quite happily: "Señor Santamaría –Alfonso, if I may- don Guillermo actually gave me a helpful hand and participated in the demonstration. I must admit it turned out very well, for which I'm so glad. I am most pleased with both of their performances: Infinity's and Guillermo's."

Guillermo countered: "Dr. Osborne, it was quite an honor to have helped you. I thank you for your confidence in my assistance."

Alfonso then joined the group conversation and asked Guillermo to explain what had happened at the presentation and what the cognitive demonstration was about. Guillermo was glad to give the details to Alfonso, while Dr. Osborne listened carefully, as he always evaluated and analyzed the feed-back from meetings for use in future experimental planning.

They continued to chat while savoring their food, especially the *Ajiaco* soup. Guillermo and Alfonso explained this is a favorite local dish made with chicken, corn cobs, three varieties of potatoes, garlic, onions, rice and - for those in the know - some *galinsoga parviflora* herb commonly called *guasca*. In the U.S. and United Kingdom that herb is considered a weed, named *gallant soldier*. Alfonso further explained Colombian cuisine is influenced by indigenous Chibcha cooking, and Spanish, African, Arab and some Asian styles.

While enjoying the appetizing variety of local dishes, the group continued their exchange of ideas and experience in the areas of science, art, sculpture, cognition, history and societal evaluation. Finally, after discussing so many different subjects, Dr. Osborne had a chance to ask his special guest Alfonso Santamaría what was the main mission of the University Museum of Science and Games.

In response, Alfonso was glad to explain that the main objectives of his Museum, which operated within the Department of Sciences of the National University of Colombia centered primarily in the educational development of young people across the country and even internationally.

He commented: "My Museum's principal mission is to carry out plans, programs and projects to a wide variety of our young citizens, regardless of their social condition and economic situation, by bringing scientific knowledge and exposure to them and by involving them in interactive games dealing with a variety of scientific stimuli."

Guillermo Olivera intervened: "The Museum has been in existence since 1986. It has very successfully accomplished its intended tasks by utilizing many different recreational educational interactive games about science in a free and spontaneous manner."

Dr. Osborne commented: "I find it most interesting that you are involving young people of all social levels in the didactical progress of your nation. Gentlemen, you know very well that today's youth, in every country, represents tomorrow's strength and future leadership in the world. I am most impressed. Permit me to congratulate you both, Guillermo and Alfonso, for your successful involvement in the wonderful Botero Museum and the progressive Museum of Science and Games." He smiled. "I don't want this remark to sound like a speech."

His guests acquiesced and proudly accepted Dr. Osborne's genuine compliment. They both knew they were sharing their expertise and professional accomplishments with a highly respected and world renowned international scientist.

Guillermo Olivera turned to Dr. Osborne and asked him: "Dr. Osborne – John – are you aware that the independence of my country originated from a discussion over a flower vase that took place in 1810 between a Spanish colonialist born in Spain and a group of native criollos or local Spanish descendants born in Colombia?

"Over a flower vase? Are you really serious, Guillermo? No, I wasn't aware at all, this is the first time I've heard that story."

Alfonso replied: "Yes, indeed. Do you remember you mentioned before that you had visited Plaza Bolivar this morning?"

"Yes, certainly, I did. I went to the Cathedral and Museo Santa Clara."

"Doctor Osborne, did you also visit the Museo 20 de Julio – the 20th of July being our National Holiday?"

"No, I didn't. I had not planned it. Actually I was not aware of it."

Alfonso explained: "That museum is better known as *La Casa del Florero* – the House of the Flower Vase, located at the 6th Avenue corner of Plaza Bolivar with Calle 11. It's a colonial house which displays the now famous flower vase. It was here that on the 20th of July, 1810 the Creole rebellion against Spanish rule broke out. All because the owner of that vase, Jose Gonzales Llorente, a Spaniard, refused to lend it to native *criollos*; as always, showing superiority and keeping supremacy over the native population, thumbs down."

"Who are the *criollos*, Alfonso?"

"They are Creoles, or Hispanic persons born in Colombia of Spanish or European descent and of course looked down by the 'genuine' Spanish conquistadors. At the time all they wanted to do was borrow the beautiful vase for the central decoration of the main table at an event honoring a well-known prominent 'Creole:' Antonio Villavicencio.'

"Was that man very well-known?"

"Yes, in fact now the city of Villavicencio is named for him. However, this incident was used as a pretext by the Creoles to rebel against the Spaniards; the beginning of a revolt which eventually led to full independence. Of course, there were a few other complexities."

Guillermo continued: "The building that is presently known colloquially as the House of the Flower Vase – and formally as the Museum of Independence – dates from the end of the XVI century and beginning of the XVII."

Alfonso added: "Its construction style is Arabian, actually from Andalusia, also known as Mudejar, an architectural style which is typical of our colonial architecture. It's characterized by its white walls and its green doors, rectangular windows, balustrades and balconies. Now they may be dark grey or black."

Dr. Osborne asked: "Excuse me, gentlemen, what exactly does the word *Mudeja*r mean?"

Guillermo answered: "*Mudejar* refers to Muslims who were permitted to remain in Spain from the 8th to the 13th centuries after the Christians returned to their country victorious from their Holy Crusades.

Dr. Osborne commented: "Thank you. A little bit of history never hurts. I knew that many Muslims stayed in Christian Spain. Now I know that their special kind of art and architecture is called Mudejar."

Alfonso complemented that description: "Mudejar art developed primarily in architecture by applying to Christian buildings in Spanish-Muslim areas some of the construction designs and materials used by Muslims for their own buildings."

Guillermo backtracked to the Flower Vase Museum: "Please allow me to give you some more details about the Flower Vase Museum because this particular building is of great socio-political interest to us Colombians. It was built for the eldest son of one of the founders of the city of Santa Fe de Bogotá, Mariscal Hernán Venegas Carillo, whose family lived there until the XVII century, when it became the property of the Royal Attorney General Francisco Moreno y Escandón until the end of the 18th century. The corner balcony overlooking what at the time was known as Royal Street of Commerce was given in the XVII century by the owners, Sebastian Rodriguez Trujillo and Maria de la Oliva to their daughter, who was one of the nuns in the Monastery of Santa Clara located near this House. There are tales her soul still roams around in the church building

Dr. Osborne said: "Oh yes, it's beautiful, I was there this morning." As he said that, he saw in his mind images of the paintings on the walls; and the scene in the confessional darted through his brain. Was that the nun's lost soul which had come to see him, searching for eternal peace?

"That balcony, because of its strategic location on the old Plaza Mayor, now known as Plaza Bolivar, was rented to watch events that would take place in the main plaza. This was the center of the capital."

Alfonso cut in: "At that time in 1810 there were several stores established in the first floor. The most important one among them was occupied by a Spaniard merchant called Jose González Llorrente, the owner of what would become known as the Flower Vase of Independence."

"How did that come to pass?" said Dr. Osborne.

"Friday July 20, 1810 was a market day in the city. Luis de Rubio and a group of citizens of Santa Fé - now just called Bogotá, - led by *criollos* Francisco and Antonio Morales went to the store of the Spaniard José González Llorente, located in that corner building, to borrow a nice flower vase to celebrate the visit to the capital of a Royal Commissioner and Frigate Commander of the Royal Navy, don Antonio Villavicencio which would take place in Bogotá on the first of August. Unbeknown to the Spaniard, all this was part of a well-established plan which sought to incite a brawl with Llorente."

Dr. Osborne opined: "You mean that the whole argument was contrived?"

Alfonso continued: "Indeed. That's what happened. Since Gonzales Llorente refused their request, a tense situation developed which in the end convulsed the populace that was in the Plaza Mayor, now Bolivar Plaza. That situation, which was actually expected and desired, awoke the independence ideals of the creoles who demonstrated defiantly and protested vigorously against the Spanish government. This revolt led eventually to freedom and the independence of Colombia from Spain."

Guillermo cut-in: "Several commercial establishments were located in that house because of the market place. That's where Gonzales Llorente had his store. After the rebellion of July 10, 1810, he was imprisoned until the 4th of January 1811, when he was able to return home. This corner house had several commercial uses afterwards. It's one of the very old colonial buildings that survived the *Bogotazo* when Eliécer Gaitán, the head of the Liberal Party, was assassinated on April 9, 1948. On that date, Bogotá was set on fire for three days. Fortunately, at that time the owners of the Flower Vase property were able to defend it against the infuriated mob."

Alfonso then explained: "The Museum was founded in 1960. In 2010 it was renovated to celebrate the bicentennial of Independence of Colombia and fifty years of existence of the museum."

Dr. Osborne had listened very attentively. When his two guests had finished, he made a thoughtful comment: "All fights for liberty and freedom always seem to be tied to periods of pain and uncertainty until a final solution emerges. Oftentimes it is different from what had been planned originally. Sometime sanguinary and cruel periods of sacrifice seem to develop from the cognitive reactions of the revolutionaries and the idealists."

They all assented to that statement. They also agreed it was a good time to conclude the delightful luncheon and return to their individual activities. They ordered a special *flan* dessert – custard pudding topped with caramel syrup - and a *tinto* – the standard small cup of coffee favored by Bogotanos. Dr. Osborne asked for the check, but *señor* Guillermo would not hear of it and took care of it, since Dr. Osborne had not charged a fee to the Museum for his presentation that morning. *Señor* Guillermo had called it 'a courtesy procedure.'

They got up and slowly walked past the original hostess who again favored them with another scintillating smile, which made the three gentlemen feel most appreciated.: "Until next time, *señorita, muchas gracias;* thank you very much.

They left by the old wooden front door, saying good bye to each other with a typical Bogotano *abrazo* or hug. Guillermo and Alfonso went walking toward the Botero Museum in the direction where Alfonso had his car. Doctor Osborne walked a short distance in the opposite direction where he saw Pedro and Julian waiting for him.

****

 *Chapter 7*

Cats and Dogs

Pedro and Julian waved to Dr. Osborne. The street was very quiet and only a few cars went up Avenida Jimenez de Quesada. Dr. Osborne guessed that most people had already gone back to work after lunch. It was a chilly though sunny day.

He happily acknowledged Pedro and Julian. When he reached them, he inquired if they had had an opportunity to eat something, to which they acquiesced. They asked him if he had enjoyed Casa Vieja and the local specialties. He answered he had a wonderful *Ajiaco,* the service had been excellent and the conversation lively and interesting. Pedro informed him that Julian had brought some food for Infinity, who was delighted to enjoy her lunch. Dr. Osborne wanted to see her and greet her. Julian reached inside the car to pick up the laptop case in the back seat. He brought it forward for Dr. Osborne to see.

Pedro was calmly sitting in front of the steering wheel. Suddenly, like lightning, he lifted his right deformed hand and screamed *"CUIDADO!* Doctor! *CUIDADO!* CAREFUL!" He opened the door and rushed to assist the doctor.

Julian had picked up and turned the laptop case he was handing over to Dr. Osborne. At that precise moment Dr. Osborne felt something solid pressing against his jacket in the back. He heard Pedro's alarmed warning and quickly and instinctively turned around. A young thug no more than fourteen or fifteen years old pushed him very hard and grabbed the laptop, turned around and started to run up the street to where an accomplice – maybe seventeen years old - was waiting for him on a motorcycle. In his rush the young assailant dropped the knife he had forced against Dr. Osborne's jacket, which clanked on the sidewalk. Fortunately it had not harmed the scientist because his jacket had protected him.

The three startled men quickly recovered from their initial shock. They turned around and started to run after the thief. Then they heard a scream: as he was running, the boy had wanted to take out the contents of the laptop case and Infinity - who was highly displeased with the whole episode - ran her sharp nails down the threatening arm and scratched it badly. And to complete her defensive action, she gave the thief on his hand a bite he would never forget.

As the young thug took his bleeding hand out of the laptop case, he gave a loud, uncontrollable howl. He swore and screamed to high heavens and dropped the laptop case, which fortunately slid down not too violently to the sidewalk. All the while the three men were trying to catch the young hoodlum. He continued running toward the motorcycle and was almost ready to climb on it, when suddenly two large long-hair shepherd dogs came running at full speed toward the thief, gracefully jumped a long distance over him and violently pushed the motorcycle down, pinning the driver under the engine.

One dog grabbed him by the shoulder. The second dog grabbed the other young thief by the arm and held it firmly while staring at his eyes with a fierce look that clearly meant: *don't move or I'll chop your head off.* The unexpected creatures were German police dogs with blue bullet proof jackets inscribed FESCO – **Fuerzas Especiales de Colombia** – and a three-color patch of yellow, blue and red. Dr. Osborne remembered having seen that icon on Captain Virginia's uniform cap.

At that same moment, two FESCO uniformed

security agents, whose dogs had attacked the thugs under their control, appeared with automatic machine guns which they pointed at the head of the two hooligans. There was no question the agents had the slightest intention of letting the two thieves get up or get away. This was their catch of the day.

Three minutes later an official dark green jeep pulled up alongside the motorbike and stopped briskly, tires screeching. A tough looking sergeant who seemed as if he had been trained by U.S. Marines, climbed down from the vehicle. With his pistol in hand he addressed the two agents and said: *"Felicitaciones, compañeros, por fin!* Congratulations, comrades! This time we've got them, finally! *Por fin!"*

By now Pedro, Julian and Dr. Osborne had reached the scene where the agents were. They were out of breath. The sergeant saluted and greeted them politely, asking them if they were hurt in any way. They said "No, gracias a Dios, no - thank God, no!"

Dr. Osborne picked up his laptop and quickly checked Infinity. She was all right but somewhat upset with all the commotion. The sergeant asked politely but firmly to see the Dr.'s ID papers. He could tell he was a foreigner. "Of course," Dr. Osborne replied. He showed his passport copy to the sergeant, who instantly said: "You must be the famous Dr. Osborne who spoke earlier today at the Museo de Botero, correct? "Yes, sir, I am" and added smiling "except the famous is perhaps out of context." He was generally a quiet intellectual scientist who did not play up his own importance and reputation.

Dr. Osborne looked down at the two misguided criminal youngsters by the motorcycle, and silently took in the whole scene, now that it was under control. The dogs had not moved from their victorious position and kept staring at their catch with deeply satisfied looks. They really were majestic in the accomplishment of their trained duty. They looked like wild jungle jaguars or fierce jungle pumas, cooperating intelligently with their masters: full cognitive performance!

The two armed guards kept their menacing weapons pointed at the two young thieves, making sure they wouldn't move one inch. While still pointing his pistol at the younger boy, the sergeant had taken a white handkerchief and ordered him to wrap it around his bleeding arm and hand. He said: "How sad, you stupid jackass! *¡Que pendejo!* You could be one of our sons. Instead of studying and learning a job, you are wasting your life doing these senseless criminal things!"

The sergeant put his pistol away and continued: "Doctor Osborne, we have been watching this street for a few days. These hooligans have been creating havoc in this area. We haven't been able to catch them until today. We were alerted this morning by Coronel Jaramillo and Captain Cosmos of FESCO that you would be speaking at the Botero Museum and you might go for lunch to Casa Vieja. They told us you were carrying a valuable laptop which might tempt the street thugs. So we put a couple of extra police dogs in the area, discreetly hiding in doorways so that we would be able to surprise the assailants. I'm sorry if you were frightened, but fortunately it seems nobody got hurt."

"Thank you, sergeant, for your timely intervention. It all happened so fast."

The sergeant's mobile phone rang. He answered, evidently talking to one of his superiors to whom he gave a quick summary of the operation. He described the situation with the motorcycle and the dogs. Then he passed the phone to Dr. Osborne: "It's Coronel Jaramillo, who has been appraised of the whole operation. He wants to quickly talk to you to make sure you're safe."

Dr. Osborne was pleasantly surprised. He picked up the phone and had a short conversation with Coronel Jaramillo. He thanked the Coronel for the timely and efficient performance by the FESCO agents and their superb dogs. The Coronel was in a hurry and started to say farewell. As he was ready to end the call, he said: "One minute, please, Dr. Osborne, Captain Cosmos just walked in. She heard about Operation Catch on her car security phone."

She greeted Dr. Osborne, and inquired if he or his driver and guide had been hurt in any way by the thugs. He replied that, fortunately, everyone in his group was fine and unhurt, though slightly shaken up. He thanked her and the Coronel again for the protective measures they had taken, which apparently had paid off. He then added, as an afterthought: "The

FESCO German shepherd police dogs were beautiful." She said: "*Me alegro mucho* – I'm happy no one was hurt. Now you'll excuse me, I have to go back to work." As she said goodbye, he quickly replied very casually: "Until later." Dr. Osborne was aware this was an official call, not a personal exchange. Who knows who might be listening? He gave the phone back to the sergeant and thanked him for his courtesy.

The sergeant then said to Pedro: "We have to prepare an official crime report since you were witnesses. It is not necessary that you come with us. If we need information, we can call you or Dr. Osborne. When we have the report ready, you can come by or send someone to our FESCO offices to pick it up. You can sign on behalf of Dr. Osborne if he is not able to come. By the way, we will also send a copy to Coronel Jaramillo and Captain Cosmos, since they were directly involved in the planning of Operation Catch."

He turned to Dr. Osborne and said: "Now we have to drag these two young thugs to their new home. Isn't it sad, sir, that they are throwing their lives away by committing crimes in the street instead of educating themselves? Unfortunately we don't have sufficient schools or jobs to help them." He saluted the doctor and proceeded to finish his job. The proud and magnificent dogs sat next to them. They kept their eyes on the two hooligans; no way were they going to get away anymore.

Infinity peaked out of the bag and gave a last

dirty look to the guy she had scratched. She meowed to Dr. Osborne as if to say: *'He deserved it, that's for sure!'*

When they got back to their car, Dr. Osborne said to Pedro and Julian: "Let's go to some casual place you know to have a *'tinto.'* We certainly could use one after the scare we just had. We need to recover our calm and thoughts. Does that sound okay? I want to thank you both for your help." Pedro and Juan both assented.

Pedro drove the group to a nice local café where they sat for a while near the San Diego colonial church and discussed their recent experience. Dr. Osborne reminded Pedro that maybe they should call the FESCO office after they had finished their coffee, to find out if the crime report was ready, so they all could go together to pick it up. That way Pedro wouldn't have to go there all alone by himself. They called to check and fortunately the report would be ready in a short while.

Later on, after they had been able to pick up the report, they drove back toward the Four Seasons hotel. On their way they first dropped Javier near his apartment building by Avenida de Chile, the well-known avenue in the northern part of the city.

A short time thereafter they arrived at the Four Seasons hotel. Dr. Osborne asked Pedro if he could pick him up around five. He would need his services that evening to take him on a private errand.

He got close to him and whispered while smiling: "Confidentially, Pedro, just between you and me and Infinity, I have a very special appointment tonight. I need you to drive me to pick my friend at her grandmother's house, then to the special restaurant at Casa Medina. While we are having dinner you can go out and have something good to eat. After dinner you can pick us up again. If there is a moon as promised by the weather reports, you'll take us to Monserrate for a trip on the cable car. I read there is going to be a full moon and the view of the city should be spectacular. The weather is going to be unusually beautiful and mild tonight. Then we'll go back to her house. I'll escort her in while you wait for me. Finally we'll return to my hotel."

Pedro listened attentively, as if thinking deeply; he was memorizing his instructions. He was a very serious and responsible person. Finally, he broke into a big happy smile and said with a very sincere voice: "Of course, Dr. Osborne; that's my job." Then, half kidding, he added: "Perhaps romance is in the air? Like the *bolero* of many years ago: *Quizas, quizas, quizas*....Perhaps, perhaps, perhaps... Oh, please excuse my reaction, sir! I guess after this morning, we all can use some lighthearted distraction. You know, of course, that I'll be more than happy to drive you around, anywhere. What about Infinity?"

"She'll stay in my hotel room resting from today's exertions. I may even leave the television on so the noise will distract her until I get back. She doesn't really care for news as we know it is mostly negative.

Who has ever heard of a news station with only good news?"

A couple of years before, Pedro had taken care of Dr. Osborne on his previous trip to Bogotá, la Zona Cafetera and Villa de Leyva. He felt he knew Dr. Osborne well enough to ask him questions which were not too personal in nature. Now, somehow, he couldn't hold back his curiosity. This was something he would never dare to do with more conservative and socially class-conscious Colombians, and especially even more so, *Bogotanos*.

He respectfully asked: "Pardon me, Dr. Osborne, I hope I am not being too forward; but I feel I've known you for a while now. Would it be very impolite on my part – I am just dying of curiosity to know – to ask you who is the lucky señorita? You said we are picking her up at her grandmother's? You know, sir, that I would never dare to ask that question to a Bogotano. They would consider it insolent."

Dr. Osborne waited a few seconds before answering Pedro, after first looking at his eyes and then at his deformed hand: "Pedro, I will tell you, since you have to know anyway and you are a very trustworthy person; but in exchange, you will have to tell me what happened to your right hand."

Pedro weighed his answer. Then he said without hesitation, but with a deep touch of sadness and hate: "The *FARC* guerrillas, Dr. Osborne. Yes, the blood thirsty *Fuerzas Armadas Revolucionarias Colombianas,* The Colombian Revolutionary Armed

Forces. They did this to me." He raised his deformed hand. He didn't offer any further details.

Dr. Osborne continued: "Pedro, my personal plan is very confidential. and I trust you will keep it that way. My friend's name is Capitán Virginia Cosmos Quesada. She is a captain in the FESCO National Security Organization and she works for Coronel Jaramillo."

Pedro was startled for a minute, almost amazed. He knew the extreme high standards and professional reputation of FESCO personnel – not easy to penetrate that circle.

He commented: "That's wonderful, Sir. I don't know if you are aware FESCO is the most professional and well trained national security organization in Colombia. Like NSA in the U.S.A. and MI5 in England. They are above the usual secret service. They are known as *Los Incorruptibles* – the Incorruptibles. Their honor is their God, above any commercial, personal or political bribe. They represent the best in my country. Our police force, army, officers, politicians and even business people are often fine too, but there are many instances of money corruption, connections, favoritism and even collusion with the drug trade."

"Where did you learn all that, Pedro?"

"From my parents first, and then when I was a Law student at Universidad de Los Andes. This was before my parents and I were kidnapped by a FARC group of revolutionaries and their drug cartel partners."

"Oh no!" exclaimed Dr. Osborne." I'm so sorry to hear that, Pedro!." He continued calmly: "Thank you for being so frank with me. I appreciate it. And I congratulate you for your individual honesty and your feelings of patriotism."

They remained silent for a minute, then both smiled sincerely at each other, more like friend to friend than driver to a superior employer. Life has many moments which are not planned or anticipated.

Pedro finally said: "*Señor* Dr. Osborne, I want to confirm the answer I gave you before to your question about tonight. *Estaré muy contento.* Of course I will be very happy to pick you up at five at the hotel. In fact I am sure you will have a marvelous evening tonight: *You couldn't have made a better choice."*

******

 Chapter 8

A New Moon, A Million Stars.

When Dr. Osborne finally got back to his large comfortable hotel room, decorated in a modern functional elegant style rather than with heavy wooden colonial Spanish furniture, the first thing he did was to take care of Infinity.

He let her out of her private laptop cage, so she could freely move around the room. She bounced happily on the bed and jumped to the floor like a kitten released from prison. He prepared her special 'nature retreat,' as he called her privacy area, checked the inflatable toilet 'container,' made sure it was filled with yellow rice and lentils, made a note to order more supplies and plastic bags later from Room Service, and filled her water dish.

Finally, when everything was set, he laid down for a short rest on the tempting bed which had been impeccably made up by the room cleaning ladies – room supervisors, as described on a tip-reminding notice from the hotel, discreetly placed on a cupboard by the window. He had given them clear instructions earlier in the morning to have the room and amenities prepared for Infinity so that everything would be ready when he came back in the afternoon. They had done as ordered. He commented to himself: 'That's what I call good service. Don't forget to tip them when you leave.'

Actually, he was rather tired from so many things – the extended walk by Plaza Bolívar, the large antique Cathedral, the colorful colonial art-rich Santa Clara Museum; followed by the lengthy Conference at the Botero Museum and the scheduled lunch at Casa Vieja – social, professional and pleasant. Add to that, the city's high altitude. All of that without even taking into account the dangerous crime episode, like a Hollywood gangster movie, in the Candelaria district, which luckily had not hurt anyone and especially not precious Infinity.

By sheer accident, he had seen Virginia's FESCO forces in action. That had impressed him considerably, especially since he was very conscious now of the involvement of his evening companion with the security intelligence organization that she and Coronel Jaramillo worked for so assiduously. He was confident he would find out much more about Virginia and her occupation during their coming dinner. He just would have to be very tactful in his questioning as he did not want to impinge on her professionalism, or even appear to be overly curious about her activities, and for that matter her personal life.

He felt almost like an inexperienced high school boy or a freshman college student who only knew about women from Playboy magazine. Was he so completely disconnected now with someone from the second sex, to use Simone de Beauvoir's description? He was actually feeling slightly nervous at the prospect of being with a girl, -*no, not a girl; a woman* - he barely knew, except for the positive waves he had perceived between them, from her to him and seemingly mutually from him to her. While resting his head on the fresh pillows he remembered the confessional scene at the Santa Clara Museum and he was almost embarrassed by the frankness of its content. He could almost ascribe it to a message from destiny or even perhaps some divine source which he could not yet identify.

It helped calm his uncertain feelings and actually made him look with positive interest to what appeared to be developing ahead into an extraordinary evening. He admitted to himself that he was looking forward immensely to being with Virginia Cosmos, and he already missed her without even having been with her. He also recognized deep in his mind that his interest was not at all sexual. It was deeply romantic: the beauty of a female human being rather than just the physical attraction of a subtly seductive woman.

Still, it had been a most unusual occurrence. While he was evaluating the meaning of that metaphysical experience, he remembered the flash scene of a sudden smooth leg and a disappearing feminine creature. He had not clearly seen nor been able to identify the face in the vision projected in his mind, but at least he knew without any doubt that the indefinite vague spirit-like image was not Virginia Cosmos. He didn't spend much more time dwelling on this occurrence which he considered probably just one of those quick fantasies that often flash through a person's mind without rhyme or reason. And yet, as he casually looked at Infinity, now sleeping soundly after the difficult day, he wondered out of curiosity: why did he see that image again? Was there a meaning? He then thought it was ridiculous, nothing to waste his time on; he turned the television news on to seek temporary relief of his streaming thoughts.

As soon as the screen opened up, it hit a commercial which he could not avoid watching. It was an advertisement for energy pills: An old man with a white beard appeared on the TV screen. For a few minutes Dr. Osborne was reminded of his grandfather up on the Swiss mountains. Once when Dr. Osborne was a very young child he had gone to visit him with his parents. Even though he was only four or five years old, he remembered seeing his grandfather give a small piece of paper to his grandmother.

He never knew what is contained until one day, when he was already a grown teenager, he saw a piece of paper laying on the small work counter in his parents kitchen. Piqued by curiosity, he looked at the paper and he recognized his grandfather's writing. He then remembered the scene when his old relative had given the note to his mother. It had a short poem the old man had scribbled in his own weakened hand. Dr. Osborne had copied down the words which had stricken him as deeply meaningful within a family association; even in external social relationships. For a long time he had carried those words in a note stuck in his wallet, until he finally decided to memorize them.

> When I was young and beautiful
> I could reach the sky
> To touch the silky clouds
> Soft as the breast of Venus.
>
> Now that I am old and grey
> I can barely touch the ground,
> When my feet come around.
> Slow and hesitating.
>
> Life came once rich and full;
> Life passed swift and hushed;
> But my deep love for you
> For all time has remained.

At that time the old man was 78. To the young child he seemed as old as one could ever get, like the people he had seen in pictures with dinosaurs or old men that lived in the Middle Ages. That's what he had heard adults say, though he really didn't know what they meant. Grandmother had passed away when she was a very old lady of 74, or for him close to 200. Since then his grandfather had lived alone, with a pleasant steady housekeeper, who was younger and cheerful and even painted her nails bright red. She looked after the house and his personal needs. He also had a middle-aged cook, silent as a nun, but fortunately with a nice disposition, who fed him adequately, and cooked in questionable French style.

John the child had come to stay overnight at

his grandfather's, as it happened to be a holiday and his parents had gone to visit one of their relatives out of town. The little boy was told to behave, eat his dinner, let grandfather read to him, and go to sleep in no case later than eight thirty. John remembered he had gone to bed, and as he was ready to fall asleep, he needed to go *'pinkeln müssen'* as mother said at home. So he got out of bed and went to the bathroom to do his *pipi*.

Grandfather was taking a shower and happily humming as he soaped and stroked his manhood. This was the first time John had ever seen a grown man – *a real adult, imagine that!* – completely naked. He didn't fully absorb the scene as he was not concerned; he was too young and too sleepy. He wondered, though, if that's the way he would look some day when he would be older. He climbed back into bed and promptly fell asleep. The child was very happy staying overnight as he loved his grandfather and always had a good time visiting him.

While the above reminiscences passed through his head, Dr. Osborne kept watching the news with only half-hearted interest. There had been a guerrilla attack somewhere in the interior wilderness area of the country and several children and women had been killed, after being tortured and raped. The news anchor also mentioned casually and almost as if it were unimportant, among other items, that two gang hoodlums had finally been caught downtown when they tried to rob a foreign tourist at knife-point. This report hit him but it was not the moment to get depressed or sentimental, so Dr. Osborne changed the news station. He got the weather report for that night. Fortunately it was going to be fairly mild: There would be a spectacular and unusual full moon in the sky. Actually, that sounded very romantic.

Dr. Osborne closed his eyes for a few minutes; but instead of relaxing, he thought he should slowly get ready for his evening date. He would try to get Virginia on the phone to synchronize plans after the visit to her grandmother's. He knew he had to get up shortly and get dressed; well groomed but not overly formal. Men wore conservative clothing in Bogotá, especially if accompanying a lady – wife, mistress, girl friend or even grandmother - to an elegant establishment.

He would need to reserve space for dinner for two people - maybe three if Virginia's grandmother came along - at an exceptional restaurant. He had thought they would go to the Casa Medina. He would ask his Concierge in the lobby to call and make reservations for him. He would instruct him to request a special cozy table for two, - perhaps three after he talked to Virginia - located in a quiet area at the Castanyoles Restaurant, the elegant eatery at the select Four Seasons Casa Medina hotel.

He hoped that his choice would please Virginia and her grandmother. The older lady might not accompany them; on the other hand it might not be a bad idea, it could be a good way to get to know Virginia and her family better. He would ask her, of course, if the choice was a good one for her; if not, he would immediately change the selection if she had another preferred choice.

He had read the Castanyoles Restaurant was comfortable, with its Mediterranean style, warm colors and Spanish tiles creating a chic and inviting atmosphere. After all, now Casa Medina was owned by the Four Seasons deluxe international hotel chain, so it should be good. He had read it was considered a superior restaurant. The property had been built in 1945 by a wealthy Bogotano architect, Don Santiago Medina Mejía as his personal mansion. It was designed using the remnants of the colonial Convent of Santo Domingo, which had been demolished in 1938. Casa Medina was declared a national monument in 1985 due to its unique Spanish and French-inspired architectural style.

The second choice was Casa San Isidro on Cerro de Monserrate, a supposedly outstanding French restaurant on the very top of that mountain. It claimed to have the backing of the French Embassy in Colombia. One would have to take the cable car to get there. A few years earlier you would not even have considered that choice because of the insecurity with crime and kidnappings, but that situation had changed quite dramatically in the recent past. At the present time it was considered quite safe.

Dr. Osborne also made a mental note to ask Pedro to go with him to a flower shop to select an out-of-the-ordinary floral arrangement for Virginia's grandmother, and a beautiful bouquet - perhaps a selection of deep crimson or vibrant bright red roses –

for Virginia herself.

Later on, after he had spoken to Virginia, she suggested that maybe they should go to Casa San Isidro restaurant on Monserrate because she liked French food, and she hadn't been there in a very long time. Besides, the moon would be shining over Bogotá and that was a very unusual situation. She said the view from that high point at night would be truly extraordinary. She did not go as far as saying it would be very romantic.

They could decide later if her grandmother *Carmencita* would be interested in joining them for dinner. Meanwhile they might have *té and galletas* - tea and home-made cookies - at her home.

As far as security at Casa Medina or Restaurante Casa San Isidro on Monserrate was concerned, Virginia indicated there would be an undercover presence at either place, once they had decided where to go. The armed security guards would be located in the vicinity of Casa Medina or in the cable car area below the Cerro of Monserrate, near the restaurant.

****

Chapter 9

An Evening of Anticipation

Punctually at 5 o'clock Pedro the driver called the room phone at the hotel. Dr. Osborne asked him to wait five minutes while he organized Infinity, her private relief area and dining bowl, and put some music on the radio to provide adequate entertainment for the feline assistant.

He left a couple of lights on. He knew the room supervisors might come in to turn the bed down and put a small chocolate on the pillow, as done in European five-star hotels. Then he checked the door of the safe, put his tie and jacket on and finally left the room, squeezing the electronic key between his fingers as if to utter: 'Here we go, John Osborne.' And then he pondered: 'Has it been so long since the time of Madeleine's tragedy that I've been incapable to enjoy a warm personal female relationship?' He told himself: 'But John, this really isn't the time to think about those feelings.'

When he came out into the lobby, he noticed Pedro was wearing a suit jacket to be more in tune for the occasion. He signaled to him to acknowledge his presence, then went by the hotel boutique to purchase a box of chocolates – prefer- ably Lindt or one of the best local brands - for doña Carmen.

Pedro actually looked quite pleased to be going on this special assignment. Dr. Osborne guessed that the whole thing had a touch of mystery and romance which Pedro obviously was enjoying. Normally the relationship between a driver and his boss is more formal, but Pedro and Dr. Osborne had interacted together for a considerable length of time. Pedro appreciated Dr. Osborne's attitude of comradeship without familiarity, devoid of any airs of social superiority or condescendence like some of his other Colombian customers.

He greeted Dr. Osborne with his deformed hand, gave him just a very light unobtrusive handshake, and then opened the car door. Dr. Osborne instructed him to go directly to a flower shop before continuing on to Virginia's house.

Pedro knew a store nearby, where they drove to and parked, while Dr. Osborne went in and selected what he thought was the proper bouquet arrangement for the beloved grandmother and special fiery roses for *Capitán* Virginia.

Would she be wearing a formal FESCO uniform for the occasion? She hadn't said anything when he had spoken with her on the phone before. She had only confirmed that a normal outfit would be appropriate, nothing formal or fancy. She pointed out she looked forward to unwinding while getting to know each other better.

While the helpful attendant who had suggested the best choice of flowers for the bouquets was wrapping them in an exquisite presentation, as he had requested she create something extra special, he saw an image of Virginia's face in his mind. He felt an indefinable warm sensation of anticipation for the evening; a soft tremor of eagerness crossed his heart. For some ridiculous reason he pondered: Is Virginia's name a reflection of her womanhood status or just a coincidence? Is Virginia still a virgin? 'Stop, John! he told himself. What difference does that make! What a preposterous thought to have at this moment!' But he remembered her soft and sensuous lips; how he would love to touch them, to kiss them. He put that hypnotizing image away, realizing that actually he could - that he wanted to - have a serious responsible love affair with Virginia Cosmos Quesada.

He gave the colorful flowers to Pedro as he confirmed rather formally what the latter knew very well: "Pedro, now please take me to the grandmother's house of Capitán Cosmos. I'm anxious to get there." Pedro asked him if he knew the grandmother's full name and address: "Yes, Pedro, Captain Cosmos gave them to me a while ago when I called her. Her grandmother's name is Carmen de Jaramillo, on Carrera 5A and 95th Street.

After a short pause Dr. Osborne added, as if it were an afterthought: "Virginia calls her grandmother Carmencita. Why? I'll probably find out later." Pedro quickly but politely opined respectfully: "Dr. Osborne, everybody in Bogotá, in fact in the country, uses the diminutive '*ita*' and '*ito*,' to make everything and everybody feel informal and closer to each other. It stimulates faster friendships in people's relationships." *That* was a succinct and valuable cultural explanation, Dr. Osborne observed to himself. "Thank you, Pedro." Pedro quickly added: "Dr. Osborne, if you allow me, you probably should call the older grandmother *Doña Carmen* until you get to know her better." Dr. Osborne answered him: "Thank you for the hint." That advice couldn't have been more appropriate culturally; it would certainly avoid an undesirable faux-pas by not seeming too familiar.

He sat back in the comfortable car seat – and then it struck him: Virginia's grandmother was a Cosmos; but doña Carmen had married a Jaramillo. Was there a direct connection between her granddaughter Virginia Cosmos and Coronel Roberto Jaramillo? Virginia didn't use the Jaramillo name. Oh well, he would certainly find out soon enough. Maybe during their dinner conversation Dr. Osborne would learn if perhaps Coronel Jaramillo was actually her uncle. Whatever the story was, John Osborne the man - separate from the prominent and renowned scientist - liked her sensuous lips and her crystal-clear penetrating eyes. He was anxiously looking forward to seeing Virginia again and finally meeting her grandmother – if he guessed right, she called her *abuelita,* her beloved grandma.

They would be at her house shortly, maybe after a fifteen minute ride. Pedro was driving toward the residential area at the foot of the oriental mountain range in the northern part of the city where numerous buildings and new modern apartment complexes had been built among a few imposing mansions left over from the past, when the city's elite lived in that neighborhood of El Norte, showing off their prized residences before the era of guerrilla insecurity, drug trade and plain street crime took over and changed the demographic arrangements.

They went past several official-looking buildings with names emblazoned on oval signs, indicating the Dutch, German, Swiss and English embassies and even past well-known private schools like Colegio La Salle and the French Lycée Pasteur.

Shortly thereafter Pedro said: "Dr. Osborne, we will be at Captain Cosmos's house in five minutes," as if to prepare him for what seemed to be evolving into a quixotic interlude. After all, the adult couple would be alone. There would be no chaperons, a Hispanic custom that had disappeared long ago. Infinity the Assistant was resting at the hotel; but would Virginia's grandmother join them for dinner? Dr. Osborne didn't know if she might stay home, thus letting the couple get to know each other and explore their lives by themselves. He figured that if doña Carmen the grandmother loved her granddaughter so much, she might be quite happy to let a new relationship foster in her life.

Unbeknownst to him, Virginia had hinted the night before to her grandma Carmencita that she would be bringing home a nice looking widowed European scientist she had met a couple of days before in Coronel Jaramillo's airport security office. At the request of her superior she had also attended a select private conference at the Botero Museum given by that cultured gentleman of Swiss-British extraction.

Virginia Cosmos had also told her grandmother – confidentially, of course - that she liked that man a lot, perhaps more than she should, as she really didn't know him yet, but she was rather impressed by him; and was hoping her dear grandmother Carmencita would enjoy meeting him too. Would she perhaps like to go to dinner with them?

After a couple of curves Pedro's vehicle reached a flat street. There were apartment buildings on both sides, behind tree-laden sidewalks. Here and there remained interspersed a few stately homes concealed behind protective walls. Pedro said: "The American Ambassador lives at the end of the street, where you see several armed guards and two armored cars in front of the gate."

Dr. Osborne countered: "I'm sure it must be quite an expensive property. The Americans always go all out for it, since their Ambassador's residence represents their country overseas."

To which Pedro expounded: "Yes, indeed, it's a beautiful property which the U.S. government has owned for many decades. Once, I was able to see the inside gardens when I took a couple of American visitors from Washington to a traditional Fourth of July Independence Day party. Captain Cosmos and her grandmother were there, as doña Carmen was invited because her husband was a well-known Colombian military general. By the way, her house is the third one on the left."

Pedro drove a few more feet, stopped the car and said: "Here we are, Doctor Osborne. Good luck. Don't worry too much about the special guards. They will carefully check us, verify our identities and inspect the car before they let us in through the large gate."

The car had in fact stopped in front of an imposing gate, consisting of two decorative iron halves with an icon or family coat of arms in the center, with the letters J and C emblazoned in the middle. There were two daunting guards in front -one on each side of the driveway - brandishing black intimidating machine guns, and wearing impeccable uniforms with an embroidered patch that read:

* FESCO *
FUERZAS ESPECIALES DE SEGURIDAD DE COLOMBIA.
HONOR – LEALTAD – PERSEVERANCIA

Dr. Osborne recognized the uniforms from his morning experience. Mechanically he translated the message: *'FESCO* Special Security Forces of Colombia * Honor–Loyalty-Perseverance.'*

Pedro stepped out of the car and opened the door for Doctor Osborne. The two guards saluted him automatically and asked him and Pedro to move aside so they could inspect the vehicle. One held on to his machine gun pointed at the automobile, while his partner slowly moved a circular metal detector under the chassis, motor and trunk. Next, he asked Pedro to open the trunk, which he promptly obliged. Having completed their inspection and obtained the necessary identification from the two passengers, one of the guards proceeded to a small security post at the end of the driveway to pick up a phone and alert the inside staff as to the arrival of Dr. Osborne. They told him he was expected.

Dr. Osborne climbed in the back of the car and thanked the guards properly while Pedro got in the front. As soon as the portal gates were opened they proceeded to slowly drive into a large lighted courtyard. The house and gardens were not visible from the street or through the gate.

The mansion was truly monumental, elegant and impressive; yet did not seem overwhelming because of its clever classical architectural design. The gardens were spectacular, with flowers and immaculate bushes. Dr. Osborne thought: 'At last I'm here. It seems unreal. What an extraordinary property!' His heart skipped a beat at the thought he would shortly see Virginia again. Suddenly he realized he hadn't felt that way in a very long time. He knew, deep in his heart, that he was affected and slowly falling in love with her. He smiled at the afterthought: 'A mysterious woman in uniform.'

Pedro carefully parked the car on the curved driveway around an illuminated fountain spewing water from three lions' jaws. He opened the door for Dr. Osborne and said, in a calm and professional voice: "Dr. Osborne, we are finally at the home of Dona Carmen de Jaramillo. If I may say so very respectfully, have a nice time. I'll be waiting for you here by the car whenever you are ready for me to take you and your guest to the restaurant."

At that moment a maid wearing a black uniform with a scalloped white apron and a small bonnet covering her hair, came out of the house front door – a solid wooden double door, in heavy Spanish ornamental style - and greeted them very politely. She said her name was Leonora. Welcome. Pedro mentioned his name to her and introduced Doctor Osborne as *Profesor Osborne*. He then gave her the two flower bouquets and the chocolate box for Doña Carmen and Señorita Virginia. Leonora said he could go the back way into the kitchen area to wait there if he wanted to have coffee and something to eat. He assented and waved as Dr. Osborne and Leonora walked toward the house front entrance.

Leonora opened the heavy door for Dr. Osborne and led him through a remarkable long hallway to a large living room. On the way he noticed the floors were covered in sections with colorful Belgian, Persian and native rugs. There were paintings of different styles and sizes hanging on the ivory-colored walls. For a moment it reminded him of the Museo Santa Clara earlier in the day.

They went past exquisite *parador* style doors – like in the old castles in Spain -that were open and permitted a view unto a formal dining room. Dr. Osborne observed through the wide opening, a long dining mahogany table in the center, maybe twelve or fourteen feet long, around which were twelve hand-carved dark caoba chairs covered with red leather and two arm chairs at either end. Obviously, this elegant décor and old Spanish colonial furniture gave him the inescapable impression of having stepped into the long established affluent residence of a traditional cultured Colombian family of considerable means.

Dr. Osborne followed Leonora as she slowly escorted him into the spacious living room. There she was, grandmother Carmen, celebrating nobility, sitting at the end of the room, reading ensconced in a comfortable deep leather chair, facing an enticing log fire in the impressive fireplace decorated all around with hand-hewn stones; bringing to mind the picture of a charming and imposing imperial dowager from the past, like nineteenth century Queen Victoria in the United Kingdom, but instead an impressive Colombian symbol of a free Colonial Queen, a native *Doña Carmencita*, Virginia's beloved grandmother.

Leonora stepped forward and introduced the visitor: "Doña Carmen, *el Profesor* John Osborne is here.' The grandmother turned around and got up from the chair. She looked at him, with a preliminary look of maternal curiosity, then she greeted him with a natural friendly smile, saying: "I am Virginia's grandmother: *Carmen Martinez Cosmos de Jaramillo*. I am delighted to meet you Professor Osborne." He moved closer to greet her, bowed his head in an old fashioned European greeting, took her right hand and bent down as if to kiss it, all the while looking into the grandmother's shining intelligent eyes.

He introduced himself: "Doña Carmen, I am Doctor John Osborne Mounier." She answered: "I am truly delighted to meet you, Sir. Please excuse me for one second while I tell Leonora to bring us some tea." She turned to Leonora and gave her instructions to bring tea for Dr. Osborne. – was that ok? or would he prefer coffee or whiskey? She explained to Dr. Osborne: I'm sure you know that in Bogotá when we say whisky, we mean it in the English sense: it's Scotch not American type whiskey like Rye. And she told Leonora to advise the driver that he could go to the kitchen and drink some coffee while waiting, since it was somewhat cool outside. Leonora said she had already done so. And the grand lady then asked, where was her darling grandchild Virginia? Leonora told her Miss Virginia wasn't quite ready yet as she had arrived a while ago from work and was still changing her uniform and getting dressed for dinner. Then she disappeared to carry out her instructions.

Doña Carmen asked Professor Osborne to sit down next to her as she wanted to enjoy a moment of private conversation before her granddaughter came down and tea was served. First she asked him if he was a Professor as introduced by the maid, or did he go by another title? He replied that normally they called him Doctor Osborne, since he was a Research Scientist at the Zurich Politechnikum, but he occasionally gave lectures on Brain Electro Cognition and Neuron Spectrograms, in which case his students, already normally advanced in their careers would call him either one or the other. But she could simply call him *John*, if she wished to – though he instantly realized that could only happen at a future time when such familiarity might be more proper.

She elucidated to Dr. Osborne who was sitting next to her admiring her charisma. My full name is: *Carmen Martinez Cosmos de Jaramillo.*. She paused for a minute as Dr. Osborne stated: "Doña Carmen, that is quite a combination of names. Is that the normal and traditional way?" She observed: "If you allow me, Doctor John, let me clarify: Carmen is my given name. Martinez was my mother's family name. Cosmos was my father's family name. My mother became a Jaramillo when she married her husband Francisco, at that time a captain in the national Army. When I got married, like all women I took on my husband's family name which we place at the end of all names, with a *de* before it, like *de Jaramillo*. This can be confusing to foreigners and speakers of languages other than Spanish but it reflects our traditional social and cultural custom." Dr. Osborne thanked her for the explanation, which indeed explained succinctly the established norms.

In the meantime, Leonora came back with a

stunning silver tray and a complete tea service which she set on a marble centerpiece in front of them. She told the grandmother that Virginia would be coming down forthwith. Carmen thanked her and told her to come back in a couple of minutes to serve the tea. Leonora assented and left.

Shortly thereafter they heard a door closing on the second floor and then Virginia's steps coming down the main stairway. She was holding on to the graceful marble banister as she made her appearance. "*Abuelita, por fin!* Finally, I am here! Doctor Osborne – John – *I'm so sorry.* Please excuse me for taking so long." And she gave a disarming happy smile as she looked at them. "I was getting ready for our dinner adventure."

Doña Carmen smiled back, so proud at the sight of her granddaughter. Virginia slowly came down the stairs and first greeted her grandmother with a kiss on each cheek. Then she turned to John and likewise gave him a gentle kiss on both cheeks. This was the Bogotano custom. John was speechless at the sight of his companion: Virginia was not wearing her captain's uniform from FESCO. It was the first time he had ever seen her not in her uniform.

Virginia was simply stunning in her fashionable simplicity and beautiful warmth. Her hair, now free for the first time since he had met her, came tumbling down to her shoulders on a cascade of glorious abandonment. Her elegant black dress modestly but sensuously hugged her upper body and sinuous hips like a sculptured statue. Almost as if hypnotized by the sight of Virginia's tranquil beauty, John said without thinking: "Virginia, I'm sorry if I seem to be staring, but I am admiring your beauty."

He was thinking in the depth of his heart how her overwhelming loveliness was almost beyond his normal capacity of perception. It had been a long time since he could pay such a sincere compliment to a woman. He added: "You look ravishing in that black dress, Virginia." She was unequivocally beautiful, like perhaps Helen of Troy might have been. At first she didn't say a word; but then broke into another captivating smile and said with disconcerting simplicity: "John, you are much too chivalrous and kind. I guess my uniform must hide me well." And she gave him another gentle kiss on the cheek while she placed her hand on his upper arm. He just couldn't take his eyes away from hers. It was an enchanting exchange.

Doña Carmen had followed that entrancing scene. In her heart she was secretly pleased by the tender embrace. Trying not to break the magical moment – as she found John to be a most charming and cultured gentleman – she asked the couple to sit down around the marble tea table. She picked up and rang a small artistic golden bell to call Leonora, who appeared without delay. She checked the porcelain cups, went back to the kitchen for a steaming tea pot, came back without a sound and carefully served the searing tea.

Still recovering from John's unexpected warm salutation, Virginia had an infinitesimal touch of crimson red on her cheeks, testifying to her surprised reaction to the sincere compliments by John Osborne. She commented – changing the topic as if to avoid lingering on the previous unexpected scene - that Colombia also produced fine tea and cocoa besides coffee. She had once visited a plantation owned by the *Carulla Supermarkets* family. Irrelevant, perhaps, but it put everyone at ease.

While sipping their tea, in the elegant Limoges porcelain cups, recognizable by the golden and heavenly blue strip near the top, they chitchatted about various mundane things, including the weather, the full moon that was forecast for that night and whether doña Carmen would like to join Virginia and John for dinner. She was silent for a moment; then she asked John to please put a log in the fire and said she would love to come along, but much preferred if Virginia and John went out by themselves and got to know each other better – or, as she said, more deeply, quietly and genuinely.

They continued to sip their tea while sitting by the fireplace. They talked about that morning's scary event with the robbery attempt successfully interrupted by Virginia's FESCO armed personnel. They also talked about John's morning luncheon at Casa Vieja – a rather traditional restaurant, very well known for preserving native recipes, as the grandmother said without meaning to be negative – and the Conference at the Botero Museum. This brought up Botero's particular peculiar artistic creations. Doña Carmen described his paintings and sculptures as bloated and colorful though not necessarily unpleasant, overweight or gross.

She pointed to the painting of a fat cat on one of her walls and indicated in a casual way: "That's an original Botero. Looks like his cat in Barcelona." Doña Carmen concluded her comments by saying: "Next to the cat is an original Grau, a cross between French and Dutch styles, but typical Colombian in its execution, called *La Mujer del Sombrero* - The Woman with a Hat. It shows a beautiful woman's head, with flowing hair and an astonishing large hat covered by colorful native flowers."

Virginia told her grandmother: "*Abuelita*, you should see Infinity!" "And who is that?" asked Doña Carmen, a little alarmed. Virginia explained she was Dr. Osborne's – John's - feline assistant in his cognitive research. Doña Carmen smiled, relieved. For a minute she had expected a different answer: Another woman, perhaps?

Virginia explained in detail the demonstration John carried out at the Museum. John also gave a succinct explanation of the cognitive performance by Infinity. Virginia concluded by saying Infinity was safely back at the hotel.

John had been holding back his curiosity. He finally asked Doña Carmen, very respectfully, about the large painting on the wall. She looked at it slowly and thoughtfully before she finally answered him. She said: "I am the widow of Virginia's grandfather, Comandante General *Francisco Jaramillo Pinzón* whom you see in this commemorative large painting on the wall. This extraordinary painting portrays my beloved Comandante Jaramillo in full dress uniform at his promotion to General. He is proudly holding in his hand a silver officer's sword, symbol of his official promotion that day."

Virginia interjected: "My grandfather is standing next to my *abuelita* Carmen who is wearing a long formal grown and a lovely pearl necklace around her neck. They had celebrated with the Minister of Defense at the Jockey Club, after first attending the official formal military gala at the *Club Militar de Oficiales,* the Officers Military Club."

It was a most impressive picture that commanded both attention and respect. John turned to Virginia and her grandmother, and inquired further about the painting. Virginia said: "John, my grandfather Francisco was a very well-known general in our Colombian Armed Forces."

She continued to explain that the Central General Command of the Military Forces is the highest level entity of strategic planning and direction for the Armed forces of Colombia which include the National Army and the Air Force. He was a graduate and a professor in Military and Exact Sciences at the Advanced School of War, with a Master's in Defense and National Security.

The picture was painted to represent the memorable occasion when he was promoted to General in the Armed Forces, a culmination of his long and loyal service to his country. Her voice got emotional and she slowed her expression, taking a sip of tea to gain greater control and composure.

John said: "The canvas is truly an impressive work of art. It's hard to tell if it was painted long ago. Was it, doña Carmen?" Grandmother Carmen cut in, with a rather casual but loving voice: "It was about eleven years ago."

Virginia continued in a quiet voice: "My grandfather was a very well-known military officer and highly regarded educated man. His family had served in the Armed Forces for three generations. Besides, they were large landowners that grew fruit trees of many kinds, sugar cane and bananas and had an extensive coffee plantation. They made a substantial fortune over several generations. But sadly, my beloved grandfather Francisco died a few years ago when I was only sixteen years old. I was still in high school, in *bachillerato*.

John immediately said: "Captain Cosmos - Virginia- I'm so sorry to hear that. How sad." They sat silently for a couple of minutes, while the fireplace flaming logs cracked and spurted colorful sparks in the hearth. Then John said, very gently: "Virginia, you were a very young lady; it must have affected you a lot. May I ask, without being disrespectful, or curious, what happened to your grandfather?"

Doña Carmen interjected: "Allow me to answer, since he was my husband for thirty-six years.

He passed away at sixty-one. His death was really unexpected – as many demises are – but it was not the result of any military activity, though perhaps the weight of responsibility and dedication may have taken its toll." She sighed and paused for a minute. "I was fifty-six at the time. My dear Francisco had gone with one of his Army Battalions to oversee operations against the guerrilla and drug lords in a wild area of our country. Getting ready to come out of his campaign tent, he apparently had a seizure or blood clot that paralyzed him. He fell like a log. He was alone at that moment. The Commander's dead weight hit the portable wooden desk in the corner and his head splintered in two. In two minutes it became blackened by the shock. His aide-de-camp found him sprawled on the floor twenty minutes later, laying in a small pool of blood. He had lost too much blood and it was absolutely impossible to do anything to revive and save him. It was devastating. It was so sad, John. But we had had a good thirty-six years together."

Virginia added: "There were newspaper headlines and television reports all over the country. The military funeral was a national affair. It was a terribly sad occasion for my grandmother Carmencita, my parents and all our family." John noted this was the first reference Virginia had made to her parents, but he didn't interrupt or comment.

Virginia continued: "Worse of all, John, they had made a secret autopsy before his burial, the results of which were known and discussed only at the highest commanding levels. It indicated there were traces of strychnine poison in my grandfather's blood, which pointed to a silent conspiracy against him, most likely by drug cartel elements rather than some disaffected military colleagues. The fatal poison had led to the disastrous blood seizure and fatal fall which ultimately killed him. There are antidotes to strychnine poisoning, but in my grandfather's case it was useless, as he had hit his head against the table corner in his fall and there was no possibility of recovery."

"To this date, the Armed Forces Command, the Military laboratories and the Secret Service agencies have been unable to trace the exact origins or sources of the strychnine that killed Comandante Jaramillo. But they detained two young cooks in the military encampment who had disappeared after the distressful event, and were found in the proximity of Medellin hiding among suspected drug dealers. Eventually they confessed to their ignominy. Virginia paused, and then added a somber note: "As you can see, Dr. John Osborne, I have many reasons for having joined FESCO a few years ago."

Grandmother Carmen wiped small tears in the corner of her eyes. She said: "Now, let's not dwell anymore on past sad stories. I want you two to go out and enjoy a lovely dinner together. Dr. John, is your driver reliable?" John answered positively. He had used Pedro many times in the past. "Then go now and don't waste any more time with this old widow." She smiled sweetly but resolutely. Virginia and John both got up and slowly approached doña Carmen. They thanked her for the tea. Virginia told her she would be back later but not too late. Grandmother Carmen added smiling: "Virginia dearest, you are a grown woman of twenty seven, you don't need me to tag along. Go enjoy yourselves. I'm going to eat dinner at home. *Hasta luego.*" John knew that farewell greeting: 'Until later.'

Carmen held up again the golden bell – perhaps an antiquated symbol of authority - and let it ring its pristine alert. When Leonora appeared almost instantly, the elderly grandmother told her to ask Pedro the driver to get the car and bring it to the front of the house where the couple would meet him. Had he had something to eat or drink? Leonora assented. Then Virginia and John escorted Doña Carmen toward the dining room. They both kissed her goodbye, affectionately on each cheek, and proceeded to the front door.

While Virginia and John waited outside by the entrance, he looked at her and said; "Your *abuelita* is an extraordinary, wonderful and kind lady." He paused and added: "And you, Captain Virginia, are breathtakingly beautiful. I am so thankful you accepted my invitation tonight. I assure you it won't be the last time, if you so allow me. I like you immensely." She smiled appreciatively and simply said: "Thank you, John." She put her hand around his arm.

As they were standing on the porch entrance, before walking to the car, she said: "I just want you to know that as part of my FESCO security regulations, I must carry my loaded pistol at all times, in my holster, in my purse, under my shawl, strapped to my thigh, wherever it is not conspicuous. Nobody will notice it." She smiled mischievously but firmly: "Especially if you behave, Dr. Osborne." His heart was boiling. He looked at her lips and felt their magic emanating toward him. He saw the full moon over the clipped bushes. And he saw Pedro waiting for them.

They walked to the car, Pedro greeted them, opened the doors and they got in. As they passed the open gate, the guards formally saluted Virginia and she saluted them back. She knew them well. They were carefully selected to guard Carmen's house. No lightness or the slightest familiarity there; all serious business and professionalism. Security meant life or death, honor and loyalty. The full moon witnessed the whole exchange; the shadows were reflected on the wall.

* * * * *

Chapter 10

Full Moon Hypnosis

    You could touch the large white naked moon. It seemed suspended in the sky. You could actually see the dark land masses where Man had landed and a vehicular rover had rolled on the surface many years ago. The entire chronological adventure seemed prehistoric, unreal and close to a dream. This was an unusual moon, which the weather geniuses had predicted for two nights. Tonight was not a routinary repetition of every day's evening performance. It was a hypnotizing magical circle that hung in the air, almost close enough to stroke, floating only a few miles away or so it seemed, protected by blinking stars in the heavens of our overwhelming universe.

John confirmed to Pedro what he had earlier instructed him to do after the visit to Doña Carmen: "Please take us to Casa Medina, we have reservations at seven thirty at the Castanyoles Restaurant." Pedro answered: "*Con mucho gusto* Dr. Osborne – with great pleasure, we'll be there at the prearranged time." "Thank you, Pedro."

John and Virginia sat in the back of the car silently contemplating the heavenly spectacle of moon and stars. It was dark. John wondered if he would dare to reach for Virginia's hand. Gently he did so. She did not move it away.

Out of the blue, quietly and unexpectedly, John saw again the image he had previously perceived in a couple of undefined and disconnected occasions: a flash of brightness in his mind, projecting the picture of a turning white skirt which sensuously revealed a smooth soft warm thigh; but then, just as swiftly, it had disappeared and there was only a sudden blank in his mind. This time, as before, he couldn't quite figure the reason for such an image bursting into his mind, especially at this sentimental moment; but he knew unconsciously that the reflection he saw was not Virginia's or anyone else he knew. John held on to the warm hand of Virginia which for only a second seemed transformed from a confident independent woman involved in intelligence work into a tremulous little bird seeking warmth and protection.

Virginia addressed Pedro. She indicated that he might notice a black vehicle following them very discretely. She told him not to worry, as it was actually carrying out Central Headquarters orders from FESCO to guard the Captain's car unconditionally.

She mentioned to John that now he probably understood more what his involvement with her could represent. He said he was ready to do whatever was needed, as long as he could have the pleasure and honor of her company. As an answer to him she gave another one of her disarming smiles, with her magnetic lips lightly covered in soft red lipstick. She actually squeezed his hand very gently, much to his surprise, and sat silent again. John realized he had a couple of lingering questions that he would ask her later at the restaurant.

As they were driving down a few steep curved streets in the direction of stately Casa Medina, Virginia commented that it was a unique occurrence to have a full moon over Bogota. It happened only rarely and she was so glad it was occurring for two nights, including this night when they were going out to dinner together. She was happy it would also be out the next evening, though John would already be gone to Villa de Leyva.

Shortly thereafter, they finally arrived at Casa Medina. The lights on the building highlighted the architectural details of the post-colonial style mansion. Pedro stopped the car by the front entrance. The uniformed valet opened the doors to let Captain Virginia Cosmos and Dr. John Osborne out. They thanked him. Dr. Osborne told Pedro they would probably be in the restaurant for a couple of hours more or less, when he should be ready to drive them to Monserrate as they wanted to look at the moon and the city from on top of the mountain. Dr. Osborne noticed from the corner of his eye that a small car had parked about a 100 meters back, and turned off its lights. Virginia followed his eyes in the same general direction; she too noticed the escort car.

She put her hand on John's arm as they started to walk up the stairs toward the main entrance. Her beauty and charm were hypnotizing. John sensed the feeling of magnetism that she projected around her, so sleek and elegant in her black dress, and commanding attention from onlookers – like the living room painting of her grandfather Francisco.

When the doorman opened the door, they entered a large foyer. Virginia kept her shawl around her shoulders as it was slightly cool – and it also helped to disguise the personal weapon she was carrying in her purse.

There was a sign on an easel stating that that night only the restaurant was having a special celebration. There would be two classical guitarists and a violinist playing excerpts of Concierto de Aranjuez. The Concert had been written in 1939 by the romantic Spanish composer Joaquin Rodrigo six years before Casa Medina had been remodeled and part of its building modified by adding components from the Convent of Santo Domingo. It seems he had stayed there once on one of his tours.

The concierge at Hotel Casa Dann had informed Dr. Osborne of the unique musical presentation that night and readily concurred they definitely should go for dinner there, just as Dr. Osborne had wished to do. He had exerted special effort with the manager to secure a reservation for a quiet romantic table for which Dr. Osborne had given him a well-deserved *propina* – or tip. The scientist was most appreciative as he wanted to go to a select place with elegant atmosphere to please his special guest. He wanted to be able to talk privately to her in order to find out more about her and also tell her about himself.

They were greeted very respectfully by a friendly Maître D' who accompanied them to their table. They were seated in the back of the dining room, which was cozier and better as it was distant from the small stage which had been set up for the two guitarists and the violinist. The sound would be less audible, but they still could hear the music and converse more comfortably. John asked Virginia if she liked the table, to which she assented, and they told the Maître D'. The lightning was subdued and the atmosphere conducive to a relaxing exchange between two people obviously enjoying each other's company. They were offered a complimentary glass of Freixenet Cava from Cataluña – which the Spanish Maître D' considered as good or superior to French champagne like Moet et Chandon.

The couple settled down and looked around. The place was packed but the Concierge had been able to secure the perfect intimate table. Both were pleased. There was a gentle diffused light shining on

Virginia's hair and John was enthralled. He had seen beautiful women before, and his own Madeleine was one of them, but Virginia had a unique soft quality about her which differed from most. He realized she really was quite unique, definitely special. How lucky to be with her tonight! He couldn't stop looking at her eyes and enjoying her sensuous inviting lips. It was almost embarrassing but he controlled his feelings. He knew how to be a respectful gentleman.

They looked at the extensive menu which included Spanish style tapas. They selected their preferred choices and decided to enjoy a glass of Malbec Mendoza from Argentina with their entrées. Neither John nor Virginia were great drinkers, she especially because of her position in FESCO and he because he had gotten used to avoiding alcoholic consumption after some of his friends had seriously abused American-style cocktails while visiting Zurich.

After they had ordered, they talked about their professional careers, their education, and their basic values. They conversed about John's visit at her grandmother Carmen's house. By now the three musicians had began to play, which fortunately they did by gently adapting the Concerto and its Spanish soul to the occasion, emphasizing the melodic adagio and its mournful expressions of romanticism. The combination of two guitars and one violin was perfectly fitting for the layout of the place, which after all was a restaurant and not a concert hall. The efficient and knowledgeable waiter commented that apparently the score for trio had been arranged by one of maestro Paco de Lucia's students in Seville, Spain.

While eating at the same time as enjoying the Aranjuez melancholy sounds, the couple continued talking about themselves, their experiences and feelings. Virginia knew John was a widower. After all, she was an intelligence expert and worked for Coronel Jaramillo in the FESCO Special Services Group. She asked him about his marriage; what had happened, how long ago, did he mind telling her?

He became pensive and exhaled a subdued sigh. He explained to Virginia that his wife Madeleine had worked for the United Nations in Geneva. Eventually she had been sent to Nigeria, Kenya, Congo and other countries in Africa as part of a UN humanitarian relief program due to the constant civil fighting between different political parties and tribal conflicts. The mission aimed to help civilians, especially women and children involved in the savage fighting. It had lasted relatively well for a period of time; but then there was a sudden burst of hate and savage retribution that brought the mission to a halt amidst a chaotic stoppage.

He continued: "Many women, female students and children were kidnapped and detained forcefully by various fighting groups. Madeleine opined in her letters that many African male natives seem to retort to savagery and primordial behavior when fighting for causes they didn't fully understand or could control. Her UN Mission staff was left unaided for several weeks."

"In the meantime, the rampage by black natives went on. Women were beaten and raped. The young students, boys and girls were kept in unsanitary quarters, undernourished and often naked. Soldiers took advantage of them, molested them and used them for cruel and sadistic games. Young children were treated inhumanly. Most U.N. staff members were beaten and pushed around without mercy."

"Madeleine and a few of the white female U.N. personnel were herded apart because they were more valuable for ransom, being both women and white. The uncivilized bandits would choose one at a time to pursue their satanic games. Madeleine spoke French with some of the natives and this helped to delay her forced and cruel situation."

"She was always hoping the U.N. would send armored personnel carriers or tanks to rescue the endangered adults and children. She herself was beaten and raped by one of the tribal leaders who fancied himself the next President of his country. When the United Nations peace keeping forces arrived, it was too late. The rebel forces managed to disappear into the wilderness, but not before leaving behind them a disastrous and unimaginable hell. The U.N. Peace keepers rescued some of the kidnapped victims, but the staff members had been annihilated. Among them was my wife Madeleine. She was found half naked; she had been tortured, raped and shot with a bullet in her forehead. The U.N. sent her back to me for burial in Zurich, with a cold official note: *'Thank you for your help. We send you our heartfelt regrets.'* As you can see, that was an overwhelming expression of sympathy by the representatives of the World Community."

John sat silently while Virginia dried tears in her shocked eyes. They stayed quiet for a couple of minutes; then she said: "I am so sorry, John, it's a terrible story." And she took his hand, squeezed it gently, held it and put it up to her lips.

She smiled kindly and said: "Let's go on, John; you and I are still alive." While sipping their Cava, they looked at each others' eyes. Hers were crystal clear, joyful and sincere. His were full of wonder and the seeds of love. She broke out into an impish smile, putting her hand on his and saying, after a momentary pause: "I could like you, Dr. Osborne." He looked at her, respectfully and warmly, and countered: "I could like you too, a lot, Capitán Virginia; in fact, I know I do and perhaps even more. My feelings are very genuine and I don't want to hold them back."

She remained quiet; then answered very sadly: "But John, it will never work out. You live so far away, in Europe, in Zurich. That's the end of the world for me. That's a very difficult situation for us. How can we have a normal love affair?"

"Virginia, since I met you, my heart has been in turmoil. I know what my feelings are. I've been evaluating my present state of affairs and I have decided to drastically change my life."

"You'll be going back in a few days, after your week in Villa de Leyva, and you will probably never see me again." A cloud of sadness passed over her pupils as she gazed at him, her crystal clear eyes fogged with apprehension. He felt a terrible pang in his heart.

He responded: "Virginia, please don't be saddened. I've been doing a lot of thinking. I believe that you should come with your grandmother Carmen to spend next weekend in Leyva. Thus we can enjoy a few more days getting to know each other."

He continued: "When I'll get back to Zurich, I will immediately request a sabbatical at the Politechnikum, as I want to return to Bogota within one month, to meet your parents and explain to them the seriousness of my intentions. I don't think they will object to our long term relationship or even a union. If necessary, you can then come to live with me in Switzerland, or I'll move to Colombia since you are so well established and your grandmother lives here. I don't want to interrupt your career. In fact, I am mulling the possibility of organizing The Osborne Cognition Research Center here, to continue my official research near where you are, so we both can be together."

"I am sure your mother and father will be happy for you. I intend to make of my life a serious, permanent and responsible relationship with you, Virginia darling."

He lowered his voice: "I know I'm falling in love with you." He looked profoundly into her eyes, trying to transmit the feelings he had deep in his heart and mind: he did sense he was falling in love, an unfathomable feeling from which he couldn't come back. She squeezed his hand very gently and looked at him. She absorbed every word he had said.

John sat silent for a moment. Then he added: "I promise I will make your parents very happy."

As he looked at Virginia, he saw furtive tears streaming down her eyes, very discreetly since they were surrounded by people. But the latter may have thought the Aranjuez melancholy music had affected her sentiments. The adagio had that effect on listeners.

John asked Virginia if he had said something wrong; perhaps he had upset her by freely expressing his sentiments? Maybe it had been too soon or sudden to open his heart. She gently moved her head to signify that he hadn't said anything wrong.

She asked him to listen to her side of the story. They were still eating and enjoying their dinner. They still had time and the table was very private. She swept away the last tears, gave back to her eyes the clarity of a mountain lake and told John to relax. Her story was long and would make things unambiguous, since they were just getting to really know each other.

First, she thanked him for his loving thoughts which she had enormously appreciated. She was deeply sorry to learn the sad story of Madeleine. She was saddened by it; she wasn't crying because she was disturbed by anything he had said.

It was essential, necessary and unavoidable to explain her personal situation. She punctuated slowly and firmly that he would never be able to talk to her mother for she had passed away when Virginia was only nineteen years old. Her beloved mother had died very young when she was merely thirty nine, of an acute attack of pancreatitis which could not be controlled or stopped. Her name was Mariana Sanchez Uribe de Jaramillo. She was nineteen when she married Rogelio Jaramillo Cosmos, who was 21 at the time. Then he was only a young officer in the Armed Forces. "My father eventually rose to the rank of Brigadier General. I was their only child."

She continued: "One day my mother was rushed in the middle of the night to the Emergency Section one of the best hospitals in *El Norte*, I believe it was *Clinica Marly*. They quickly determined it was her pancreas, but she didn't survive more than two days. John, my dear Dr. Osborne, it was a disaster, a tragedy. My grandmother Carmen almost fell apart. My father was distraught to no end. I was so overwhelmed, so shaken, so broken down; my mother was so young to die at thirty nine. I was the same age – nineteen – that she was when she married my dad. She died only eight years ago. It seems like a hundred."

She stopped for a few minutes, sighed softly and then continued:

"My grandfather Francisco had died three years before my mother. My grandmother Carmencita told you what happened at that time.

Now I had lost both my grandfather and my mother within a space of three years. Life is full of sadness, occasionally interspaced with moments of great happiness – like now." She again took John's hand in hers and squeezed it gently. "I am so glad you are here with me tonight."

John had listened attentively and felt deep sorrow for Virginia. He told her so and kept her hand in his.

She continued slowly and steadily: "My grandmother Carmencita and my dad decided that I should finish my high school *bachillerato* in Bogotá. I needed about two years to recover from my shock. When I reached twenty-one they insisted I travel to Paris to study at La Sorbonne University, perfecting my French and getting involved in Literature, History and Philosophy. After that time I was a little over twenty-two years old, spoke French and English fluently and had a good educational background. And I was in Paris."

She hesitated a second and continued haltingly: "By then, my dear Dr. Osborne, I had a relatively serious affair with a French *bon ami,* –a young boyfriend about my age. I was still very much affected by my mother's death so I refused absolutely to sleep with him, which was pretty much contrary to the norm among young students; but we agreed he could come to Bogotá to meet my father and grandmother."

"The following year he came to Bogotá. He was twenty four, intelligent and well-educated. I was twenty-three and perhaps within a short time, we could consider marriage here. Or possibly even go to live in Aix-en-Provence or Bordeaux where his family had a pharmaceutical enterprise. His name was Jean-Pierre, same as his father, and his mother was Pierrette."

John had paid close attention to Virginia's story and carefully followed the developments in her life. He sighed, at the thought that she was no longer free, probably now married to her French fiancée. His feelings were contradictory and his mind was running in different directions.

Finally, he commented: "Virginia, I have followed everything you have said and I appreciate your frankness. Perhaps you should be home with your husband; I really don't mean to interfere with your lives."

She looked at him straight in the eyes, with an expression of concern, and then firmly stated: "John, my friend, don't misunderstand me: *I was never married*; *I don't have a husband.* Otherwise I wouldn't be here with you. I will explain that situation; but first let's take a short break. Let's finish our meal and listen to the guitars and the violin."

They continued eating silently. They slowly savored their glass of Malbec. The Concerto of Aranjuez was enthralling and hypnotic. She continued: "We were never married. It's a very long story." She paused.

Suddenly her eyes darkened and slowly grew somber. She clutched his hand. "Actually, John, I am really getting very tired. It has been a very emotional evening. Perhaps we should skip the visit to Monserrate tonight, as I must go to work early in the morning. I have an important project with Interpol. It's too bad you are leaving tomorrow for Villa de Leyva."

John reacted instinctively. "Please wait a minute, Virginia. While we were enjoying our dinner together, and I was listening to your story about your mother and your subsequent trip to La Sorbonne, I was actually thinking that I should not leave for Villa de Leyva until the day after tomorrow. As you say, there seems to be not enough time to continue our conversation." He stopped. She waited for his decision, while he glanced pensively at his hands.

Finally, he looked at Virginia's languorous eyes and resumed: "Listen, Virginia: it's all set. I have changed my plans for us. I've decided that I will definitely not leave tomorrow. I will depart the day *after* tomorrow. If you allow me to invite you tomorrow night, we could eat at Casa San Isidro which you say is a fine French restaurant at the top of Monserrate. We'll have so much more time to peacefully be together, and still enjoy the *luna llena*, that gorgeous full moon that has illuminated our blessed evening tonight."

Virginia gave John a grateful look and, squeezing his hand in hers, answered him: "That would really be wonderful. I agree with you. That's a perfect idea. I'll be able to finish my story and explain without rushing what happened with Jean-Pierre. It will be much better and we can get to know each other even better. I want you to know I am very comfortable and happy to be here with you." She smiled and again gently squeezed his hand. Her lips were like magic in the night, and John didn't hesitate. He had already made up his mind.

He would leave for Villa de Leyva the day after tomorrow. In the meantime he could do some work in the hotel room, maybe visit the National Museum and then have the enormous joy of seeing Virginia again in the evening.

He told her that it would a much better plan. They would be together once more. He would pick her up at Doña Carmen's house like today. Virginia agreed, and softly smiled.

Now it was late; the Aranjuez interlude was over. A flaming *Crema Catalana*, that special Barcelona custard with a burnt sugar top was served to conclude a delicious meal. They both ordered a *'tinto'* coffee and remained quiet for a few more moments, tenderly holding hands. The stories Virginia and John had told each other were intense and meaningful. They both had absorbed their intended powerful and evocative revelations. Virginia had a clear picture of John's very personal anguish and he had learned that Virginia had lost her mother through unexpected circumstances.

Perhaps most important of all, for their private relationship, John had learned she was not married now and in fact had never been married. He admitted to himself that he was enormously relieved to learn that after the Sorbonne interlude when Jean-Pierre had come to Colombia to perhaps finalize their relationship into a permanent liaison, there seemed to have been an interruption in Virginia's plans. He still didn't know what had happened. He was careful not to upset Virginia. But his heart had skipped a beat. Now it was calm again.

He would probably find out more details tomorrow evening. Surely she would explain the whole situation. But what about her father? She hadn't said a word about him. Perhaps he had left the family after the unexpected death of his wife, leaving Virginia all alone in the care of her grandmother Carmencita. Anyway, he was glad to postpone his trip by one day. His sentimental feelings were more important than scheduled travel times. He also insisted that Virginia and doña Carmen come visit him over the weekend as his guests at Villa de Leyva, when Virginia was officially not working. They all could have a few peaceful days together.

John asked for the check, told the waiter to alert his driver, and thanked again the Maître D'. Afterwards, when he saw Pedro, he informed him that tonight's plans were modified; they were not going to Monserrate until tomorrow night. There would still be a full moon.

Pedro would drive Dr. Osborne to Villa de Leyva the day after, and maybe pick-up Doña Carmen and Captain Cosmos over the week-end and drive them to Villa de Leyva as his guests, unless, of course, they preferred to use their own transportation. In any case, John would be there with Infinity von Braun.

They got into the car and drove back directly to the grandmother's house. The guards inspected the car with the metal detector, but recognizing the Captain, saluted and didn't ask the passengers or Pedro to get out. They called on the security phone and opened the gate. Once in the circular driveway, Dr. Osborne and Virginia got out by the garden entrance to the house. Pedro pulled the car a few yards away.

Leonora had arrived at the same time to open the front door. John escorted Virginia up to the main door. They both looked at the moon and gently kissed each other on the cheeks, Bogotano style, though he lingered a bit. They said good night. Virginia whispered: "Good night, my dear friend John, thank you so much for a wonderful evening; I'm so glad we have been together." "Good night, Captain Virginia, I am so deeply grateful for your company." Smiling, he added: "And your beautiful eyes. Until tomorrow." Leonora was patiently and politely waiting by the open door.

As they left the driveway and passed the gate, the two gate guards saluted Dr. Osborne formally. He replied with an informal and friendly wave, as he was not a military man.

Pedro drove him to the hotel. Without hesitating, Dr. Osborne asked him if he would enjoy being his guest for lunch tomorrow after his visit to the National Museum. He wanted to thank him for his help all day long. Pedro accepted Dr. Osborne's invitation – normally not extended to a driver – and suggested they could go to a rustic, unpretentious restaurant called Las Margaritas, not far from the National Museum.

As Dr. Osborne went up to his room, he looked forward to seeing his assistant Infinity. It had been a very emotional evening.

In the elevator he wondered: '*Where is Virginia's father?*' They had not mentioned him.

****

 *Chapter 11*

A Momentous Day

On the following day, after a peaceful breakfast downstairs in the hotel restaurant enjoying his favorite *huevos pericos* - scrambled eggs with chopped onions and tomatoes - Dr. Osborne stayed in his hotel room most of the morning, reviewing research documents, looking at the news, and keeping company to Infinity von Braun.

He took time to check his valuable laptop for any damage from the Candelaria incident. He noticed with relief that no harm had been done to it, except for a very minor scratch that would serve to remind him of the uncertainties of life in a colonial street at the most unexpected moment. He turned it on and was pleased to see how well his equipment had recorded and saved Infinity's performance at the Botero Museum in a special memory drive.

Then he was truly startled to also see a video of the attempted robbery attack on the street after lunch at Casa Vieja. He checked his laptop settings to find an explanation, but everything was normal. He concluded therefore that the only possible reason for that video having been accidentally filmed was that the on-off mechanism on his assistant's black collar had been activated while the laptop had fallen from the attacker's hands when Infinity had scratched and bitten him. It triggered the power and transmission function while it slid down to the pavement, fortunately without causing any damage or breakage to the screen.

Although imperfect, Dr. Osborne was still able to see the film taken through Infinity's cage opening. Although not always focused because of the on-going commotion, it had filmed the two thugs trying to escape before being cut down by the two trained security German shepherds, their arrest by FESCO Special Forces and the jeep sequence with the officer in charge. Dr. Osborne thought of showing both videos to Virginia, as she would be the only person that could be told about the confidential wireless communication between Infinity's black collar, her master's laptop and its subsequent memory drive. Then he briefly thought how lucky he and his companions had been to come out unhurt in that morning's episode.

He was to be picked up by Pedro at ten thirty and driven to the National Museum. On the way out of the hotel he went to see the Concierge in the lobby and asked him to make a special reservation for an early dinner at the Restaurante Casa San Isidro on Monserrate: like the night before, a table for two, beautiful, quiet, cozy and romantic. The Concierge assured Dr. Osborne he would get him an excellent table as he personally knew the manager, the maître d' and the sommelier. How was it the previous night at Casa Medina? Excellent? Wonderful. It would be equal or better tonight. He liked Dr. Osborne whom he found to be a truly honest genuine and *simpatico* gentleman, in spite of his renowned scientific reputation. He was not a show-off oligarch. The concierge got rewarded for his good thoughts. He got another good *propina* – the convoluting tip of necessity.

Dr. Osborne had learned from an English tourist book that at the National Museum he would be able to view indigenous archeological artifacts, Afro-Colombian art, miscellaneous cultural objects, and paintings by Fernando Botero, Alejandro Obregón and Guillermo Wiedermann. He had inquired who was the last artist and found out he was a Jewish artist persecuted by the Nazis- who had settled in Colombia. There were many Germans and Swiss who had moved and adopted Colombia as their permanent home. It had mountains like Europe.

The collections in three floors of the country's oldest museum span its history from the pre-Hispanic era. He found it interesting that the exhibitions were housed in a *British* designed building that dated back to 1823. At one time it was the city's main prison, made of old stones and bricks in a fortress-style architecture that included arches, domes and columns. It was shaped like a Greek cross. Until 1946 more than 100 prison cells built behind a solid exterior façade, still impressive today, were used for male and female prisoners. Then the building had been transformed into the present national museum.

Dr. Osborne spent a couple of hours meandering around undisturbed, playing the unusual role of being an average tourist and enjoying the museum's displays. Nobody recognized him in spite of the fact that his face was on the TV news showing the attempted robbery in the Calendaria section of town on the day before and the opportune FESCO intervention - rather than just the local national police- since it involved a well-known foreign scientist. His visit to the Museum had been a worthwhile cultural interruption of his normal intense research activities. While being busy observing the enlightening displays, he had also realized how much he missed Virginia's company. He whispered her name to himself.

At about one o'clock Pedro picked him up in front of the Museum. As previously agreed, they were going to have lunch together. Normally a client would not eat lunch with his driver; the chauffeur would go to some eatery by himself. But Dr. Osborne had made a direct and personal invitation which Pedro could not refuse – or rather, he figured he should accept it to avoid being rude to his amiable client, making an exception to his customary routine. Actually, Dr. Osborne wanted to reward Pedro for his superior and trustworthy professional standards.

Pedro had suggested the Restaurante *Las Mar-*

garitas on Calle 62 with Carrera *Séptima* – Seventh Avenue - a family-operated eating place which had been in uninterrupted operation since 1902. It was considered to be the oldest restaurant in Bogotá. It had started with the sale of *empanadas* or traditional small meat or chicken fried pies or turnovers to the ladies of Chapinero in Santa Fe de Bogotá when they came out of Mass on Sunday morning. Originally, it was called Las Marias de Sal, but this name was changed to honor the original owner: Margarita.

Since Pedro knew Dr. Osborne had a Swiss-English background he had also suggested a Swiss restaurant like the *Divino Swiss Home* on Calle 70, if that would please him more. It was a small place with a good reputation if you were looking for a European restaurant. Or perhaps Dr. Osborne would rather go there alone with Capitán Virginia? He explained to Dr. Osborne that *divino* was not a religious metaphor. In Bogotá the word *divino* – which does mean divine – was used as an exclamation of something wonderful and positive that would be most welcome: '¡*Ay, es divino!* – it's wonderful!' Dr. Osborne had even commented then that if they went there, he would treat Pedro to a *cheese fondue* – had Pedro ever had one? No? That would be fine; he would enjoy it for sure. It was prepared in a special Swiss communal casserole of cheese and white wine, heated over a small flame, and eaten by dipping bread in the pot using long-stemmed forks to pick the bread cubes.

However, after visiting the National Museum Dr. Osborne had thought that the first recommendation – Las Margaritas Restaurant - would be better and less complicated for lunch. Of course Dr. Osborne was continuously thinking of Virginia. He could hardly wait until that evening when he would see her again. They had a dinner engagement; but in the meantime a distracting luncheon would make time go by faster. Besides, that way he could practice with indigenous fare and get to know more native dishes. He would be eating only local foods for the next several days.

Pedro was a special individual and Dr. Osborne had become rather fond of the young man. He was punctual, pleasant, professional and quite well educated for a driver. Dr. Osborne was aware that Pedro had studied one year at the University of Los Andes; why did he stop? What was wrong with his hand? What had happened? That had awakened the Dr.'s curiosity. He told Pedro he was very glad he had accepted his luncheon invitation as he wanted to show him he appreciated his responsible and proficient company. It was actually like a reward for all his attentiveness and dedication to the Dr.'s activities.

The restaurant was simple, rustic and inviting. After they had settled down and ordered a local beer and an appetizing combination platter of *papa, carne y arroz* – potatoes, meat and rice - the three basic staples of Colombian food, Dr. Osborne asked Pedro if he could ask him a few personal questions. Would he mind? He explained it was not out of morbid curiosity but rather as an expression of intellectual interest in his background and career.

"No, sir, that would be all right."

Dr. Osborne had already been considering an idea that had crossed his mind the evening before when he was with Virginia: if he ever moved to Bogotá and set up The Osborne Research Center, perhaps Pedro could be one of its staff members.

"Pedro, you told me that at one time you were studying Law at Universidad de Los Andes. You said that was before your family -your parents and you - were kidnapped by FARC and their drug cartel partners. Did I understand you correctly?"

"Yes, Dr. Osborne."

"Did you learn your English at Los Andes University?"

"Partly, sir; and also at home with Mr. William Crown, a private tutor from the Colegio Americano in Bogotá,."

"That's splendid."

"Plus my parents, with help from the International Rotary Club, sent me for three months to England as an Exchange Student to improve my language skills."

"That's fantastic! What a smart thing to do: God bless them. No wonder you speak so well!"

"I will always be grateful to my parents for their help." He paused. "But now my father is no longer with me."

"Oh, Pedro! What happened to your dad?"

"Those FARC murderers took him from me forever. I hate them and despise them. They claimed they were helping the poor and the country and instead enriched themselves with drugs, gold, politics, girls and corruption."

"Pedro, you don't have to talk about them if it is too painful for you." He paused again for a short while.

"I really don't mind talking about them with you, Dr, Osborne."

"Then, Pedro, tell me what happened."

They stopped for another pause. After a quick, friendly toast -*salud,* to your health – Pedro spoke slowly, relating his story:

"My parents had a small country farm, really more like a modest finca – a country home not far from Bogotá, near the town of Facatativá, where they grew anthurium flowers and roses. It's a good area with the right cool climate for growing flowers. They sold them regularly to a Bogota exporter who shipped them mostly to Florida. My father and mother were not what you would call affluent people by wealthy Colombian standards, but they managed quite well."

"One day, a couple of years ago, after I had finished my second semester at Universidad de los Andes, my parents decided they wanted to visit my aunt Marta who is my mother's sister and lives near Medellín, to celebrate her fifty-fifth birthday. However, we had a serious problem: My father refused absolutely to drive our family car and my mother would not fly under any circumstances – so the only alternative left was to go by bus. It was considered a safe enough choice, in spite of occasional news on television and newspapers about FARC attacks."

"Please continue, Pedro; I am listening attentively." said Dr. Osborne.

"I'll try to make it as brief and quick as possible." He paused and then continued: "On the specific day of our trip, we took a scheduled bus leaving early from Bogotá to go to Medellin. The long distance buses are actually quite comfortable. We were told there was a new highway, at least part of the way and that the old road had been improved. It should take us only approximately eight hours. Of course, Dr. Osborne, you must keep in mind the distance is only about 450 kilometers or 250 miles, but it's full of curvy roads and up and down mountains."

"Anyway, about halfway to Medellin, in a relatively quiet wooded area without much traffic, the bus was suddenly ambushed. The driver was forced to stop. A truck had passed us and halted right in front of the bus. A group of hooded criminal guerrillas got out, armed to their teeth, and opened the bus doors. All passengers were told to 'get out, quickly' and not to resist. The assailants asked for everybody's identification card, name and home address. Doctor, you can imagine how quickly one moves when you are staring at the menacing nozzle of a machine gun! They pulled out several laptop computers and entered all the information therein, to determine which passengers were good candidates for ransom; I mean which ones looked like good potential victims for obtaining higher ransom money."

"To the few cars going by it must have looked like the bus had broken down, something not unusual, and the truck was helping to fix it. Besides, if anyone realized it was a kidnap situation they definitely would not want to get involved. On the contrary, they certainly would continue faster on their trip and even accelerate. They knew it would take the police at least forty-five minutes or more to arrive on the scene.

After a relatively short lapse of time, perhaps only twenty minutes which seemed like one hundred years while the guerrilla did their homework by the side of the road and gathered the desired financial information, they reloaded about two-thirds of the passengers into the bus and ordered the driver to take out the bags and get going, quick, *rápido,* fast, take off and don't look back or we shoot you, all the while pointing their machine guns at him and the frightened passengers."

"The remaining people, which included my parents and I were blindfolded roughly and both hands tied behind our backs. Subsequently we were loaded, pushed and shoved in the rear of the truck which had the side tarpaulins down and only enough room in the center between coffee bags for the kidnapped victims. We were being taken God knows where; women and children were crying and asking for *piedad, señores* –pity, please, don't hurt us."

Pedro took a breather. He and Dr. Osborne forced themselves to eat some food and sip some beer. He continued:

"After a couple of hours driving us blindfolded we finally stopped again. We were in the middle of nowhere, in a forest, nothing around us except for a miserable camp with a couple of campaign tents where they pushed us in, took our blindfolds off, freed our tied hands and gave us a speech about not trying to escape, as we would be shot on the spot. They stated they wanted to keep us alive, of course, so they could collect their programmed ransoms, one of their means of support besides trafficking in drugs, illegal gold mining, prostitution and other criminal activities."

Dr. Osborne reacted, upset and concerned. A picture of Madeleine quickly crossed his mind. "Please continue, Pedro, this is a terrible story."

"My parents' family was unable to get the ransom money. We were kept captive in the same tent for about three months. When we went to the bathroom - an outside latrine - we were always surrounded by soldiers."

"My mother was 'asked' to help in the kitchen, unless she preferred to be raped and abused; my father was taken at gun point to work in the fields;

and I was forced to chop wood and keep the cocaine laboratory fires going."

"That's awful, Pedro! I'm so sorry you had to go through that ordeal." said Dr. Osborne.

"I was also forced to work operating a *fique* shredder, to shred *agave* leaves. They assigned *Luisita*, a young peasant girl to help me by passing the cut fique leaves to me which I would then insert into the rudimentary shredder. On one occasion when the armed guard was rushing and jostling me, I fell down and slipped because I was very tired from lack of food and sleep. Unfortunately, as I slid forward my right hand got caught in the machine. The thickness of the plant leaves was the only thing which helped to protect my arm. I screamed so loud. It was terribly painful. The young *campesina* Luisita reacted quickly and helped me, gracias a Dios, God bless her. She actually saved my hand by stopping the machine and pulling me and my arm back. The armed guard had actually turned around; he couldn't watch. It was too much for him. He was only a young boy, maybe fourteen or just fifteen; even if he had a rifle, he was just a child, *un niño*."

He continued: "Maybe you didn't know, Dr. Osborne, that the FARC guerrilla criminal organization would recruit poor young children, promising them food and shelter and even education, for the purpose of turning them into future soldiers, brainwashing them into believing the FARC guerrilla mission of overthrowing the legitimate government was good for the country and they were training them to become vicious guerrilla fighters to get rid of the corrupt government. That's just like the Nazi Youth groups or perhaps worse, because in Colombia they were also playing with drugs."

"You asked me a question about my hand. That's how it got messed up; to this day it's painful and deformed. It's also embarrassing. I have never recovered its full use." He lifted his arm and showed his hand to Dr. Osborne, who winced instinctively.

Dr. Osborne had been listening attentively and was greatly saddened by Pedro's story. He said: "Pedro, how did you manage to be freed? How did you and your parents escape? Did they finally manage to pay a ransom?"

"Dr. Osborne, it seems implausible, almost unbelievable; it was like a miracle, though a sad one. We had been in that jungle-like camp close to three months. My dad had not been able to obtain the money for the ransom; besides, it was illegal to cooperate with the guerrillas. One day, my friend the young *campesina* Luisita who was my helper whispered to me there was a rumor among the peasants, the *campesinos*, that the regular Army was nearby and they were probably going to attack the camp to liberate us. I told that to my parents, but they wouldn't believe it. It seemed impossible."

"The next day, at about four in the morning, there were screams in the air and firing of machine guns. There were Army soldiers giving orders, running around and creating complete confusion among the FARC operatives. It lasted maybe twenty minutes. When it was over, several *guerrilleros* – guerrilla fighters - were lying dead; but most of the camp had escaped. They had taken my dad and a few other prisoners with them. My boy-soldier guard was one of the victims. It was a pathetic sight, all bloodied on the ground." He paused; and then went on: "To this day I have no idea what happened to my father or the other people."

"My mother was shaken but unharmed. The young campesina Luisita was safe but terrified, crying her heart out. She came to my mother's side looking for protection and huddling for comfort. She didn't know where her parents were; she couldn't locate them anywhere. My mother helped her, even though she herself had gotten very thin and lost weight. I thought she had caught tuberculosis over the past few weeks as she was always coughing. Perhaps she was sick with pneumonia. I was praying to God she would not die. When the whole military operation was over, they took us – my *mamá,* the young girl Luisita and me to some sort of military hospital where they checked us over. They took x-rays of my hand, but couldn't treat it. They said someday I would need extensive surgery in a regular hospital in Bogotá. Eventually, after a couple of days the Army sent us back to our home."

"There was no trace of my dad; the Army officer in charge said they would notify us if they found or heard anything. To this date, there hasn't been any news." He stopped. "That, Dr. Osborne, is my family story. Sad and depressing!" He wiped away a few painful tears that were rolling down his cheeks.

Dr. Osborne remained silent for quite some time. The beer and food didn't seem too appetizing anymore; but gradually Pedro grew calmer. He interrupted the melancholy situation and said: "Thank goodness, Dr. Osborne, my mother is much better now and the young girl Luisita helps her at home. I have sort of gotten used to the situation. And I sincerely appreciate your kindness and paternal interest in me and my family."

"Now it's time to put these things out of our minds, we cannot change them; let's finish our lunch. Don't forget you have a wonderful evening ahead for you and Captain Cosmos." He smiled.

Dr. Osborne looked at Pedro. He thought for awhile, and then stated: "Pedro, you may be only my driver but you are a very exemplary human being and a strong young man. Who knows if in the future your circumstances may change and your position could be different? Make sure you keep in touch with me." He didn't say anything further. He was just planting future seeds. There was a lot of uncertainty in the air. Virginia was the most complex situation in the universe.

Although not too enthused anymore, they finished their lunch and beer. They sat quietly for a long while. Dr. Osborne was pensive. Suddenly he heard like a firecracker in the distance and saw a picture of his beloved Madeleine laying down on the ground, shot in the head, in some God forsaken country in Africa. The cruel image crossed his mind. He vividly sensed her fear and suffering during the last minutes of life in her ungrateful African mission.

Calmly, he paid the check, still meditating over the events which Pedro had described during their rather intense lunch. After they got back to the car, Pedro started it silently, and slowly drove Dr. Osborne back to the hotel. As he dropped him off, he automatically reminded him he would pick him up around five o'clock to drive him to Doña Carmen de Jaramillo's house to pick up Captain Cosmos for dinner.

He also suggested Dr. Osborne contact the Concierge at the hotel, to reserve a table at *Restaurante Casa San Isidro* at the top of Monserrate. It usually was quite crowded, as it had an excellent reputation for quality and service, complementing the extraordinary view of the city below, especially on a romantic moonlit evening like tonight.

Dr. Osborne thanked him for his care and suggestion, and told him he had done just that in the morning before going to the National Museum. Pedro respectfully smiled and said: "With all due respect, Dr. Osborne, while I was in England a professor taught me that two heads are always better than one; especially, as my teacher said, *if one of them is from an Englishman.*"

****

 *Chapter 12*

Full Moon over the City

Dr. Osborne was glad to get back to his hotel room and check on Infinity von Braun. She was used to being alone and behaved accordingly, but she always was happy when he got back home. It was almost as if she sensed the concern he had for her, and she reciprocated by being a soft, intelligent and affectionate feline. She had been trained since birth and she was without a doubt Dr. Osborne's favorite assistant in his laboratory and companion in his travels. Perhaps that could change in the not too distant future.

He had thought about taking her to Virginia's grandmother's house that evening but then it occurred to him that such an idea would complicate matters, as he would have to bring her back to the hotel after leaving Doña Carmen for his dinner engagement with Virginia. On the other hand, leaving Infinity with Doña Carmen for the evening might not be wise, as the gentle but independent cat preferred her own familiar surroundings unless she was on a research mission. Besides, what about if Virginia's father showed up at Doña Carmen's house? No, even if he loved Infinity, he was convinced it would not be very practical.

He rested quietly, going in his mind over Pedro's dangerous adventure. He was thankful that the young man's mother was better and Luisita, who seemed like a smart young girl, was now helping her. Who knew if in time Pedro might not become sentimentally attached to that young girl? There might be a problem, though; would they be considered 'socially compatible?' After all, Luisita was a campesina, a modest creature from the fields, even if she had saved Pedro from a worse fate during his calamity at the agave shredder.

Pedro now had a very serious problem with his incapacitated hand; it would need to be operated someday. That would probably cost a lot of money. Besides, he still had to finish his university studies, if at all possible, before he could get a decent job in a first-class firm. Only time would tell what his future would be with or without Luisita.

Dr. Osborne thought he could have fallen asleep for a short while, because an hour had gone by when he next looked at the clock on the night table. He thought that wouldn't be surprising after such a long trip from overseas, the high altitude of this huge metropolitan city, the dangerous robbery attempt in La Calendaria and especially the emotional feelings pervading his heart; that sentimental journey which floated all the time in his mind.

Now it was almost time to get ready; except that at that precise moment, a flash of light had crossed his mind. Forming gently and unexpectedly, he saw again the undefined image he had previously perceived in similar occasions in the past: the background screen became the picture of a whirling white skirt which sensuously exposed a silky tempting thigh; but then, just as promptly, it had banished. There remained only a grey blank left in his psyche. As before, he couldn't quite figure why such an image should burst forth in his intellect. Unfortunately or for the better, it seemed he had no other choice but to forget about it.

Presently, Dr. Osborne's thoughts were completely different. He was looking forward to another delightful evening with Captain Cosmos. He knew she would not be wearing the uniform of her FESCO Intelligence organization. Tonight, like the previous evening, was not a mandatory occasion that required Virginia to carry out a difficult or even dangerous mission. It was just the continuation of what was becoming a tender interlude which he wished would never end, as he was thoroughly enjoying it; and Virginia too, seemed to be warmly partaking in it.

Once he was ready, he fixed Infinity's area and food for the evening. The smart cat probably was thinking, in her cognitive experience, if my owner goes out with a beautiful companion, the least he can do for me is to leave me happy and settled for the evening. I bet he will also put on some music for me; which is exactly what Dr. Osborne did. Plus he alerted the floor room service attendant that Infinity was alone in his room: 'Please check on her once in a while. Thank you.' He left her a nice *propina* again. Out of habit and professional experience he also locked the laptop in the safe, where his passport was protected and secure.

At precisely five o'clock the room phone rang by the bed, breaking the silence and almost startling John. Pedro had arrived and was waiting downstairs. "I'll be down right away." His heart skipped a beat. He almost felt Virginia's presence in the air. He said goodbye to Infinity, patted her soft head and closed the room door.

He bought a small blooming flower plant for the grandmother as he passed the hotel store downstairs, said hello to the serviceable concierge, greeted his driver Pedro, and off they went to see Doña Carmen and her granddaughter.

When they reached the Jaramillo property gate, Dr. Osborne knew the routine with the armed guards and prepared to get out; but they recognized him from the night before and signaled for him and Pedro to stay in the vehicle. They were expected. However, the guards did the explosives search under the car and around it with the sensitive metal detector, as this was mandatory. Cleared after inspection, they called the kitchen on the inside phone, opened the heavy wooden gate into the private driveway, waved Pedro in and saluted Dr. Osborne. John greeted them properly and gave a short courteous smile.

As John turned his head, he noticed from the corner of his eye the small escort car from the previous night, parked not far from the entrance and reflected in the moonlight. It was ready to accompany them later on their journey to Monserrate. John thought: 'What a pain in the neck; is this really necessary? Maybe someday I will understand all this extra security better.'

Pedro drove around the courtyard circle by the illuminated fountain, parked in front of the main door as usual, and almost cheerfully – or so it seemed to Dr. Osborne after the earlier serious episode at lunch – opened the car door for him and said: "*Hasta luego,* Dr. Osborne." 'Until later, Dr. Osborne,' when he and his guest Señorita Virginia Cosmos would come out to go to dinner at the Casa San Isidro Restaurant.

The moon was rising in the horizon over the house roof. It brightened the gardens with a soft ethereal glow. Dr. Osborne was fully aware of the visual enchantment around him as he stepped on the front portico where Leonora had come out to receive him. She waved at Pedro, who returned the greeting and automatically started to walk toward the kitchen entrance using the back way. Leonora entered the house and escorted Dr. Osborne to where Virginia was waiting for him by the side of her grandmother *Carmencita*.

He had to hold his breath. There she was, Virginia Cosmos, his FESCO captain, dreamlike in a beautiful midnight blue dress, slinky and elegant, with two thin white stripes in the front running the length of the dress, past a short, elegant, but oh! so sensuous and enticing slit which discreetly showed a couple of inches of her leg above her knee. She was smiling at him, with a devastating exquisite expression of pleasure, control and anticipation. His heart was thumping. Her smile alone would take down the mightiest walls of a fortress. It penetrated like a tornado deep into his spirit and for a few seconds left him speechless. He quickly reacted, however. He went over to her and greeted her with the customary *abrazo* – the Bogotano embrace – and a gentle kiss on the cheek – maybe staying a moment or two longer than necessary. Then he greeted Doña Carmen, who remained seated and received him cordially and almost affectionately. After all, wasn't he aiming for her granddaughter's happiness?

The wooden logs were burning on the hearth. The decorative hand-cut stones around the fireplace reflected softly but evenly the reverberation of the friendly flames. Carmen and Virginia asked John to sit down. Would he enjoy a cup of tea or would he prefer a whiskey with water or soda or on the rocks, the usual Bogotano social custom?

They talked about the previous night and the

enchantment of Los Jardines de Aranjuez. During their honeymoon Carmen and her husband el Comandante Jaramillo had visited the Royal Palace of Aranjuez and impressive grounds in Spain, 50km south of Madrid, started in the 16th century, finished two centuries later. It is now open as a public legacy to the Spanish people. At one time only the nobility was allowed to travel to those areas. "Can you imagine that, Dr. Osborne? The rest of the people were not good enough. Spanish nobility was a display of irrepressible oligarchy. What right did they have to talk about Colombian oligarchs?"

She glanced subtly at the extraordinary painting of her beloved husband and she, imposingly hanging on the wall. They respected their country, their environment, their social status and the populace that had to struggle daily for their living and education. She said: "Our responsibility as educated members of the wealthy social class is to respect every single human being, and value every person irrespective of their social standing."

It all made so much more sense to John tonight. He couldn't stop looking at Virginia and her simple but imposing demeanor. A flattering thought crossed his mind and he couldn't resist saying it aloud: "Virginia, may I say what I am thinking?" She hesitated one second and said: "Please do, John." He proceeded: "To me, you are more enchanting, beautiful and charming than all the Kings and Queens of Spain and their glorious royal palaces like Aranjuez." Virginia blushed slightly, and flashed John an appreciative thank you smile while Doña Carmen broke into a proud and maternal sign of affectionate approval.

During their conversation Dr. Osborne commented, among many other things, about the sad story he had heard the night before in relation to Virginia's mother and the unforgiving sickness that took her at a relatively young age. They all exchanged thoughts and philosophical ideas about life, death and even Christ's necessary resurrection, based entirely on loving your neighbor. Dr. Osborne also mentioned his wife Madeleine's cruel suffering in Africa while accomplishing a humanitarian task. Is this what the world expected from people serving humankind? To be executed?

They got into a more serious philosophical but friendly discussion. John said: "What kind of retribution is that, when you are applying the Lord's commandments of Love, following the Christian Bible, respecting the Moslem Qur'an, abiding by the Jewish prophet Abraham or obeying the Muslim prophet Muhammad? Were their teachings perhaps too complex and maybe set up too many multidirectional rules?"

Dr. Osborne further commented: "Some scholars pointed out that Muhammad had led 27 military campaigns against innocent villages and caravans, and planned 38 more. Apparently he was following the Islamic Hadith teachings that say: 'I am the prophet that laughs when killing my enemies.'"

John then pointed out that, on the other hand, Christians and Jewish martyrs say: '*I will die for what I believe,*' while a Muslim martyr has the opposite philosophy: '*I will make you die for what I believe.*' "So how can there be peace on earth with such radical differences?"

"Look at your own beautiful country of Colombia, fighting FARC, FLN and other guerrillas and paramilitary groups for more than half a century. This struggle and other political conflicts have killed approximately a quarter or perhaps a half a million people. Is that necessary to achieve progress, harmony, peace and economic development? I'm afraid, Virginia and Doña Carmen, that we have a very long way to go."

There was silence. Grandmother Carmen remained serene for a moment, but eventually assented. Virginia also agreed, but had a pensive air about her.

After a while, Virginia eventually broke the silence, saying: "We cannot solve in one night all the world's problems. So, John and I better get going to enjoy our dinner. Carmencita dear, do you want to come along? Or are you too tired?"

Abuelita Carmen answered: "Another time, *mijita*. I think it's much better if the two of you go out alone to enjoy each other's company." John looked inquisitively at Virginia.

Virginia explained to John that *mijita* was a diminutive for daughter; like 'my little daughter.' She continued: "Very well, Carmencita; then we will go now to our dinner because John has a reservation. We'll take a rain check. John invited us to Villa de Leyva for the weekend. We'll have a nice dinner there during our little trip, all right? You'll finally get to meet Infinity von Braun when we are there." Doña Carmen agreed. She rang her little golden bell. Leonora appeared, always as if by magic, almost like a Pavlov's reflex.

She was told to 'please go fetch a black overcoat for Virginia' and was instructed to 'advise Pedro that *la señorita Virginia* and *el profesor Dr. Osborne* were ready to leave; please tell Pedro to get the car ready. Thank you.' John realized she was used to giving orders.

Virginia stood up, kissed her grandmother goodbye and put on her black coat with help from Dr. Osborne. As he stood behind her helping to put her coat on, he perceived the fragrance of her hair and whispered: "Virginia, you are so beautiful and your perfume is hypnotizing." She answered: "John, you are flirting with me all the time; but do not stop. I'm flattered and I enjoy it." She reached for her purse which contained her obligatory weapon, and carefully put it around her shoulders. Life's reality must always interrupt dreams.

They left Grandmother Carmen comfortably ensconced in her leather armchair, waving good bye and smiling very contentedly at the young couple. Earlier she had learned that Dr. Osborne was only 35, definitely unmarried, actually a widower, highly educated, economically on solid ground and therefore a most acceptable candidate for her 27 year old single granddaughter. Perhaps Destiny would bring them together while she, the surrogate mother, was relatively young. That would be a blessing she had been wishing for a long time, after so many painful events in her life.

The lucid and round moon was out in full glory like the previous evening. The weather was cool and calm. The night air was clean and refreshing and the clear visibility made it possible to see the Sanctuary Church on the peak of Monserrate mountain from the far away El Norte area - the northern section of the city. One could easily distinguish the famous steeple and symbolic lighted place of worship from a long distance; that was not always the case. It was an especially beautiful night.

Pedro drove in respectful silence. It was a pleasant unrushed trip in the moonlight to the base of Monserrate. There was not much traffic. Dr. Osborne and Pedro, and surely Capitan Virginia, noticed that the official escort vehicle followed at a safe inconspicuous distance.

John had gently taken Virginia's hand into his own and occasionally caressed it gently and affectionately. Her hand was pliable and warm. John felt almost overwhelmed by a sweeping feeling of tenderness toward his companion. Was this really happening? It had been such a long time since he had felt this kind of affection invading his heart. What about

Virginia? She seemed to feel likewise, comfortable and relaxed by his side.

Could he really be falling in love? He had forgotten what it felt like. Could she also feel the same way? What about Jean-Pierre, her boyfriend. Where was he? Why wasn't Virginia married? And where was her father? Would he object? Where were they? What was going on? He reflected on these matters, and expected to ask her all those questions once they were settled at their table at the restaurant. He felt a bit anxious; he didn't want to lose this extraordinary person, this alluring woman. There were many female individuals in his professional world; but he hadn't felt attracted like this to anyone since Madeleine's tragedy. In fact, he realized without vacillation that he really hadn't met anyone like Virginia.

Virginia had reminded Pedro of the presence of the unobtrusive escort car. He had taken due note, so as to avoid losing it. Fortunately, the moon was shining brightly and the luminosity was clear; Pedro could check occasionally through the rear and side mirrors.

They would need to take the cable car to the the top of the mountain to reach the Restaurante Casa San Isidro. Fortunately, there was not a great amount of people milling around when they got to the base of Monserrate where the cable car and the funicular departed for the trip up to the Sanctuary. It was just as well there were not many tourists; it was safer and more relaxing. The funicular was not running at that time of night.

The escort car had parked unobtrusively. The two occupants, not in uniform, had stepped out discreetly, and walked toward the ticket area pretending to be waiting for a trip. Virginia acknowledged their presence in a very succinct manner, inclining her head and giving the undercover individuals an almost imperceptible smile. They were wearing a black jacket and pants that made them practically indiscernible in the crowd.

Pedro had dropped his two clients off and safely parked the car. The escort vehicle was also all set. Virginia and John had their tickets for the next cable car. They were fortunate as they didn't have to wait long: the system ran every half hour.

They stood close to the front window of the cabin to enjoy a good panoramic view of the city as they went up over the trees. The moon shone over the lighted capital as they moved smoothly suspended from a steel cable that in fifteen minutes brought them to their destination. One could feel as if standing on the top of an Alpine resort but without any snow. The only other alternative was the funicular which was not running at that hour of night. Dr. Osborne had read in his room, that it had been built between 1926 and 1929 by Lowis von Roll, a Swiss company. It was inaugurated in August 1929 and could carry 80 people. The cable car system they were traveling in was inaugurated in September 1955. It had two cabins with capacity for 40 people.

Virginia looked very serene and satisfied. She glanced at John a couple of times to give him her magical smile and her penetrating clear look. Every time she did that he felt a magnetizing sensation within his chest.

When they stepped out of the large cable car, Virginia held on to John's hand. "I haven't been up here in a long time. I'm glad we are together, John,"

"You have no idea, Virginia, how delighted I am. Are your sure this is not a dream?"

"You're as real as this mountain, John." She gave him a disarming smile, and she squeezed his hand.

He asked Virginia if she was cold, as they were considerably higher than Bogotá, and she replied negatively. She brought her coat closer around her to feel warmer and said: "John, let's walk quickly to the church even though the building is already closed for the night. I know the young sacristan. He is waiting for us as I called him earlier to do me the favor of opening the church for ten minutes. Let's hurry. I want you to see it with me, and I want to say a special prayer."

She explained to John that she had met the young man at the FESCO headquarters, when he was a witness during an investigation of robberies by foreign tourists and local visitors of the modest '*Charity Box for the Poor*' placed at the rear of the church. "Can you imagine that, John? People stealing from the modest charity box for the poor? *Para los pobres?*"

The young sexton was indeed waiting for them. He greeted Captain Cosmos and John, and locked the door again as soon as they were inside the building. Once within the church they walked to the front, and knelt down by the communion rail facing the main altar. They prayed silently for a few minutes, each one asking for their private needs. Were they perhaps searching for a mutual love destiny in the future?

Afterwards, as they strode back toward the main door, John looked at the side altars, the white walls and a few old paintings. He thanked the sacristan and gave him a small donation which the young man much appreciated. Virginia thanked the young fellow again for the big favor of opening the doors so they could visit the church. He said good bye to Captain Cosmos and Dr. Osborne, and locked the doors behind them.

When they stepped out, the moonlight hit them in its full splendor. They were going to the restaurant but took a slight detour to look at the magnificent sight of Bogotá, spread in all its glory from South to North and East to West, with a cluster of high skyscrapers in the center, and avenues and cross streets creating an extraterrestrial electric puzzle. It was a celestial scenery.

The moon was so close you could caress it. They walked in silence gazing at the enticing panorama before they stopped to look at the magical view while standing by the edge of the curving path. Virginia turned her face toward her escort, and gently closed her eyes. Her long lashes covered her usually sharp and clear pupils while she stood immobile in front of John. He was attracted to her like a heavenly magnet to another cosmic body. He felt like a hypnotized honeybee from outer space, reaching a multicolored open flower to taste her precious nectar, to inhale her womanly scent. Then he gradually inched his mouth closer to hers. Her lips were softened by the moon rays and their reflection attracted him even more. Finally, his lips softly touched hers. She didn't move. She tenderly but firmly put her hand behind his neck to hold him close to her. It was a passionate clasp which sealed their fates.

They remained locked and warmly glued like that for a long time, as if their feelings were being cemented into an eternal embrace. Virginia finally opened her lids very tenderly, looked at John, and disconnected the clinch while saying: "I know I could *really* like you, John Osborne; even love you." He was so taken by the whole momentous exchange that it took him a minute to react.

"It's a mutual feeling, Virginia. I'm afraid I have already fallen in love with you. I cannot backtrack. And I don't want to."

He held her in his arms until she finally said: "John, we have to go to the restaurant now, as I'm sure they're waiting for us. You said the reservation was for eight o'clock.'" And she rewarded him with one of her disarming smiles.

They looked back at the Church bathed in the

moonlight. At that precise moment, the spire bells of the Sanctuary of the Fallen Christ began to ring; one, two, three, up to eight intense and crystalline strokes which, in the silence of the night, reverberated above the trees, seemingly all the way up to the stars and down the mountain to the precious glow of the myriad lights of the city below. It was difficult to conceive that the bright light from the moon was actually the sun reflected by the moon's naked surface.

They walked silently hand in hand like first-time school children going to class, and reached Casa San Isidro only five minutes away. John turned Virginia's face toward him, looked straight into her eyes with his piercing and intelligent gaze, smiled warmly and said: "I want so much to talk to you because I care a lot about you. Let's go have a good dinner."

The maître D' was pleased to see them. He was expecting them; the reservation was in order. He escorted the couple to what he said was the best table in Casa San Isidro, overlooking the entire city of Bogotá with its gigantic multitude of lights blinking in the *Sabana* Valley. He expected, of course, a small pecuniary reward for his professional performance.

After they got settled, they carefully studied the menu and followed the Chef's suggestion. A very accommodating and obviously experienced head waiter recommended the special *Sole de Pompadour,* the Chef's *fish creation* of the evening. It was named somehow after Madame La Marquise de Pompadour. Surely the nice waiter had no idea who she was. Neither did the fish; but John and Virginia did.

The server then signaled the Sommelier, who came over and greeted the guests in a friendly, impeccable and slightly snobbish *style français*. Since it was a French restaurant, he recommended a vintage Pouilly-Fuissé with their *fantastique* fish selection. That was a good choice, as John was very fond of Pouilly-Fuissé. His mother and godfather had introduced him to its perkiness when they celebrated his eighteenth birthday at the renowned restaurant of La Tour d'Argent in Paris.

John and Virginia were not sure if they could finish this choice selection; if not, the staff would do it for them. A full bottle might be too large for them. The Sommelier agreed, of course. Besides, John told him he would get a nice *propina*.

When he left, Virginia remarked to John how amazing it was, that such extra contributions like *tips, propinas, pourboires, Trinkgeld* and the like, make the world go around, although the difference between gratitude and corruption is very thin in government and business circles. John smiled and agreed. It was a concise and pertinent observation.

They commented leisurely on the beautiful ride up the cable car, the special church visit, the enchanting moonlight, the mesmerizing ringing of the Church's bells in the night air, and especially – very special, indeed - the private magic moment of their delicate kiss. He could still feel the softness of her lips under the hypnotizing moonlight. They were very much at ease with each other, in their own romantic orbit.

John decided this was the moment to ask those few questions which he had been harboring in his head. He still couldn't figure out certain answers or make head or tail of unknown situations.

"Virginia, can you please tell me more details about Jean-Pierre? For a while yesterday I thought you would have married him when he came to see you in Bogotá after your stay in Paris studying at the Sorbonne."

He paused and added: "And what about your dad, Mr. Cosmos,? I've noticed you never mention him or talk about him, not even at your grandmother's house. Does it upset you to tell me about him? Would you prefer that we don't discuss that part of your family? I've been wondering all this time what may be the real story behind your silence. Am I being too forward or impolite in asking for details? I have such deep feelings for you that I need to know you better to understand more completely your mindset. We need to be always on the same friendly wavelength, don't you agree, Virginia, *mi futuro amor*?"

Did she mind his intimacy? He immediately paused and took a sip of his white wine, while looking at her. He loved her sincere magical eyes, her enticing lips, her delicate face, her magnetizing personality. She didn't quiver negatively. Instead, she fixed her penetrating eyes on him for a couple of minutes before answering in a slightly tremulous voice: "*Sí, mi futuro amor,"* she punctuated slowly, looking back at him,

"John, it's all rather complicated. That's why I haven't given you many more details about my father and Jean-Pierre. Actually, it's very painful and it hurts me to dwell on them. Perhaps not on them as individual human beings, but rather on the circumstances surrounding their lives. However, I agree you need to know certain details if we are to have a long and meaningful relationship; especially since I feel we both are falling in love."

John acquiesced by slightly moving his head and looking at her. He gently squeezed her hand.

****

Chapter 13

Tête-à-Tête in Casa San Isidro

"John, dear Dr. Osborne, let me tell you the whole story. First, I'll talk about my friend Jean-Pierre; and then about my father, an Army officer of high rank, Brigadier General Jaramillo Cosmos. That is the next grade above Colonel, but below a full Major General. You met my uncle, Colonel Roberto Jaramillo at the airport. He is my father Rogelio's brother."

John was surprised and somewhat confused: "Jaramillo? And not Cosmos? I thought your last name - your family name - was Cosmos, and not Jaramillo; now you say Jaramillo should be your family name after your father and uncle. I am somewhat confused. Can you please tell me what is the relationship here? Virginia, dearest, can you explain it a little more?"

Virginia went on: "John, as I said before, it's a complex story. You have to listen to all of it before you can really understand." She gave him a gentle smile, but he noticed a sad cloud in her usually bright and crystalline eyes.

"Let me start first with Jean-Pierre, to explain that situation. His family name was Durand. He was French. We would probably have gotten married but for many circumstances that didn't let that happen, and that I'll tell you shortly. We had a decent relationship and we were in love, the standard love that leads to marriage. I was not passionately in love. To fall keenly in love with someone would be very exceptional for me, as that means giving your entire self and perhaps even your soul to another person. That would be a very unique and rare occurrence in my case. It hasn't really happened yet; but it is possible, John, if the right knight appears on his white horse." She paused for a few seconds, and faintly smiled. "We seem to be going in that direction."

"All in all, Jean-Pierre and I had a friendly, warm and clean rapport. He had been very kind and correct while I was at the Sorbonne. He was a good friend. It was a difficult time for me, after my mother's death. I was pretty much without enthusiasm and devoid of any will to do things. That's when I met him and developed a special friendship while trying to study."

"Eventually, after my school year was over I returned home to be with my father Rogelio, my grandmother Carmen Martinez Cosmos and my uncle Coronel Roberto Jaramillo Cosmos who you met at the airport. I was about 22 years old then. Roberto is my father's younger brother by almost 5 years. My father Rogelio was always extremely active carrying out his Army obligations, often traveling out of town, usually on dangerous missions. He was acutely involved in the struggle against the FARC guerrillas and the drug cartels in Medellin and Cali. Those people hated him."

She paused. "For this reason, I lived almost all the time at my grandmother's house, especially since she was alone after my grandfather, Comandante General Francisco Jaramillo, had passed away. I'm sure you remember the whole story which my grandmother told you when we were visiting her."

She continued: "Jean-Pierre came to Bogotá to visit me. He was here for about two months, getting to know my grandmother Carmencita, my uncle Roberto, his wife Blanca, and their two children who are my cousins, Juan and Blanquita."

"While Jean-Pierre was here, my grandmother Carmencita decided to take advantage of our National Holiday on the 20th of July when we have a few extra days off, to go visit her sister Adelita who lives in a small plantation, actually a banana and fruit tree country farm near Bucaramanga. That is beyond Villa de Leyva, which is about four hours away from Bogotá by car; plus another three hours from Villa de Leyva via San Gil, a town very much involved in the promotion of a variety of advanced extreme sports activities like rafting, climbing and the like.

We all thought it was a good idea for Jean-Pierre to drive with my father. By driving from Bogotá to Adelita's plantation near Bucaramanga, Jean-

Pierre could accompany my father Rogelio and see the magnificent countryside, especially down the impressive Chicamocha Canyon area between San Gil and Bucaramanga. However, since the aggregate driving time between Bogota and Bucaramanga is about 8 hours, which is a long way for my grandmother, she and I decided the two of us would fly from Bogota to Bucaramanga as flying time is only around one hour, bypassing the mountains and curvy roads."

"Go on," said John. "I don't want to be impolite and interrupt, but let's not forget to eat something, Virginia my friend, and have a sip of this special Pouilly-Fuissé."

She agreed. She paused a couple of minutes to eat some of the appetizing French cuisine. Then she sighed before going on. "Jean-Pierre was really enthused with the idea and my father too, as he was glad not to have to drive alone to see Carmencita's sister Adelita. The road between San Gil and Bucaramanga is exceedingly mountainous and curvy. Grandmother would always get car sick. They decided her son Rogelio – my father - would pick my grandmother Carmen and me at the airport in Bucaramanga, and drive us afterwards to Adelita's country estate."

"On the scheduled morning of the trip my father drove Jean-Pierre and I to Carmencita's house very early, around seven o'clock, to drop me off and say good-by to his mother. As was the norm with an officer of my father's rank, an army jeep with three armed soldiers would follow my father and Jean-Pierre as a security escort."

"They followed us to Carmen's house. When we were leaving my grandmother's house, one of the servants came running out to my father's car carrying a box with a variety of flowers." She said" General, please wait one moment. The florist just delivered this gift box of flowers which *el señor* Jean-Pierre had ordered for *Doña* Carmen's sister *la señora* Adelita. Please take them with you, so that Doña Carmen and *la señorita* Virginia don't have to carry them on the plane." Jean-Pierre was delighted they had arrived on time, thanked the maid and told her to put the box in the back of the car with the suitcases, which she promptly did."

"They said goodbye to my grandmother and I. We would see each other at the Bucaramanga airport. It was a fairly nice day; only a light drizzle was falling. Jean-Pierre and my father should have a good trip and enjoy the countryside. They left smiling and waving. Outside the gate they were saluted at full attention by the gate guards. The escort jeep pulled up. When they were ready, they all left for the trip to Bucaramanga. Grandmother Carmen and I went back into the house to get ready for our flight later on."

"When they arrived in Villa de Leyva, it was around eleven. They called us, saying they were having a coffee at a small food stand by the side of the road. They had made good time, it was around eleven thirty. They called us again when they got to San Gil. I got the call as we were on our way to El Dorado airport."

"The road from San Gil to Bucaramanga via the Chicamocha National Park varies from a double separate roadway to a single roadway used for traffic both ways, depending on the location going down the steep mountain. There are many motorcycles, trucks and buses. This road stretch which climbs 600m offers outstanding views. Cutting through the mountain there are truly fearsome drops down to distant rivers. A long cable car cuts across the canyon. Chicamocha National Park is very popular, but it's actually on the other side of the road from San Gil to Bucaramanga and that's why you have a long cable system."

Virginia suddenly stopped talking. Her composure changed slowly from relaxation to tenseness. Her looks portrayed a feeling of incredible pain. A tear came down her cheek. "Excuse me, my love, my dear John, I can't help feeling this way. Allow me a minute to recover, to get control of myself."

Dr. John Osborne sat silent and felt great anguish seeing Virginia's obvious suffering. He took her hand in his and gently brushed her tears away with his white handkerchief. He knew she was holding on through the sheer power of her indomitable will. When she felt back in control, she continued:

"Sometime after one o'clock, about one hour after they had left San Gil, they were descending the curved mountainous road, now only a two-way thoroughfare, oftentimes reaching the very edge of the road bed which on occasion was protected by flimsy metal barriers."

"When they reached one of the most dangerous curves, where there was practically no visibility on the left side of the road because of the tightness of the curved angle, there was a sudden screech. At that very moment a huge cargo truck appeared coming up on the left side and crossed the highway going full power, even accelerating on purpose, hitting my father's car with full force, pushing it like a bowling pin against the metal barrier, crashing it through the barrier and shoving it in the air. The truck's front tires remained turning in the air as the truck front section was suspended by the side of the road, over the metal barriers. The front wheels were turning uncontrollably. But the car was gone. Suddenly, as it tumbled down in the air, an explosion took place like an infernal firework, spraying sparks and flames all around the car, throwing out the occupants, disintegrating their bodies into a free for all down the side of the mountain."

"The escort jeep had managed to stop barely two feet away from the front side of the truck, whose huge engine was still running. The three soldiers had immediately jumped out to try to help their commander. But there was no possibility of survival for the Lieutenant General – my father, his army driver and my friend Jean-Pierre who could have become his son-in-law." Virginia stopped. She was so upset and distraught that John felt a tremor going up his own spine.

"As one of the soldiers opened the truck door, he saw through the other open cabin door that the driver was running away from the truck, going the other way down the road, and had climbed on a waiting motorcycle which had turned around from the climbing lane and was facing down toward Bucaramanga."

"Then the alert soldier saw a wireless control on the truck seat. He immediately and suddenly understood. He screamed to the other two soldiers: 'We have been ambushed, they have assassinated General Jaramillo and the other two occupants. Call the Bucaramanga airport right away and alert all the forces in the area!' It was impossible for their jeep to go around the truck as it was completely blocking the width of the roadway. They looked over the section of what was left of the metal fence. As they glanced over the parapet, they could see down the mountain, almost by the flowing river, the charred remains of the General's vehicle."

Virginia stopped, morbid and silent. "That, Dr. John Osborne, was the end of my beloved father, his loyal driver and my unofficial fiancé Jean-Pierre."

She became silent, crying discreetly and painfully onto John's shoulder. He too sat quietly, transfixed, shocked and overwhelmed. The moon shone on the balcony and on Virginia's face. She was pale and distraught but somehow slowly managed to contain her tears. The pain was expressed by the cloudy pupils in her precious eyes.

When she recovered, she looked at John and tried to smile, a feeble movement of her sensuous lips, saying: "I am glad I was able to tell you that sad and painful story of my life, here alone, privately, just the two of us."

John couldn't say much. He whispered: "I too am glad to be here with you, Virginia. Now I understand what your heart has been going through all these terrible years."

Virginia said: "From the plane above the canyon, as we were overflying the area, we saw smoke and people running on the road. When we arrived at Bucaramanga, the airport was cordoned off. The passengers were left out first. Then several officers approached us and escorted us to a private office where they gave us the awful news. My poor grandmother fainted and almost had a heart attack. She had lost her son. I was so dizzy I couldn't breathe normally for a long time. I had lost my father and the young man who might have married me.

After a short while, the officers drove us to Adelita's home. You can't imagine the scene there. No point talking about it now."

"When the intelligence network put all the pieces together, including the valuable information from the soldiers who were escorting my father and Jean-Pierre and had witnessed the whole drama, they confirmed the whole thing had been carefully orchestrated by the FARC and drug cartels. The remote control found in the truck cabin had been used to activate a bomb which apparently had been placed in the car, most probably in the flower box that had been carried in at the last minute by the innocent maid and which in the rush to pack it had not been carefully checked by the Security guards at the house gate."

Dr. Osborne said: "Virginia, shall we continue with our meal and wine, or shall we leave? We need to comfort our hearts and souls. This has been a shocking story. I feel so sorry for you and your grandmother Carmencita. No wonder she never mentioned anything. The mere idea of reviving those thoughts is devastating."

She suggested they calm down and finish their meal. While eating quietly, they continued to exchange thoughts about a multitude of things. John was obviously intensely interested in knowing what happened after things returned to some sort of normalcy, if that were possible, after what had happened to Virginia and her grandmother. How did this terrible trauma affect her career after her father's demise? How did she get involved in intelligence work, something so understandable in her case but not so easy to accomplish?

Virginia explained, saying: "As you can well imagine, John, the ambush against my father and Jean-Pierre, plus the innocent driver, created a stir in Colombian political and social circles and within the entire Army. It left my grandmother and I devastated. My uncle Roberto pressed for an investigation, which concluded what we already had surmised. The attack had been financed by drug dealers and involved FARC's strategic support."

"The two guys on the motorcycle who had fled from the truck after the crash and explosion were eventually captured after the soldiers had alerted the army control center in Bucaramanga. They confessed to their participation in the crime and divulged they had been paid for driving the stolen truck and ramming my father's car. They stated they were told by those who paid them that the attack was in revenge for the many drug arrests the Lieutenant General had made and to pay back for the capture of imprisoned drug dealers. The two fellows were not fully aware of what they were doing; they only saw the opportunity to make some good money by driving a stolen truck which had already been 'acquired' by the criminal group."

"My uncle Coronel Roberto Jaramillo recommended that I use my grandmother's family name of Cosmos instead of Jaramillo which already was so well known in military circles, by FARC and the drug world. So that's why I go by my grandmother's Cosmos name, as you have been wondering. It gives me some protection."

"My uncle Roberto suggested I lay low for six months and then join the Intelligence Command at FESCO, where he had good connections, provided of course I could pass the required test and training."

"Subsequently he arranged for me to get additional background schooling and preparation with the

British Secret Intelligence network at MI5 and MI6 in Cheltenham and London in England. So eventually I was sent to Cheltenham where I was meticulously instructed in the affairs of Secret Intelligence and Spying Techniques. While there, I met a nice young American agent. She helped me tremendously on a personal side to overcome the terrible tragedy of my father and my boyfriend. As I told you before, I did not love Jean-Pierre passionately, but I did love him for his genuineness and respect. As I mentioned, dear John, I never went to bed with him, and he was murdered before we were married."

She continued: "The young American agent in Cheltenham commented she was born in Colombia but her Security Agency in the States - I think it was NSA - would not let her travel there for security reasons. I seem to recall she had some Swiss relatives that owned a chain of tea rooms in our capital. Though I stayed only one year in Cheltenham, my friend had been four years in England, so she knew all the ropes and was most helpful in getting me approved by MI5 and MI6, which in turn made it possible for me to get back home into the very exclusive FESCO group as a Special Inspector Agent with the officer grade of Lieutenant. Eventually, after a couple of years, I was promoted to Captain on my own merits."

"My uncle and I kept our family name connection very discreet. Occasionally, I help on intelligence matters that involve important airports such as l Dorado. That's why I happened to be there the day you arrived, although we knew you were on that flight." She paused, smiled at him and whispered: "And I am so glad you came in that day, because now I think of you all the time." She gave him a look of infinite warmth.

John sat silent for a minute and answered: "Virginia, I also think about you night and day. I think it's very simple: I have fallen in love with you." He kissed her hand and looked at her hypnotic eyes. "Your magic has overpowered me. Tomorrow I am leaving with Infinity to Villa de Leyva. Please do not change your mind to come over the weekend with Doña Carmencita so we can spend a couple of days."

He added: "Afterwards, I'll see you in Bogotá when I come back from Villa de Leyva. I will then go to Zurich, stay there thirty days and return to Bogotá to see you. You know very well what will happen then. The day will not be far away when you'll have to change your last name again, using Osborne, - except you can keep Cosmos for purely professional matters. All this if you want, of course. We won't let that interfere between the Researcher on Intelligence and you, the beautiful Intelligence Specialist." He got up, went around her chair, and gave her a light kiss on her sultry lips.

When they had finished their dinner and enjoyed the mandatory *tinto*, they called Pedro on the phone to alert him they would be down fairly soon. John paid their check, thanked the waiters, the maître D' and the Sommelier- who smiled and gave them the half-full bottle of Pouilly-Fuissé for Carmencita;

he stated she would no doubt enjoy it better than the staff, who actually preferred local beer.

As they left the restaurant, they looked once more from their table at the lighted city below, shining like a million stars, reflecting the moonlit universe above them, and left arm in arm. They could hear in the background, through the restaurant's speakers, a melodious French song from a distant past, which both could understand from their knowledge of the language:

> Plaisirs d'amour
> Ne durent qu'un moment.
> Chagrins d'amour
> Durent toute une vie.

John said: "That's French philosophy." Virginia smiled and said: « Pleasures of love last only a moment." John countered with the rest of the lyrics: "Sorrows of love last a whole lifetime." They hugged briefly.

Virginia was so warm that John could feel her tenderness flowing through her black coat. They looked again at the church, resplendent in the bright light of the majestic moon. John touched her lips with his hand. They walked into the cable cabin which was still empty. He took her in his arms and kissed her softly but warmly on her inviting and slightly parted lips. Slowly the cabin got crowded and the cable car returned to the base where they saw Pedro waiting for them, Not far behind him were the escort guards. Now John understood the reasons for all the precautionary behavior.

They drove quietly back to Grandmother Carmen's house, holding hands in the back seat of the car. Pedro made a comment about the beautiful moon and the special glow of the church atop the mountain *Cerro of Monserrate*, to which Dr. Osborne acquiesced.

They reached Carmen's residence at a leisurely pace without much traffic, although John noticed Pedro would not linger at the red lights, out of habit, he said, as it was a common occurrence in the past that the thieves would take advantage of that momentary delay to either steal your watch, grab your jewelry or snatch a woman's purse, especially if the driver made the mistake of having his window down.

The house was well hidden behind its protective wall, and the street itself was adequately lit at night. You could see well enough to walk on the well-maintained sidewalks - though nobody was walking. You could distinguish the night guardians, most carrying a rifle, in front of the houses or apartment buildings; or military guards keeping an eye for suspicious activity in front of the larger residences of more important people. John observed that oddness to Virginia who remarked, rather casually, that street crime in that area was rare and had now practically completely disappeared. Half-seriously, she pointed discreetly to her holster and gave John a disarming smile. He thought to himself: if her pistol won't stop hoodlums or worse kinds, her disarming smile will.

After the usual inspection by the military guards at the gate and the checking for explosives under the car, Pedro was allowed to proceed. Captain Virginia instructed the guard not to call on the security phone as it was too late and Leonora was no longer on duty. Virginia had the front door keys anyway, since after all it was her house. The guard obeyed and opened the exterior gate. Pedro drove into the circular garden past the lighted fountain. Captain Virginia told him to park a couple of car lengths past the house door to avoid waking up her grandmother.

Pedro left them out of the car and said he would just wait there, to which Dr. Osborne assented. He told Pedro they would leave after a while for the hotel as the next day they would be traveling to Villa de Leyva with Infinity.

John escorted Virginia up to the main entrance. He held her arm and guided her up to the mansion's door by the foyer entrance. She opened it without hesitating and asked John to come in. Would he enjoy a cup of coffee or tea? She told him she would prepare it herself. He told her it was very kind of her but it wasn't necessary. She had had a long day and surely was tired. She reminded him that she wouldn't see him until the weekend as he was leaving the next day, and she already missed him. She looked at him with one of her pervasive looks and turned around so he could help her take off her warm black coat.

She then faced him, moved a step closer as if to pass in front of him, and before he could react, she put her arms around him and said: "John, my dear friend, I think I have fallen in love with you. Thank you for such an enchanting evening, I'll be seeing you in a couple of days. I can hardly wait."

She pressed her moist lips against his and remained thus for a long while. Then she took his hand and put it against her chest, between her breasts, and looked at him with a tender look. She whispered: "John, we are adult people. Sometime in the future I will let you love and play with what you have in your hand. You may play with my lips, hands, breasts and whole body; but remember, my dearest John, please never, but never, play with the heart that is beating under your hand tonight." And she kissed him with her moist and parted lips. Through her silk blouse he felt the soft roundness of her breast and the steady beat of her heart. After a long moment, they separated and he said: "I promise you, Virginia, to do just as you have said. This is not a game for me either. I am a loyal lover."

He thought it would be better to say good night and go back to his hotel. She agreed and hugged him in a mutual promise. She opened the front door; he touched her lips again, and stepped out. He heard the door being locked behind him.

****

 *Chapter 14*

Boyacá's Bridge of Freedom

Pedro had advised Dr. Osborne that next morning it would be desirable to go away relatively early to avoid the traffic build up on the roads leaving the North of Bogotá in the vicinity of the *Autopista*. That was the turnpike which had been built over the last few years, expecting to modernize and accelerate transportation in the northern area of the capital, as much within as on the outskirts, but principally in the outlying residential and industrial districts.

When Dr. Osborne commented to Pedro that they had had a long night the previous evening, he replied that his profession required dedication and time to comply with his customers' needs and not to worry about his personal comfort. Besides, he wasn't married yet. He still had to complete his university studies first before walking down the aisle, probably with the young campesina girl who had saved his right hand, certainly his arm and undoubtedly his life too.

Dr. Osborne had asked Pedro if he meant Luisita, the country girl he had met during his captivity by the FARC. He smiled and assented, adding: "I would give anything to complete my university studies soon and get a relatively good paying job to get married to Luisita and continue my career."

Dr. Osborne had already contemplated the foreseeable future and his anticipated return to Bogotá to set up the Osborne Research Center, perhaps with the backing and cooperation of the Zurich Politechnikum. He had already thought of the possibility of engaging Pedro as one of his potential employees and even assisting him with the planning of a serious operation of his damaged hand. That would be the most practical and valuable way, yet unbeknownst to Pedro, to thank him for his assistance, truthfulness and overall human quality. And yes, why not, also helping to synchronize the budding romance with Dr. Osborne, that unexpected love developing with Captain Virginia Cosmos.

He had found out from his attractive and intelligent companion that she was none other than the *niece* of Colonel Roberto Jaramillo who had first greeted him when he arrived at Eldorado Airport in Bogotá. It seemed all these events had happened long ago, and yet, it was only a few days in the past.

After previously reserving accommodations for his return in about a week or ten days, Dr. Osborne checked out of his hotel. He personally carried his assistant Infinity in her laptop cage He told the hotel service desk that he would call and confirm exactly his return date, but it was better to reserve in advance as all hotels were normally quite busy and fully occupied in the metropolitan capital. The thought already had crossed his mind that maybe he could spend two weekends in Villa de Leyva as it was already mid-week, provided Virginia, either alone or with her grandmother Carmencita, could come to spend those extra days in the colonial city. He might also get bored and decide to return earlier to Bogotá. Time would tell what the future held in store as far as his travel plans were concerned.

He would synchronize by telephone with Virginia if she would prefer to drive from Bogotá with Pedro or by herself. He ventured to guess that, since it would be a personal visit, she might not need to travel in her uniform and would not require to be escorted by FESCO security guards; but he didn't know what FESCO regulations would demand. Obviously, she was highly regarded and respected within the FESCO organization and had a highly responsible position within the upper officer staff that stipulated mandatory consideration. For all he knew, she may have been assigned security protection at all times, especially keeping in mind the poisoning episode with her grandfather and even worse, the truck ramming and subsequent explosion of her father's car with all its occupants.

Dr. Osborne remembered that Virginia had commented at Casa San Isidro, when relating her father's tragic story and the aftermath decision by her uncle Roberto to send her to train at MI5 and MI6 with British ultra secret operatives, that she had come out second in her overall training group and first in her pistol target shooting category which included several experienced English agents. She mentioned her achievements in a very casual way, without emphasizing the tremendous degree of success they represented. He had noticed she was not a boaster, like some people who are die-hard show-off persons; that included members of the privileged high society classes, be it Paris, New York, London or even Bogotá.

Dr. Osborne told Pedro he would prefer to sit in the back of the car, since traveling that way he could let Infinity out of her laptop cage for the lengthy trip to Villa de Leyva. Pedro clearly understood and even suggested that, traveling that way, he would be able to concentrate better on the driving, since there were always many cars, trucks and dozens of motorcycles to watch for on the road. They weren't always careful drivers, nor did they at all times follow the rules.

Dr. Osborne found the surrounding country area of the large capital city of Bogotá geographically interesting and quite diverse. Pedro commented that the northern region encompassed three departments or provinces: Boyacá, Santander and Norte de Santander which are considered the breadbasket of Colombia. Dr. Osborne would certainly enjoy the ride.

Pedro would take short detours to show Dr. Osborne some detailed pastureland.

Indeed, Dr. Osborne observed the farmland was picturesque; the countryside was colorful and often just magnificent. The green rolling pastures were broken up by small red-tiled fincas and *campesino* shacks – humble peasant huts often protected only by rustic straw roofs.

Dr. Osborne noticed what Sarah Woods, a travel author for British Bradt travel publications, had penned when describing small roads that occasionally weaved through a lush landscape of flower fields, edged by stalls weighted with slabs of cheese and churns of cream. He could see sombrero-wearing herdsmen ushering goats through pocket size villages, and machete-holding farmers tending to vast maize crops growing between broken-down farm machinery. At times, chubby sheep could be seen scrambling up steep grassy banks navigating large piles of pumpkins and potatoes. Chickens roaming freely would be pecking at scraps of corn under apple, pear and peach trees; and horses with worn saddles were tethered to the fruit trees or fences protecting domestic cattle munching on the grass. Cows would lie down in shady spots near small watering holes.

Amidst this bucolic country scene, children would be running through bloom-filled meadows while grain stores were guarded by weathered old women, probably of Indian origin, wearing ponchos woven from cheap grey wool. Pedro mentioned that further north this peaceful panorama was often shattered in some areas by mountain peaks overlooking gushing rivers and deep rocky gorges. Woods had stated that this northern heartland region was renowned for its genuine anti-colonial revolutionary spirit.

This was the country region through which Dr. Osborne was being driven now by an affable Pedro and accompanied by his loyal assistant Infinity who was peacefully sitting next to him. He was enjoying the panoramic display and the cultural features of the surrounding countryside.

They still had a couple of hours left before they would reach the famous *Boyacá* Bridge where they would stop for a break and a quick lunch prior to continuing to Villa de Leyva. After dropping Dr. Osborne at his hotel, Pedro would then turn around to go back to Bogotá.

Dr. Osborne couldn't deny that all this was very interesting and the views most enjoyable – but deep inside of him he missed his new female companion: where would Captain Virginia be at this time? He wanted her smiles, her magnetizing looks, her piercing clear eyes and the softness of her lips; and yes, perhaps the sensation of her soft bosom. He searched in the air for the scent of her hair and feminine magic. He said her name to himself: '*Virginia, Virginia*'. And he added: 'If you only knew how much I miss you already!'

He had phoned her earlier when he had left

the hotel. She had wished him a safe trip, and had ended the call by saying: 'I miss you, John; but I'll be seeing you soon.'

His thoughts were interrupted when, after a while, Pedro announced they would reach the Boyacá Bridge in a few minutes. He suggested that once he was safely parked, Dr. Osborne should walk around the monument's exhibit area while Pedro stayed with Infinity.

John reflected that many people, especially foreign tourists, probably imagine that the Bridge of Boyacá, which crosses the small Teatinos River – *el Rio Teatino*s - is going to be a spectacular overpass, awe-inspiring in size and projecting superb engineering like the Eiffel Tower - which was actually planned along the lines of an inverted railroad bridge - spoiled as we are today by modern bridge designs with sophisticated suspended spans crossing rivers, mountains and even ocean bays. This beautiful and modest bridge is nothing of the sort. Actually it's very undersized, almost like a toy bridge.

The river is not wide and turbulent; but it was a physical obstacle for the Spaniards, They were carrying heavy battle gear, horses, rifles and the rest of the superior Spanish armory. Simón Bolívar, without a trained army and no weapons, put together through bravery and inspiration an upstart force of peasants from the fields and surrounding villages. Against overwhelming forces, his 3,000 campesino troops were victorious fighting the great Spanish forces. It was a crucial battle eventually leading to independence from Spain. The small bridge had managed to cut-off the great Spanish army; on top of that victory, the peasant army captured 1,800 Spanish prisoners.

Royalty has its perks but not when men are fighting for their freedom and independence. To honor this historic accomplishment by Simón Bolivar, there are manicured lawns going to the river's edge, a monument of the Liberator on top of a succession of beautiful paved and grassy terraces, leading to a perpetual flame from a cement torch burning in tribute to Bolivar and Independence from Spain. Against such a dramatic backdrop, the white Boyacá Bridge at the bottom of the grassy hill looks small and rather unremarkable.

After he had reached the top of the monument esplanade, Dr. Osborne looked down at the impressive panorama and absorbed not only the sight but the meaning of it all. Ah! If only Virginia could have been there with him! They could be embracing each other while reflecting on the meaning of liberty and love. Perhaps some other day they would be able to do so.

He went back down the grassy hill to rejoin Pedro and Infinity. "Pedro, let's go have something to eat by one of the *chozas*." Those were simple food stands by the side of the road. "I could use some reenergizing; and you?" Pedro smiled and assented. Infinity just meowed. After Dr. Osborne took her out for a short cat-break, they left to look for a place to eat a well-deserved lunch.

After their *almuerzo*, Pedro continued driving for about half an hour through some changing landscape, an interesting terrain that was like a natural mix between dry desert and wild rocky sites. They finally reached the center of Villa de Leyva, actually the *Plaza Mayor*, which is the main plaza where the hotel was located. The hotel had the same name as the main city square.

Since the area where the hotel is situated is primarily a pedestrian zone, right by the main colonial plaza, Pedro did not linger. He helped Dr. Osborne to check in and carried his suitcase up the stairs. Dr. Osborne carried the valuable laptop with Infinity in her practically indistinguishable cage. She was used to her carry-on facility.

He was most pleased with the accommodations and the friendly service by the welcoming receptionist, Maria Elena. It had been a long time since he had started to plan his vacation trip at the Politechnikum, and now he was glad to have reached his destination. He walked downstairs to accompany and say good-bye to Pedro. They would be in touch concerning Virginia and her grandmother's trip, whether the two of them or only Virginia. In any case, Dr. Osborne had reserved comfortable connecting rooms. One of them was like a suite, with a nice couch and a small living room area, which made it be very comfortable. There were beams across the ceiling and the overall construction retained the original colonial design.

From the hotel terrace he looked around Plaza

Mayor and noticed quite a few people playing with kites. They rose and fell like birds in motion. Colorful and in different sizes, the gracious kites competed with the few pigeons that maneuvered in the air. Evidently, the winds were favorable in Villa de Leyva. He had noticed a poster advertising an Annual Kite event, apparently well-known around the country as people from all over came to compete in the joyful event.

Dr. Osborne could hardly wait until the weekend. Was all this real or was it just a dream?

****

Chapter 15

Music at Colonial Cathedral

Dr. Osborne had every intention of enjoying his stay in Villa de Leyva by walking with Infinity, reading books in Spanish by native authors, sitting and eating at the restaurants in town, and actually doing nothing but relaxing and thinking; though he had not anticipated that his thoughts would dwell overwhelmingly on Captain Virginia Cosmos. He knew she would be arriving in a couple of days, and that gave him the inner peace and enthusiasm he needed to think positively and enjoy his precious time alone, especially while waiting for the weekend when he would see her again.

He realized his feelings were in disarray since he had met her, and deep inside his heart he knew he had fallen in love. It was not a question of how many days, weeks or months. He could tell that his feelings had been hypnotized, and his life's outlook had been affected irreparably. He knew true love had been locked in his soul.

As a distraction while in Villa de Leyva he planned to read a couple of books from famous Colombian authors: *Maria,* by Jorge Isaacs and *One Hundred Years of Solitude* by Nobel Prize winner Gabriel García Márquez. Also, although not written by a Colombian author, he was intrigued by a book called *La Fiesta del Chivo* by the famous Peruvian author Mario Vargas Llosa, a powerful book describing the era of Dictator Trujillo (who was known as *El Chivo,* the Goat) and his assassination in the Dominican Republic. He had purchased all three volumes at a bookstore near the hotel in Bogotá.

After Pedro had left, Dr. Osborne rested for a while in his comfortable hotel room. While doing so he suddenly was interrupted by the same vision he had seen before in his mind, without rhyme or reason: a young woman's face, a turning wide dress and the flash of a soft thigh, which then faded away into the recesses of his intellect. Nothing remained but a blank sensation.

In the middle of the afternoon he decided it was time to get up and go outside to explore the town, taking his laptop and his Assistant Infinity with him.

He stopped by the front desk and asked the attendant Maria Elena if she had any suggestions for a local eatery and other simple activities in the small city. He commented that his travel companion, Captain Virginia Cosmos, would not arrive until Saturday morning. He asked about the special banners he had noticed in the Plaza Mayor. What was the occasion? She mentioned that Plaza Mayor was decorated with special banners bearing a black cross and a funereal crown in honor of Sister Angelica, the Reverend Mother Superior of Our Lady of Carmel Convent - *Nuestra Señora del Carmen*, - the Carmelite convent near the Religious Museum of the Church of Carmel.

Mother Angelica, the most recent Mother Superior, had actually lived in the convent since she was a sixteen year old orphan. At that time she had been welcomed as a novice by the Congregation of the Carmelite Sisters. She had always been a responsible and dedicated member of her Congregation. She eventually rose from novice to assistant to executive director until being placed in charge of the Convent at age thirty-five. She remained its formal leader for almost fifty-five years.

The Convent had been established in Villa de Leyva by Royal Decree of the King of Spain in 1642. It had taken three years to build; but finally in 1645 it was opened by the first six Carmelite nuns. In recent times the number of novices and nuns usually varied between ten and thirty-five.

The night before, the well-loved but rarely seen Mother Angelica had passed away peacefully in her sleep. One wish she had always expressed was to have a funeral Mass celebrated in the main colonial church in town facing the Plaza Mayor and known as the *Iglesia Parroquial de Villa de Leyva,* colloquially called *La Catedral*, probably because it looked like the central Cathedral in Bogotá which faced Plaza Bolívar. The request had seemed simple enough, because Mother Angelica had spent her entire life at the Convent in Villa de Leyva; except that Mother Angelica was a cloistered nun and this meant she was not allowed to leave the Congregation to be on the outside with lay people.

Fortunately, because of the special situation, the Cardinal Archbishop in Bogotá had consented to Mother Angelica's request; and in turn had requested permission from higher Church Authorities. Before her death, he had obtained the appropriate approval of the Holy See in the Vatican, so she was able to depart from this world knowing her last wishes had been granted.

Maria Elena explained to Dr. Osborne that this funeral was a very special event. Exceptionally, *el alcalde* – the mayor, had also given permission for the procession from the convent to the Church and afterwards to the cemetery, situated behind the convent grounds. The burial Mass would be at seven in the morning; shops and restaurants had been instructed to remain closed out of respect until the procession to the cemetery had
been completed.

Maria Elena gave Dr. Osborne a colored map and a few suggestions about using his time. He thanked her and left the hotel. In the plaza, one of the largest original town squares in the continent, still covered with the original cobblestones from colonial times, he sensed what it must have felt in the past to arrive on your horse and see the grandiose layout. There were no modern buildings to disturb the time-frozen imagery. The feeling was extraordinary: no automobiles, no interruptions, no disruptions, no sacrilege: Only people; and here and there a few unremarkable dogs.

Dr. Osborne reached into his laptop case to pull Infinity out. He attached forthwith a black leash to her collar until he was sure she felt comfortable in the unfamiliar surroundings. She was so happy to feel free or at least be out of her cage that she curled around Dr. Osborne's feet and started walking across the plaza toward a stone fountain in the center. Dr. Osborne followed her, paying attention to the environment. When they reached the fountain, he sat on the stone edge, picked up Infinity, turned on the hidden power button in the special black collar and put her down again. He took out his laptop and set up the software training instructions.

He then took the leash off. He wanted to test how Infinity would react. He instructed her to walk a short distance back toward the hotel, sit down when signaled, remain on the spot for a couple of minutes, and then turn around and come back toward her master. He powered the camera on the collar to synchronize the screen clarity, and after that let Infinity go free. He would be checking her performance and reaction to the sounds he would transmit to her through her collar giving her instructions. He was delighted to be back in his research element. Nobody paid any attention to them, not even the few children running by or a couple of old people sitting on the steps of the sidewalk on the other side of the fountain near the entrance to the church.

Infinity carried out her instructions perfectly, while Dr. Osborne controlled her movements through his laptop screen. The transmission of the various sounds, varying in pitch and duration, indicated to Infinity where and when she should stop, turn right or left, sit down or walk back.

Dr. Osborne was most satisfied with her performance. She hadn't lost any of her trained instructions in cognitive reaction. He told her to come back and she immediately followed her orders. These were kind of sophisticated Pavlov reflexes infused with scientifically controlled cognitive commands.

When the test was successfully completed and Infinity was back by Dr. Osborne's feet, he petted her fur, picked her up gently, put her back in her caged space and told her they were going to visit the church but he didn't want her to be loose at this time since they might be decorating the church for tomorrow's early funeral of Mother Angelica. Of course, since Villa de Leyva was a small town, there wouldn't be any large crowds even if many of the residents attended the Mass while the stores and cafés were closed. The few municipal schools were showing their respect by sending their pupils to the unusual ceremony.

Dr. Osborne walked slowly in the direction of the church, climbed a couple of steps running the length of a sidewalk that stretched from the beginning of the street all the way across the Iglesia Parroquial, and quietly entered the sacred structure. It was long and narrow, with high ceiling, and relatively simple white walls without many paintings, and only a couple of side chapels, except in the area near the main altar.

On the left side there was a fairly large chapel where about twenty children of grammar school age in school uniforms were practicing choral songs in preparation for their performance the next day at the funeral Mass. His eyes wondered around the general scene and observed a fifteen or sixteen-year-old girl, probably a teacher's aide, leading the choir rehearsal. Evidently she was in charge of the group of young children. Though he didn't linger on her, he quickly noticed that she seemed very poised and was actually quite attractive. He surmised she was an auxiliary teacher or aide in the local public school or at the parish school. She noticed he was observing the scene, and acknowledged his presence by a quick respectful wave of her hand. He had a peculiar sensation that she seemed vaguely familiar, but that was impossible, of course.

He turned to the opposite side of the nave and saw a young man, maybe seventeen or eighteen years old, playing the accompanying music for the religious songs, on an antique organ which still managed to sound acceptably good. Evidently, the organ player, the young students' choir and the choir directress were all rehearsing for the funeral ceremony on the next day, as the music was rather somber and solemn.

Dr. Osborne was genuinely interested and impressed by the quality of the singing rehearsal. Since he had nothing else to do, he decided to stay for a while listening to the young people practice their musical renditions; so he quietly sat on the right side of the nave, on a pew not too distant from the preaching pulpit, but away from the old fashioned confessionals. Actually, there were two old ladies apparently waiting their turn to enter the site of Reconciliation, as Confession was presently described in modern jargon. As they used to do since they were young women in the past, the ancient communicants had their heads covered by a black laced scarf which partly hid their lined faces shrunken by age.

The privacy curtain opened on one of the confessional sides and the figure of a young man slowly emerged. He had just gone to confession. He was probably no more than fourteen years old, and looked somewhat hesitant. Dr. Osborne recognized signs of autism or mental challenge; he knew the description of mental retardation was no longer used though the description often still fit the person's appearance. The young fellow walked across the aisle and picked up a broom and bucket he had left standing against the opposite church wall. Dr. Osborne surmised that evidently he was a janitorial helper in the parish assisting in its maintenance.

Very gently, Dr. Osborne opened his laptop case and let Infinity sit on the pew. Wasn't it wise to inculcate some religious breeding into her animal life? While sitting in silence, he enjoyed questioning in his mind what priests would think standing in the pulpit, elevated above the congregation, trying to maintain its attention during the obligatory sermon, making sure their parishioners would not fall asleep while they spoke – somewhat for the same reason psychiatrists, psychologists and counselors normally require their patients or victims, depending on who they are and how much they are paying, to sit at a level below the desk or chair where the big Guru can sit to control the situation and the monetary fixation.

The young handicapped boy had a slight limp. He walked toward the side chapel where the students were singing, said hello with a big smile to the girl directing the group; he then continued in front of the altar cleaning the railing and all the way to the organ where he stopped and observed the youth playing with his deft fingers on the yellowed ivory keys. He looked at the organist, sort of keeping rhythm with his head, smiled politely and went on with his cleaning duties.

Meanwhile Dr. Osborne sat at his place while Infinity walked to the end of the pew and back; when she returned he picked her up gently and put her back in her laptop cage. By then the two old ladies had completed their sacrament and the corresponding penance – he wondered what two elderly people like them would have had to confess – too much talking about neighbors; swearing occasionally; being ungrateful; thinking about love and being unable to do anything about it; missing Mass on Sunday or on a Holy Day? Oh well, he thought, there were not a million reasons to keep them from going straight to Heaven. As they passed by him on their way out, they bowed politely to him and wished a very good afternoon –*muy buenas tarde, señor*. And they gave him a grandmotherly wave.

As he was getting ready to leave, a hand touched his shoulder. He hadn't noticed that the priest had come out of the confessional and had walked toward him. He introduced himself, saying: "Good afternoon, son. Are you waiting to go to confession? I was going to finish now but…" Dr. Osborne replied: "Oh no, father, I'm not waiting. I was just listening to the young people practicing." The relatively young priest stopped and looked at Dr. Osborne and commented: "Oh, excuse me, sir. You must not be a regular parishioner from Villa de Leyva."

He introduced himself: "My name is Father Juan Garcia Rodriguez." Dr. Osborne answered: "Padre Garcia, I am Dr. John Osborne, *servidor y amigo* – your friend at your service."

Father Garcia sat next to Dr. Osborne and they engaged in a friendly conversation. Padre Garcia was about 45 years old and had been the parish priest in Villa de Leyva for the past five years. He had been involved in synchronizing permission for the funeral Mass celebration on the next day for Madre Angelica. He hoped that Dr. Osborne would be able to attend. Father Garcia would be most pleased to have him join them at the funeral service. Dr. Osborne had a chance to explain that he was not a medical doctor, as the title might lend itself to some confusion. It was a doctoral degree from the university. Padre Garcia indicated that prior to entering the Seminary for the priesthood he had delved into medical studies as he had been tempted to become a medical doctor. However, his calling for the priesthood became clearer and stronger, and he ended his explanation smiling and saying: "You became a Doctor of Science and I became a Doctor of Souls."

He heard a meow and was astonished, wondering where the message came from. Dr. Osborne explained he was traveling with his assistant Infinity, and had all the necessary permission and mandatory documentation. He took out the beautiful and well-behaved cat, and introduced her to Padre Garcia: "Father, this is my assistant Infinity, a gift from our heavenly Father."

Padre Garcia himself kept a kitten in the rectory. He used to have a German shepherd but had to give it up as it became too difficult to take care of. He immediately loved Infinity, caressed her gently and said: "What a fine-looking and special feline!" Dr. Osborne answered: "Thank you, Padre Garcia. May I ask you, if you have a minute, to please give her your blessing?"

Padre Garcia immediately said: "Saint Francis of Assisi loved animals. Of course, Dr, Osborne, I will be more than happy to bless her." He forthwith proceeded to bless the cat. Then he stood up and excused himself, as he needed to go talk to the choir directress Viviana Angel and the organist Gabriel Santos, to finalize details for next day's ceremony for Mother Angelica.

He told Dr. Osborne to follow him as he would like to introduce him to them. He took him to the choir area to meet Viviana and Gabriel. When the introduction was completed, Dr. Osborne said goodbye and left the group discussing plans with Padre Garcia for the funeral Mass, musical strategy and the choir's participation.

****

Chapter 16

Funeral of Mother Angelica

Early next morning, before the sun had completely risen, Dr. Osborne took his laptop case with Infinity in her adapted cage and had a simple breakfast on the terrace of his hotel. It was a cool morning and there were a few dark grey clouds in the sky, but there was no rain forecast for the day. That's what the weather moguls had indicated on the national TV, but a more precise way of knowing exactly the weather situation was by simply going outside and looking at the sky. The view from the terrace was incomparable, overlooking the imposing colonial plaza with its decorative fountain in the center. There wasn't a soul to be seen. The stores and restaurants were closed, as instructed by the town mayor. The simple but somber black flags were waving in the gentle breeze.

At exactly seven o'clock Dr. Osborn heard the church bells tolling. As he looked toward his left in the direction of the monastery, he saw a slow and impressive crowd of people gathering behind a most remarkable sight. A donkey with a black mantle was leading the parade. The young man he had seen the day before in the church was walking next to the animal, guiding it toward the church across the plaza. Its mantle had a black cross in the center. There were flowers on his head. The animal was walking slowly and steadily, with its head bent toward the ground as if expounding on this serious occasion.

The noble *burro* emblazoned for the occasion with a black robe was pulling a simple wooden cart on which a plain casket had been placed. It had on it one small crown of white flowers, probably from the convent's own garden, and a single purple banner with the name of *Madre Angelica Servidora del Señor* stamped on it.

Behind the donkey and the casket containing the body of Mother Angelica Servant of God, was Padre Garcia; and a few feet behind him were twenty-four sisters from the convent, dressed in a black garb complete with a dark veil which covered their heads and fell loosely on both sides, hiding their faces and reaching all the way to their waist, in a communal disguise of shared pain and sadness. They were saying the Holy Rosary and humming a sacred ritual as they slowly walked together like one ethereal soul.

It was a grandiose sight. Dr. Osborne put Infinity at the edge of the balcony, and turned on the micro-camera on her collar. He thought he could show that special event, unique in all its painful symbolism, to his dear Virginia, who would certainly appreciate it. Oh, how he missed her, Capitán Virginia!

He quickly got up, put Infinity in her bag, and walked across the plaza into the church where he sat in the last row, without making any noise, as imperceptibly as possible. To his surprise, the church was packed to the hilt. Men were dressed in their Sunday best, wearing a dark tie. They came to pay their respects, though none of them had probably ever met Mother Angelica in person; but she had been a symbol of Villa de Leyva for the past half-century and they were conscious of her devotion and servitude to God and the people of the town.

The women had come out to wish her a fond farewell, since they realized her closeness to God and the kindness and goodness she represented for all of them including the town's children and students. During her tenure she had been allowed on occasion by her superiors to visit the schools to inspire the young people and the medical clinic to see and pray for the sick parishioners.

The local school children and youngsters were all standing in their uniforms behind a few pews reserved for the mourning confraternity. The few who were part of the choir were near the organist, with the director keeping an eye on them and preparing them for the entrance of the funeral procession.

Two of the older students were playing the violin along with the organist. Six members of the city's elders, selected by Padre Garcia specifically for the memorial service, were expecting the donkey at the entrance of the church, to place the casket on a rolling catafalque used for the normal funeral Masses of the parish.

A few minutes after Dr. Osborne, unobtrusively carrying his laptop with Infinity, had purposely sat down on the last pew so he could observe without interfering, a muffled bell sound from the church tower announced the arrival of the nuns' cortege. The six elderly men retrieved the casket and slowly lifted it up the two sidewalk steps, while the limping young boy took the burro and tied it up to a steel pole which originally had been used by people who in the past may have come to church riding their horses. Dr. Osborne read somewhere that it was still a custom on Sundays by some of the local gentry to continue that ritual.

The six bearers placed the casket on the catafalque and stood respectfully behind Padre Garcia, who dressed in black robes, had already entered by the main church door. The children's choir started their hymns as Viviana directed them and Gabriel proceeded with his accompaniment on the old organ. Dr. Osborne thought they sounded very inspiring. One could tell they had practiced a lot. It should make young Viviana and her musician friend Gabriel, very proud of their efforts.

The bearers placed the simple casket on the catafalque and followed Padre Garcia down the nave toward the altar. Everybody had stood up and a few of the elderly women were seen shedding an emotional tear. The church sacristan had joined the crowd and actually sat on a pew opposite Dr. Osborne. This way he could check once in a while on the *burrito* which was waiting outside to take the casket back after Mass to the Convent grounds for burial of Mother Angelica among her sisters.

From where he was sitting Dr. Osborne could make out Viviana and Gabriel, the young organist. In fact he thought they recognized him, in spite of being quite far, as Viviana bowed her head in a mute salute. Dr. Osborne was appreciating the lovely music, the young organist and the two accompanying violinists. After all, this was only a small country town and it was surprising to have so much talent available for Mother Angelica's funeral.

He remained at the funeral Mass until the very end. The mayor had given a short but eloquent eulogy, followed by a few words by Padre Garcia. After the Mass, on the way out of the church preceding the body of Mother Angelica, he saw Dr. Osborne and gave him a very discreet acknowledgment of his presence. After all, the day before he had personally invited Dr. Osborne to the ceremony.

The casket was returned to the front on the catafalque by the six elderly bearers, who carefully brought it down the two stony steps and placed it on the cart. The limping sacristan had retrieved the burro which was ready in front of the cathedral. The nuns' cortege followed. As they walked out past the silent people in the pews, the latter started clapping automatically and respectfully to complete the funeral celebration. When the burro, casket, padre and mayor were ready, the cart was guided by the limping boy, the nuns followed silently and most of the congregation joined the funeral parade toward the convent where they eventually put Mother Angelica to rest in the closed cemetery.

Dr. Osborne waited a couple of minutes and then walked toward the front altar. He congratulated the choir directress Viviana and her colleague Gabriel and the two young violinists. As he turned to leave, he had a peculiar sensation that the girl had a familiar aura about her but he just put that by the wayside and left the church retaining the emotional and melancholy aspect of the ceremony. The thought crossed his mind: He was sure that Virginia would have enjoyed it too. He called her on his cellular phone and though the call was short and sweet, he was immediately cheered up by the conversation and the warm sound of her voice.

The church was now empty, as most people had left. The stores and restaurants around the plaza were slowly but steadily starting to be back in operation. Life was becoming normal again. Dr. Osborne lifted his special laptop bag with Infinity and went to have a glass of freshly squeezed pineapple-guava called *feijoa*, a hot cup of coffee with milk, and a local meringue cake called *besos de novia* or bride's kisses, in a shop not far from where he was standing in front of the cathedral.

After an enjoyable pause recovering from the morning's funeral events, he felt refreshed. He could now spend some time thinking about the coming weekend with Virginia. He was uncertain as to her anticipated reaction during their personal and intimate reunion but he had felt enough waves coming from her to know she warmly seemed to enjoy his company as much as he loved being with her.

He decided to walk around the town to enjoy its many colonial charms. Villa de Leyva was an extraordinary whitewashed colonial city historically preserved through the centuries when the rest of the country was living through chaos and turmoil, from the struggle for independence from Spain to the survival of FARC guerrillas and paramilitary executioners. In the past it was also renowned for bountiful olive crops.

He could hardly wait until Virginia joined him on Saturday. Today was already Thursday. Still a couple more days left until he could again be with her and see her gentle smile, look into her clear and profound eyes, and perhaps feel again the tenderness of her lips, the softness of her bosom, the inspiration of her affection; nay, the hypnosis of her presence and the ecstasy of her female attraction.

He went toward the northern corner of the Plaza Mayor, which extended its cobbled surface wide over 14,000m2 proudly covering several street blocks in every direction, where diverse eateries were lined up under old wooden romantic balconies and peaceful buildings cheerfully adorned with flower-filled window boxes like in European villages. He planned to eat there alone or with Virginia at another time.

He turned right toward the mountain range which could eventually be reached if one followed Calle 13, the thirteenth street, to its end. It was a street where lots of stores and restaurants were located. Some sold handicrafts and fresh vegetables. There were charming cafés and small hotels hiding in the back streets. The altitude of 2,144 meters was ideal for meandering around in cool weather without suffering from high altitude like in the capital of Bogotá.

It was quite busy for a weekday; the children were still in school; and the elderly people sat by the storefronts, adding to the charm of the whole scenery. After crossing a couple of streets, he decided to turn left on San Agustin Street, as he had actually been thinking about visiting a colonial hotel which originally was a flour mill, called Molino La Mesopotamia. It had been constructed centuries before, in 1518. Many parts of the hotel and gardens dated back to the original foundation and the heavy stone design and wooden decorations were still visible to present day visitors.

He had inquired about this old hotel and found out it had a natural pool of fresh water in the back gardens. It was like an inviting pond with crystal clear water with therapeutic qualities. The street he took to get to the Mesopotamia Hotel passed the colonial birthplace of Antonio Ricaurte a great hero of Colombian Independence from Spain. As Dr. Osborne walked by, he noticed the colonial residence was located in front of a park bearing his name and a statue of his heroic death. Antonio Ricaurte had been fighting with the Liberator Simón Bolívar in San Mateo, Venezuela. While under attack by Spanish soldiers he became encircled defending an armory storing gunpowder kegs. He let the enemy approach and then ignited the gunpowder kegs to cause a tremendous explosion that killed everyone, including himself.

As Dr. Osborne continued on that street, he passed the imposing landmark of the Church of San Augustín near a small stream flowing under a bridge which was part of the street. There were residences on both sides of the street. Not far further north he saw the entrance to the *Hosteria del Molino* La Mesopotamia, with a closed gate. He decided to visit the above Flour Mill Hotel and get information and rates - for the next time, perhaps, -as he was very pleased with his present hotel on the Plaza Mayor.

He was quite delighted with the colonial style rooms and the atmosphere, wooden doors, rustic tile floors, balconies overlooking the green gardens; it felt more like a country residence than a hotel. He walked to the *Manantial* pool, the spring source of fresh water for the casual and inviting swimming pool, which was actually a large water hole where one could swim, located near the main water source for the hotel. Although there were changing facilities, there were no towels available unless you were a guest, in which case you would bring them from your room. He sat at one end of the pool and actually took off his shoes to test the water and refresh a bit from the morning's activities.

Where was Virginia? He would bring her here after she had joined him on Saturday, and they would jointly enjoy the peace and beauty of the large water hole and the surrounding gardens and stone paths, before having lunch or dinner by the fireplace in the old colonial dining room. He could taste the smell of home-cooking on the kitchen stove; but he was suddenly taken aback by the sudden perfume of flowers in the air. The aroma forced him to close his eyes and see Virginia's face. He missed the anticipated softness of her kisses against his own anxious lips.

Since he was in the hotel dining room, he ordered a simple lunch overlooking the gardens. The charming hostess asked him if he would enjoy the fireplace and he couldn't resist the thought of a bright cheerful fire for him and Infinity, al- though he sensed the absence of Virginia's embrace while eating in such a romantic place. He would come back with her over the weekend.

He enjoyed a delightful but somewhat lonely lunch - he missed Virginia so much! The hostess recommended *carne asada* and *papitas criollas*. He took real pleasure savoring the thin marinated beef steak, a typical robust piece of flank or roast meat cooked over the wood-fired grill in the old fashioned kitchen. The hostess explained that it was cooked that way to impart a charred flavor.

Dr. Osborne thought it was good but not as tender as prime beefsteak or filet mignon. Nevertheless it was flavorful and filling. He reasoned most of the steak meats in Colombia and probably in the rest of Latin America, except perhaps Argentina, are usually less tender than in other countries like the United States or Europe. He reflected that was probably due to the way cattle is fed and grown in natural grassy expanses.

Concerning the small *papas criollas* or native potatoes, he thought they were delicious when cooked as an indigenous delicacy prepared with some flavorful fresh herbs on top to augment their earthy taste. He finished his culinary adventure with a *cafecito,* which complemented in style the typical *campesino* repast. The small standard *tinto* coffee, smooth and not as strong as the Italian espresso brew, settled in his stomach like a reward from heaven.

He didn't forget Infinity. While sitting there he gave some yellow rice and ground meat to his assistant, who thoroughly enjoyed the private attention. Dr. Osborne had alerted the waiter and the restaurant manager, explaining the special situation and official permit. Dr. Osborne did not imbibe in an after-dinner liqueur as it was not his custom to abuse alcoholic pousse-cafés.

He left the restaurant feeling rested and pleased with the whole experience. He thanked the staff and the manager, and advised them he expected to return over the weekend with his beloved. And he told himself and Infinity they would return in a couple of days. Infinity seemed to concur as she gave a gentle meow that he took as feline confirmation.

****

 Chapter 17

The Choir Resonance

After his relaxing lunch, Dr. Osborne slowly walked back to the street. He enjoyed the location so much he decided to find a bench and sit for a while to write some of his travel reactions into a special file in his laptop computer. He took Infinity out of her carrying cage and secured her by her leash until he sensed she had acquired a sense of security with the new terrain. As he could not find a bench, he sat on an old tree which had partially fallen down and looked like the perfect spot to sit on.

He put his laptop on his knees, feeling like a graduate student preparing for a final test. It reminded him of the many examinations he had to successfully pass and add to the oftentimes overwhelming paperwork and disciplined applications he had to survive in his quest for a doctorate related to cognition, psychiatry, linguistics and other subjects which required deep perception, profound concentration and memorization. It was during that period of his life as a doctorate student that he had first met Madeleine, who would eventually become his wife within a few months after he graduated and received his doctorate title.

He contemplated the changing life experiences over the years and how, at present, he was sitting on a beautiful log in front of a hotel in an old colonial city, anticipating the arrival of a woman who had penetrated his heart when he least expected it. He reached into his laptop bag to let Infinity partake of the serenity of the surroundings and to enjoy the grass which grew without formal restriction along the cobblestoned street in this residential area of the old city. He actually admired the cat, such a noble animal that accompanied him during his research activities at the Politechnikum and his travel around college campuses, famous institutions of higher learning, research foundations and even miscellaneous government circles in a variety of geographical locations, oftentimes in remote and even dangerous areas. Here he was sitting and reminiscing about the past, and yet he was conscious he now had such a vibrant and challenging future with an unusual, warm and intelligent woman. It seemed so natural to think of her as a life complement of his love and sensual feelings. He missed her and wanted her near him and Infinity.

While peacefully sitting there, he noticed two people walking toward where he was resting on the tree branch. His eyes followed them automatically. As they slowly got closer, Dr. Osborne recognized one of them. She was the young choir director he had met the day before when Padre Garcia had introduced him to her and also to the organist preparing the musical renditions for Mother Angelica's funeral Mass. In fact, Padre Garcia had given Dr. Osborne an imperceptible greeting at the funeral Mass when he was walking out after the ceremony, escorting the casket and the group of twelve nuns dressed from head to toe in black veils and robes – actually, he thought, similar to the *Burka* outfits worn by many Muslim women who surely haven't realized that a lot of their customs are copied or inherited from the Christian faith which preceded their own Mohamed Muslim establishment by nine hundred years. It crossed Dr. Osborne's mind that the reason Muslims believe in Mary, the mother of Jesus, is because they consider the latter a prophet; and not what He really is, the son of God. Even Abraham is the common root of their religious development.

The other person walking beside her was an older woman, like those mothers or grandmothers one sees in the typical tourist posters promoting the kindness of cultural natives. She had a black shawl around her shoulders and her face was lined with an expression of age attained only after a long hard-working life. In their own way her aged features projected a peacefulness of body and spirit often sought by many people but not achieved in their life's quests.

When they were passing in front of him he saluted them by removing his white hat from Quindío, as Robert Jaramillo had said when he had greeted him El Dorado Airport, which he had been wearing all morning, except in Church and at lunchtime. The young girl recognized him from the day before and gave him a friendly smile and wave. Noticing Infinity laying nearby, she grabbed the older lady's arm and guided her toward Dr. Osborne. She said: "Good afternoon, sir, I remember you from yesterday, when Padre Garcia introduced you to our group. Allow me to introduce you to my mother Adelita who went with me to the funeral Mass this morning." Dr. Osborne got up and greeted Viviana Angel and her mother Adelita, extending his right hand, which was reciprocated in a gentle fashion. Adelita stated right away that she had seen Dr. Osborne on the television news the night before.

Immediately thereafter, Viviana exclaimed with a happy voice: "Oh, *mamita,* look at the beautiful cat, so soft and intelligent! *Doctór,* can I take it with me to my house to play with it for a while? I won't hurt it. *Please*? We live over there, right in front of the hotel" Viviana repeated: "Oh, please, can I keep the cat with me for a short while?" She paused and added: "And maybe you could also bring it back tomorrow, perhaps while you go to lunch?" She promised him she would take very good care of the cat; she loved animals. In fact, she had thought of becoming a veterinarian when she grew up. "Could you, please? *Please*?"

A little surprised but not shocked, Dr, Osborne replied: "Señorita Viviana, perhaps it is possible; but this cat is not just an it; it is a *she*. Her name is Infinity. She is a close element of my family and an essential associate in my research work." He stroked her fur and added: "You did such a wonderful job with the choir this morning at the *Parroquial*

Church – the Parish Church -that I think I will make an exception and let you play with my valuable assistant while I take a walk around the neighborhood; as long as your mother allows you to play with her."

Viviana turned to her mother Adelita and asked her if that would be all right, to which she assented. Adelita then asked the Doctor to follow them into the house so he could see where Infinity would be playing. Dr. Osborne made sure Infinity had her black collar on. Dr. Osborne followed *la señora* Adelita and her daughter Viviana into their house.

Viviana commented to Dr. Osborne that her mother was leaving next day for the nearby city of Tunja, the capital of the Department of Boyacá, to visit her sister Rosario until Saturday.

Their house was indeed directly across the wooden gate that opened into the Hotel Mesopotamia's garden entrance. There was another restaurant at the end of the street, where Dr. Osborne could also go and spend some time drinking the perennial coffee, unless he preferred to walk toward the plaza, sit in a café and order a *pan de yuca,* the local yucca bread he had seen advertised on a billboard.

Adelita and Viviana showed their modest but comfortable house to Dr. Osborne, while Viviana carried Infinity in her arms, where evidently she was happily set and occasionally meowed her approval.

Adelita and Viviana showed him the cozy kitchen which still had a wood and coal burning stove surrounded by light green tile. It adjoined the living room, which led to a bright entrance hall going directly into a small and quaint garden in the back of the house. It was filled with flower plants: white gardenias, blue hydrangeas and pink azaleas. Infinity walked out to take advantage of her freedom of movement under Viviana's supervision, to contribute to the garden's rich flower arrangements by dropping her signature.

The hallway opened unto two nicely decorated bedrooms, with one double bed in one and two single beds in the other. Both rooms had a wooden window facing the colonial street. They sat for a few minutes in the living room. Adelita was enjoying the visit and reassured Dr. Osborne that she too would take care of the cat until Dr. Osborne returned. They agreed that he could go for an hour to have a short promenade to see the Carmelite Convent from the outside and look at the many colorful local stores in the side streets around the Plaza Mayor. Maybe, if time permitted, he could visit one of the Museums; but he deferred that last suggestion, as he would rather do that with Virginia on Saturday.

Dr. Osborne was most pleased with the unexpected warm hospitality and obvious responsibility of Adelita and Viviana. If the girl was the choir director in spite of her young age and she had been introduced to him by Father Garcia, he had no doubts about her behavior and maturity. He felt very much at ease leaving his precious possession with them. Besides, he could sense Infinity's empathy toward these two persons. He advised them he was ready to leave for his short walk.

Adelita told him and Viviana concurred, that they would be very happy to take care of Infinity, which they promptly described as the beautiful ***GATO DE VILLA DE LEYVA –THE CAT OF VILLA DE LEYVA.***

Viviana managed to explain to Dr. Osborne, before he left and while they were still sitting in their small living room, that her elderly mother was a widow, as she had lost her husband a couple of years earlier when he was attacked by a *paramilitary* group while visiting family members in the country region near Medellín where they had travelled to see him from El Aro, in Antioquia, a town which had seen terrible murder, destruction and raping by that bloody and sinister organization. Dr. Osborne knew the paramilitary were cruel and vicious, and killing was no obstacle in their search for power, often assisted by military forces, drug lords and corrupt politicians. All these people utilized the excuse of not fighting the FARC guerrillas directly because they didn't have – or so they said as a cover-up – the necessary manpower and financial support to fight openly against the FARC. So they relegated instead that cruel task to a third unofficial grouping, considered non-existent and an invisible fluke, which terrorized the campesinos, stole their land, raped women, kidnapped children, killed government officials, all in the name of Justice for the Motherland and its 'oppressed poor.'

The latter group would be the reverse mirror of the 'rich, unkind and abusive oligarchs' who controlled the Conservative Party– or so they explained in their political presentations– against the leftist populist forces of the 'real social' political segment represented by the Liberal Party of the murdered Jorge Eliecer Gaitán who had been assassinated in the famous or infamous *Bogotazo* of April 9, 1948.

Dr. Osborne felt very comfortable with the attention and friendliness of Adelita and Viviana. Adelita somehow reminded him of his own mother, albeit she was an older woman who evidently had aged with the accumulation of time and suffering.

He agreed to go for a leisurely walk in town and return within the hour. He was escorted to the door by Adelita while Viviana held Infinity in her arms. Dr. Osborne noted the girl was very gentle while interacting with his assistant and he was pleased to let the agile feline in Viviana's care. He sensed she was a very responsible young girl. In a fleeting moment he noticed her friendly smile, attractive figure and emboldening bosom.

He walked leisurely around the streets of the Plaza Mayor, which took him past the Church of our Lady of Carmen and the religious Museum of the Carmelite nuns where Mother Angelica was now interred; and subsequently, the house and eponymous museum of the artist Luis Alberto Acuña. Finally, Dr. Osborne sat to enjoy another coffee – his constant *tinto* - at Hospedería la Roca, one of the cafés which also advertised tourist rooms for rent, around the central Plaza Mayor.

While time went by, he carefully studied the whitewashed buildings and green balconies, and he felt transported to hundreds of years ago, imagining the horses walking on the rustic pavement, ladies holding up their long dresses on rainy days to keep them from getting soiled by dirt and water, campesinos carrying fruits and vegetables to the various eateries, children going to a rudimentary school – oh well, he thought, whatever your imagination can generate. Abruptly, he wondered: Where is my Capitán Cosmos? I miss her terribly; I have fallen in love with her; there are still two more days of waiting before I am able to hold her close to my heart. So he got up and left to go back to retrieve his assistant Infinity and thank Adelita and Viviana for having taken care of the Gato of Villa de Leyva, as they now called his cat Infinity. It was a peaceful and tranquil walk back to their house.

When he arrived back at their dwelling, he knocked on the door. They came out quickly to greet him, smiling radiantly and explaining right away how happy they had been, and how content *Infinity* had been, playing with them instead of doing serious research like she probably did at her usual university laboratory. Viviana told Dr. Osborne he had arrived just in time, as she was going out with Gabriel to meet a few of their friends in a café near the church.

Dr. Osborne took Infinity from her arms and placed her back in her portable cage. He shook hands with Adelita and Viviana, thanked them profusely, indicated he might come by the next day or Saturday around lunch time to drop Infinity, and suggested he would be glad to pay them for their supervisory service; but they would hear none of it. He waved goodbye and departed.

As he went out the door he heard a motorcycle approaching and he recognized Gabriel, who was coming for Viviana. He waved to Dr. Osborne and gave him a shy smile. Dr. Osborne waved back.

As Dr. Osborne was getting ready to walk away, Viviana came out smiling, waved at him, said hello to Gabriel, and swung onto the back seat of the motorcycle. Dr. Osborne kept looking at the whole maneuver, actually thinking how lovely young friendships can be. As he watched Viviana lifting her leg over the motorcycle back seat, her skirt flipped open and rode above her knee, along her thigh, revealing a sensuous innocent flash of flesh; the turning skirt slit above the knee suddenly revealed a smooth lightly tanned thigh – or was it just the natural color of her native Indian skin, which he had seen so many times in his unexplainable visions? But this time the picture did not become a blank image as it had always happened before. The mystery of the image had been solved. He was greatly relieved.

He almost gasped as he now understood where his mental pictures had come from and felt a sudden comfort in the process of his mind: It had been a vision of destiny that evidently anticipated this moment and not a senseless accident of his brain. He quickly figured the only meaning was simply to create a connection between his imaginary perception and the real vision of a beautiful attractive enticement.

At that precise and meaningful moment, two things happened: the Cat of Villa de Leyva meowed loudly with obvious satisfaction; and Dr. Osborne's portable mobile phone rang insistently as it vibrated in his shirt pocket. It almost startled him.

****

Chapter 18

A Surprise Call

He took the cellular phone out of his pocket and answered with a slight shake of his hand. *It was Virginia calling him!* He held his breath. Instinctively, fifty things ran through his mind before he spoke to her. He wasn't any more used to romantic entanglements. Was there a sudden problem? Wouldn't she be able to come on Saturday? Did something happen at FESCO that would keep her from coming to Villa de Leyva to be with him? Then he quickly got upset with himself for thinking negatively. Why should he even feel that way?

He listened like a cougar in the jungle waiting for his prey. Oh, yes! Subsequently, paradise opened up: After greeting him, Virginia told him she had *great news*: She would be arriving Friday afternoon instead of Saturday. She was anxious to see him. She had extra time-off that she would rather spend with him than wasting it around Bogotá. She commented how glad she would be to be with him – and jokingly mentioned that would be true even if

Infinity was around. She thought he would be pleased to learn that information.

John exclaimed spontaneously: "Virginia my friend, I couldn't have heard better news today! I am so pleased! I will be counting the hours, the minutes, the seconds until you get here!"

She reminded him she had previously twice invited her grandmother to go to dinner with them in Bogotá, and she had declined; but had indicated she would be glad to go out in Villa de Leyva, as she always enjoyed that colonial town. Accordingly, Carmencita had decided to join her and John, and had also invited her cousin Susana to come along. Thus the two ladies could be with each other and do the tourist bit unhurried by themselves, while Virginia and John were alone enjoying their own company.

Virginia asked him to check with the hotel to make sure the reservations for her grandmother and her cousin were in order; she had personally called the hotel and made them under Capitán Cosmos of FESCO. That always commanded more attention and immediate respect, especially in a country with so many male chauvinists, otherwise known as *machos*.

John confirmed he had previously reserved two adjoining rooms for the two of them; should he keep that arrangement or switch the rooms over to her grandmother and friend? Virginia answered to keep those adjoining rooms for them, as she had already reserved two separate rooms for her grandmother and friend. Besides, she commented that if he didn't behave properly, she could always lock her door and let Infinity move in with her. And she laughed like a little girl, which disarmed him completely.

He asked her if he should contact Pedro, as he had told him he would confirm their weekend plans. She said that Pedro had called her because he couldn't get hold of John. Obviously he didn't know that Dr. Osborne was attending the special funeral for Mother Angelica. So she had told him it wouldn't be necessary to pick her, Carmencita and Susana up, as they would be traveling in Carmen's car, which was the official armored vehicle mandatory for her travels. She told John FESCO required a bullet-proof car for her transportation.

She mentioned to John that after their driver dropped them tomorrow at the Hotel Plaza Mayor, he was instructed to continue to Tunja, about half an hour away, to deliver some important documents to the local police office and thus take advantage of the roundtrip from Bogotá. He would return the next day to Villa de Leyva and be available to take them sightseeing if they wanted to, together with Susana and Carmen or by themselves. She suggested he call Pedro as a courtesy to him.

John said that if she, her grandmother and Susana got to Villa de Leyva at a reasonable time, they all could go to the Restaurante de la Gata, ironically so called 'Of the Cat,' supposedly a Swiss-German eatery where they could enjoy a fondue. Wouldn't Infinity be happy - another cat in the horizon!

Though most likely he would leave her behind in the hotel room.

Virginia said that sounded spectacular and she would be looking forward to dinner. Of course Carmen and Susana might be too tired after their trip to go out to eat with them, and they might prefer to stay at the hotel restaurant. Besides, she said in a languorous way, the two of them still had so much to talk about, didn't they? Wouldn't it be better to be alone? She could barely wait to be only with him. She said good bye and told John she was sending him a quick kiss until next day.

After the call from Virginia, John felt cheered up at first; but subsequently, he sensed he was alone, almost lonely. To distract himself, he went walking around town, carrying his laptop and Infinity. He looked at various stores, cafés, and restaurants all around Plaza Mayor and in the streets nearby. He visited the Museum of a well-known artist, Luis Alberto Acuña, in what used to be his private residence.

At one time, he passed Father Garcia who was crossing the Plaza Mayor with a group of old women parishioners. He greeted them and told Father Garcia how beautiful the Mass had been for Mother Angelica. He invited him to have coffee and pastries in one of the bakeries or other casual eatery. Father Garcia said he would definitely and gladly join him on the way back from his errand.

Dr. Osborne sat with Infinity in a cheerful looking restaurant where a young guitarist was singing songs from the Colombian coast called vallenatos, mixed with old time tango ballads from Carlos Gardel and boleros from Mexican artist Agustín Lara. Gardel was an Argentinean singer, songwriter and actor; he was the most prominent figure in the history of tango. He died in Medellin in 1935 in a plane crash. Lara was Mexico's greatest romantic songwriter, ugly as sin but talented as a divine angel, who died in 1970. Behind the bar counter was a photograph of *don* Agustín Lara, with his name in full, which Dr. Osborne noted for his intellectual satisfaction: *Ángel Agustín María Carlos Fausto Mariano Alfonso del Sagrado Corazón de Jesús Lara y Aguirre del Pino*, who thank goodness became known by the simpler Agustín Lara. When Padre Garcia joined Dr. Osborne for a savory snack, he commented that somehow Agustín Lara's talent in music had extended to his flair in women, as he had been married at least five time to beautiful and well-known Mexican movie stars.

The temperature was cool and pleasant. John was trying to control his emotional reaction to Virginia's call and the news of her earlier arrival. As she had said, they still had so much to talk about. Maybe he could ask a few more personal questions without offending her. None of her answers would affect the way he felt about her.

Now he knew some very personal information. She had never been married before nor had she lived with Jean-Pierre, the French friend she had met in Paris and who had been killed with her father in that terrible truck assassination attack going to Bucaramanga. Virginia had told him she had not slept with Jean-Pierre as she had been too upset about her mother's death at the time. But she didn't mention any other man who may have wooed and courted her while she was in England undergoing training at MI5 and MI6, perhaps the most select spy and security organizations in Europe. In a nutshell, MI5 concentrated on matters of homeland security, terrorism and other threats inside the UK, and MI6 operated regarding overseas espionage and international counterterrorism.

One ludicrous thought quickly crossed his mind. What about before those years when she was already a woman? What about before? Could she still be a virgin? But what difference did that make! Did that really matter, one way or another? He answered his own question: Of course not. They were mature people, intelligent adults, consenting to a love passion that seemed to be consuming them freely and genuinely. Love was evolving in a genuine burst of incandescent feelings, and there should be nothing to detract or negate any of their sentiments. He would be able to analyze these thoughts with Virginia as soon as she would be with him, starting soon, the next day, on Friday afternoon; but evidently not soon enough; very soon, hopefully, because time now seemed to pass very slowly for Dr. John Osborne. Even Infinity was very quiet and slept most of the time in her private royal chamber.

John couldn't anticipate what she would tell him during their reunion. He also wanted to ask Captain Cosmos if they had ever caught the murderers of General Jaramillo, her beloved father.

Padre Garcia had slowly meandered to the café where Dr. Osborne was sitting wondering about different things, mostly about Virginia Jaramillo Cosmos. He was somewhat melancholy being alone and waiting for what now seemed an eternity until next afternoon. John and Padre Garcia had some empanadas and other light fare to appease their hunger, and drank delightful cool fruit juices to quench their thirst, and who knows, perhaps pacify their spiritual yearnings, too.

John was delighted to get together with Father Garcia who actually looked cheerful, positive and glad to see Dr. Osborne as well. It was easy to talk to him as he seemed to be an intelligent and humble man in the service of God Almighty. He was dedicated to the local parishioners of his beautiful church; he was in charge of the students developing their lives and careers in the local school; he supervised the church choir and took care of the elderly who were slowly waiting their turn to leave this unpredictable life.

Padre Garcia further explained he also guided all the people in between who were struggling in their daily lives to survive, earn a living, eat decently, make love within the acceptable rules set up by the mother Church which were disobeyed in great part by the passions of love and ethics, the phallic impertinence of men's ego and mutual glandular activity, and the protection of the appetizing humid caverns of the female monument.

Yes! He was quite well informed of the reality of life, morality deviations and sufferings instilled by love, chastity, purity and the overwhelming pursuit of a normal everyday life within the search for the attainment of basic moral values, compounded by the deluge of pornography on the internet and the spread of topless and full frontal nudity in the networks of the world. And the saddest development of all, even the priests who were the epitome of moral guidance and ethical pulchritude, had betrayed their people and crucified Jesus every time they abused the young boys and girls when they had taught them to masturbate under the holy cloths, and the parallel sadness of tearing down young women's dreams of innocence and chaste affection.

John and Padre Garcia talked for a long while. The holy representative indicated he was glad to take a break after a heavy week of work and penance, to discuss different topics with an intelligent and unbiased doctor of Letters and Philosophy, and to discover an aura of mutual understanding and compassion that was absolutely necessary to survive in today's universe, with so many problems in the world, let alone Colombia with its hundreds of thousands of dead, tortured, maimed, disappeared, through the criminal activities of drug dealers, the cartels of Medellin and Cali and other regions, the FARC, ELN, AUC, paramilitary groups, government and military corruption at all levels, M-19, MAS, UP, and so forth.

Father Garcia's voice remained calm but John could see he was making a powerful effort to hold back tears of sufferance from controlling the painful emotions which inundated his eyes. The Doctor of Science and the Doctor of Souls communicated well and openly and exchanged fundamental ideas about the true value of existence and love, sin and recovery, patriotism and betrayal, devotion and respect for a faith given to us human beings by the only messenger entitled to do that: the Son of God who, for his effort, peace and heavenly love was rewarded with a bunch of nails pushed through his flesh to attach him to a wooden cross. But then, Padre Garcia stated with a peaceful smile, at the conclusion of their intellectual exchange: He was the only one who was entitled by his powerful Father to come back alive three days later. Father Garcia and Dr. John Osborne concluded their cordial get-together and parted feeling satisfied and reinforced in Truth.

****

 *Chapter 19*

Reunion in Villa de Leyva

In the late afternoon of the next day, John received a phone call from Virginia. She was traveling in Carmen's car, and advised him the three of them were not far from Villa de Leyva. They expected to reach the hotel Plaza Mayor within a half hour. They had already passed the Boyacá Bridge, and their driver - who had worked for her grandmother for many years - was now proceeding steadily on his way to the city. The change from green pastures to rocky and desertic panoramas was always impressive to see but it indicated they were close to their destination.

On the whole, they had enjoyed the trip from Bogotá, in spite of the occasional traffic delays, especially in the neighborhoods leading to the outskirt of the capital, where finally motorcycles, colorful buses, trucks, bicycles and even pedestrians seemed to fall into a more orderly parade that allowed almost normal driving. They had gone through a short rainstorm that sent hail as big as stones on the windshield and pelted the car's fenders; but that was not an unusual display by nature in the Bogotá skies.

The dark black vehicle was large and comfortable in normal traffic, though purposefully not overwhelmingly large. Perhaps instinctively other drivers respected the special unmarked vehicle, as they could not tell if it was an official government or military vehicle, a bigwig executive working with his mistress during an escapade out of town, a paramilitary or drug dealer's limousine coming to complete a dirty deal or leaving the evidence behind, or even a Cardinal on a holy promenade. Actually, it looked like the automobile from any well-to-do Bogotano family; and the middle class folks were not far behind in their ability to buy bigger and better cars than in the past. There was steady political and economic progress in the nation of Colombia.

Manuel, a retired loyal member of the Armed Forces, was an expert driver. If anyone should come too close to the car, like street vendors or other unwanted characters, Manuel would dismiss them authoritatively with a wave of his hand, and either a terrifying nasty look or smiling greeting, depending on the purpose of the 'offer'. If someone insisted too much, he would simply touch or point to the weapon discreetly but handily lying next to him – a menacing mean looking life-stopping AK47 auto machine gun fully authorized and loaded. At the sight of that vicious-looking gun, any interloper would instantly disappear into thin air.

Capitán Cosmos was in uniform, since she was still on duty, and they had left as soon as she had arrived from FESCO to Carmen's residence. She was sitting in front next to Manuel and his *amigo;* his friend, as he called his awesome weapon. Of course, somewhere in her uniform or hidden on her person, Virginia too carried the symbol of her authority, the special Glock 17 pistol she had been given by her English instructors at the end of her training course, as an official award for being first in her target shooting course and as a symbol of her newly achieved professional spy interrogatory clout.

Dr. John Osborne was back at the hotel waiting for the visitors. He was carrying his laptop and Infinity. If anyone had been able to put their hands on his chest, they would have felt his heart's beat accelerate at the thought that soon the woman he had irreparably fallen in love with, would be sitting across from him; and he would be able to touch her hands, see her captivating smile, sense her magical scent and permanently enjoy her overwhelming charm which had enveloped him like a magician's cape.

He smiled to himself as he imagined he was a cat and Virginia, dressed in a glittering dress and a shimmery mantle, was performing on stage as a magician, moving her wand over a big British style top hat while pulling out nervous black kittens with her white gloved hand. He thought that was a ridiculous idea: he, the famous researcher, a cat! And she, the smart intelligence agent, a magician pulling up black kittens! He must have thought of Infinity. Is that what love was doing to him? That was ridiculous! He put the whole scene out of his mind. Instead, he sat in the lobby of the hotel, ordered a *cafecito*, and drank his coffee while waiting for Virginia, her grandmother and her friend Susana.

Around five o'clock, the bullet-proof black car pulled up on front of the Plaza Mayor Hotel to let its passengers out. His heart jumped with joy as he saw the smart looking Captain Cosmos, who smiled at him in her own precious way. She was the delicate kitten he saw coming out of the top hat. That is all he needed from her: he knew instantly he had been right all the time thinking about her love. He went out to greet her and Carmencita and Susan. They were so happy to see him, too. He gave them a warm greeting, and lingered only an extra minute with Virginia, since she was still officially dressed in her uniform. But he saw her clear penetrating eyes under her formal hat. They were scintillating. He also greeted Manuel, cordially but formally. Manuel carefully carried his 'friend' while escorting Carmencita and Susan to check-in at the lobby. Captain Cosmos followed them with Dr. Osborne by her side.

After checking-in, they all said farewell to Sergeant Manuel, who would be going on to Tunja to deliver some documentation from the Judicial Court in Bogotá; he would return the following day to be at their continuing service. Dr. Osborne accompanied the two ladies with the hotel attendant, and then escorted Captain Cosmos to her room. She checked the facilities, including the connecting door to his room. And next she hugged him, saying how happy she was to be in Villa de Leyva with him. Her smile and candor melted his soul. She indicated she would need some time by herself to rest and get ready for the evening. She commented Carmencita and Susana had told her in the car they might just stay and eat at the restaurant downstairs, where they all could meet to have an aperitif and small canapés, before the young couple went out on their evening venture. Carmencita was too smart to curtail the young couple's activities. Besides, she really liked John and wanted Susana to partake of her sentiments.

That arrangement sounded like a good idea. John told Virginia he was then planning to take her go out for fondue at the Restaurante de la Gata, as he had previously mentioned to her. Would that suit her? She said yes; they could try it. He commented he had personally checked the restaurant and it was quite cozy and adequate.

She said it would probably take her half an hour to get ready; and it would also give time to Carmencita and Susana. John replied: "That's fine. We're in no rush, Virginia. By the way, I guess we'll dress sort of elegant casual, typical for Villa de Leyva. In the meantime I'll get Infinity settled. Till soon, my dear Capitán." They gave each other another warm hug, a short but inspiring kiss, and he left her via the room door. On purpose, he did not use the connecting door.

A while later on, when she was ready, she knocked on the connecting door. She did this out of habit when entering offices at FESCO's main headquarters; but her father and mother had taught her to always be polite and respect people's privacy behind closed doors. Always knock first!

John opened the door. Infinity was peacefully stretched out; but she was startled, jumped from the couch to the floor, said meow and sat immobile looking at Virginia. John too remained motionless, staring at the woman who had become his flaming love. He grabbed her hand, guided her into the small living room area, and silently turned her around. Impulsively, he joined his feverish lips to hers; they were so tempting, soft, enticing and asking for his love's caress. She closed her tranquil and clear eyes, put her arms around his neck and held him tight. She returned his emotional feeling in a reciprocal embrace. They remained locked in that position for several minutes, breathing in unison, sensing their excited emotion, and enjoying their first real moment of privacy.

There was no bright moon in the sky, but through the open balcony window they could see the incredibly hypnotizing panorama of the colonial plaza, stunning whitewashed buildings set on cobbled streets, emerald green shutters, flower-filled window boxes and ancient balconies. All around, the soft inviting lights of the restaurants, cafés and miscellaneous stores seemed to protect the historic architecture. The past was standing still; it did not move; just as the two young lovers were peacefully entwined in each others' arms.

****

 *Chapter 20*

Burundanga Cumbia

Sometime on Thursday, the day before Virginia and her grandmother were to arrive at Villa de Leyva, Dr. John Osborne had sat at a café on a side street of Plaza Mayor. He had picked up a travel magazine written in English, which had an article on special drugs. Evidently, it had been left behind by some foreign tourist or government or business representative.

Actually, Dr. Osborne had been thinking for some time about possibly using new applications for greater control and mobility of his star assistant Infinity, affecting his research of Infinity's cognitive behavior patterns. He was intrigued intellectually by the drug *scopolamine,* which however had risky applications. It was available in sheer abundance from any of three plants in the *Solanaceae* family freely growing throughout much of South America.

Coincidentally, he had seen a detailed description of *Burundanga* in a travel book – of all things - by Sarah Woods from Bradt Travel Guides in England. It explained as a Serious Warning that a derivative of the drug S*copolamine* colloquially known as *Burundanga* was administered to tourists and regular customers in bars, restaurants, dance halls and other places where people congregate in search of fun and company to pass the time away, oftentimes with disastrous results. He read this dangerous drug is shared or forced casually via drinks or cigarettes. It is colorless, odorless and tasteless and can even be easily sprinkled on to food. Victims become so docile that they have been known to hand over belongings or their sex without batting an eyelid. Others awake in a state of grogginess having been robbed of all possessions or their private chastity. You are advised to not even accept a cookie or a cigarette from someone you don't know; and even from someone you may know who might be planning, unbeknownst to you, evil things with your body or belongings.

He read that *Burundanga* can even be put on parts of the body to be licked on purpose or accidentally, for instance by prostitutes or night operators. It can be blown into someone's face so that anyone with criminal intent can guide that person and direct them anywhere like an innocent child, for example to bank ATM machines to withdraw unwittingly all their savings and cash. After the episode, the victim probably won't remember anything. Paper sheets doused with an alkaloid or plant-derived organic compound –like caffeine, atropine and quinine – may be used. Their effects may vary from medicinal to poisonous; but it is believed all alkaloids cause a physiological result on the human body. Consequences from the plant can make you go zombie. It's perhaps the scariest drug on the market. After reading the article attentively, Dr. Osborne immediately discarded it in principle. This sinister drug had no reasonable application in any of his cognition and brain research.

He put it out of his mind. Tonight was another story: For starters, it was Friday night at the Plaza Mayor Hotel and he was with Virginia. As he held her in his arms admiring her subtle and insinuating décolleté while looking at the Plaza Mayor, he gently kissed her neck. Then they agreed they should be going, as first they had to go downstairs to have a short get together with Carmencita and Susana in the hotel restaurant. They called Carmen's room. She didn't answer her room phone, which meant they were downstairs waiting for them.

They got together in the lobby and sat by the fireplace. It was a cordial and affectionate reunion. They ordered a few *canapés para piquar* -- hors d'oeuvres to munch on, two *whiskeycitos* - small whiskeys - for Susana and Carmen, and delicious fruit juice for Virginia and John.

After a while visiting and talking about their earlier trip today and in previous visits to Villa de Leyva long ago, Carmen suggested that Virginia and John leave for their dinner, as she didn't want them to linger and lose their time together at the Restaurante de la Gata. They got up, kissed Carmencita and Susana good-bye and left happily to celebrate their fondue evening at the Cat Restaurant. John said he would introduce Infinity to Virginia's relatives at another time, maybe the following morning.

They walked slowly on the cobblestones across the Plaza Mayor, holding each other. Virginia had entwined her arm around John's; for any curious onlooker they looked like an old married couple.

The restaurant was relatively near; a few blocks at the most. The unhurried walk was romantic under the diffused lights from the street lamps and local stores illuminating the colonial town square.

When they got to La Gata they were greeted most cordially by the owner and his wife. They were seated at a corner table which gave them plenty of privacy to talk. It was a romantic setting, though the place was casual with a European touch. While selecting their fondue, they decided to try a glass of local wine. This was a rarity in the country, as Colombia is not known for its wines like Argentina and Chile.

The owner described the wines from the two local producers. One was from the vineyards of Marqués de Villa de Leyva, which to the surprise of the couple was an unusual business operation that had been started at least over twenty five years before. He told his guests that most Colombians do not even know it exists. The grapes are grown in a high altitude climate, which makes them special. The waiter explained there was another local vineyard which was two hours away, called Marqués de Puntalarga. The light white wine they ordered to accompany their cheese fondue was quite enjoyable and the quality very acceptable.

John kept looking at Virginia; she looked so feminine and warm that he felt his heart thumping with pleasure. Her hair, normally hidden by the captain's hat and now free like a condor, fell over her shoulder in rivulets of scented glory, so naturally and sophisticated at the same time. His love was uncontrollable and he was hypnotized by the poetry of her eyes and the sparkle of her friendly smile. What a fortunate man he was to be sitting with Virginia in this small and cozy restaurant in Villa de Leyva! She looked at him with her piercing and tranquil eyes as he sat momentarily quiet.

He told her what he was thinking; and she responded by squeezing his hand and flashing her eyes which she opened wide as if to let him penetrate her being to the deepest corner of her heart. He could feel his soul mingling with hers in a communion of earthly love and ethereal feelings. Was it possible that Virginia was still single and virginal? He knew she was not presently married nor had she previously been. Ah, love has many facets, uncertainties and anguish! To love, you must suffer. To suffer, you must love.

They talked about many things: their jobs and responsibilities; their own relationship; their future together. She asked what he had done since he had arrived in Villa de Leyva. He commented about Mother Angelica's funeral, which he had partly filmed through Infinity's minuscule camera on her collar. Later he would show her the short video.

He also told her about the church choir, the girl conductor Viviana, the young organist Gabriel and his convivial get-together with Father Garcia. He asked her what she had been doing since he had left Bogotá. It seemed like a century ago, as he had missed her that much. So in turn, she told him what she had been doing since he had left her, primarily working on her security projects, without divulging any confidential information, of course. She was genuine and open hearted.

He told her that the next morning they could walk to visit the Mesopotamia Hotel and maybe have lunch there. He mentioned he had indicated to Viviana that Infinity could have a short visit with her. The girl had asked him for that favor since she had enjoyed Infinity so much the previous day, saying that her mother would be going out of town by bus on Saturday at dawn to visit a cousin in Tunja, and would not be returning until the evening. Her mother always left a copy of the house keys with Father Garcia as a precautionary measure.

They were enjoying their superb fondue when Virginia looked at John and asked him a direct question: "John, can I ask you something important?"

He replied: "Of course, Virginia, that's why we are here; to search our hearts."

"John, my friend, would you sleep with me for one night just to make love to me?"

He answered: "No. Even if I would like to, I would not."

She looked at him and said: "Do you like me as a friend or only as a woman?"

He said: "I love you both as a friend and as a woman who happens to be very beautiful."

"Do you want to know more about me?"

"I want to know everything you want me to know about you. You too can also ask me whatever you want."

"Are you curious about my love life, my love feelings for you, and probably whether I am a virgin? Does that make any difference to you?"

"No, my dear Virginia; life is made of many events, and we cannot control all of them or plan what destiny has in store for us. No, it does not make any difference to me if you are a virgin or not, since I love and need you for what you are, not what you could have been or should be."

She asked: "Then when will you go to bed with me?"

"Whenever destiny unites us."

"Will you sleep with me tonight?" she murmured.

John answered without hesitating: "Yes. We'll sleep together; but we are not going to have full sexual relations. It will happen soon; but I feel tonight is not the night."

Virginia looked at him with her scintillating eyes and smiled with her sensuous lips, saying:
"I'm glad to hear that, John. I wasn't ready either. Somehow a silent hand is holding me back. I'm tender and ready; but I would rather wait. Tonight is not the night. It would be an evening of irreparable damage."

"It's okay, Virginia; destiny will grab us by the hand when we are ready."

They looked at each other silently for a couple of minutes as they continued to eat their sumptuous cheese fondue. They had a sip of the local Marqués de Villa de Leyva white wine and she smiled again at him. She loved his gentle manners and unrushed sexual impetus. She preferred the sense of love over the rush to penetrate. She caressed him gently with her eyes, crystalline like a mountain lake, and asked: "What else exciting did you do during the last couple of days?"

John answered he had had a very pleasant, intelligent and friendly get-together with Padre Garcia. He couldn't recall an earlier occasion in his life when he had ever sat alone with a relatively young man of the cloth and exchanged intellectual ideas on a variety of subjects, all realistic and pertinent to today's style of living, wisdom, philosophy and unfortunate sexual scandals by some priests.

Virginia asked if he had had time to read any of his books or anything else. He answered that he really hadn't had that much time to read, except for *La Fiesta del Chivo,* by the famous Peruvian author Mario Vargas Llosa. She commented that she too had read it, during her last year while training with the British Secret Service in Cheltenham. It had been a peculiar distraction.

Out of sheer curiosity, Virginia asked John if he had looked at the news or read anything else. He said that he had actually read an interesting article related indirectly to his research, but he had discarded its application as too risky, dangerous and uncertain: the use of the drug *Scopolamine* colloquially known as *Burundanga.* Was she or FESCO familiar with it?

John looked at Virginia's face; it had become pale and her eyes had lost momentarily their usual iridescent shine to become opaque and troubled. He asked her if he had said something wrong. She shook her head to indicate a negative answer. Then he saw two tears swelling up against her closed pupils. When she opened her eyes they were bathed in a watery expression of immense sorrow.

Virginia looked at John, straight into the depth of his heart, saying: "John, your question is perfectly fair and intelligent. *But my answer is very complex and painful.* I'm so glad we are here in a nice private corner so that I can fully answer without interruptions. You must listen to me very carefully." She grabbed his hand and held it tenderly; almost as if to protect herself. She actually moved a little closer to him, so as not to be overheard by anyone. John had a moment of uncertainty as he looked attentively at his dearest companion Virginia.

She stated: "I am going to tell you a very private story that nobody has ever heard, except my beloved grandmother Carmencita."

"John, my beloved friend, *mi amor*, we were talking a while ago about love, making love, sharing love and indirectly about relations that may affect a woman's virginity, her very own private natural protection of body and soul. You commented the possibility of using a certain drug in your research endeavors for Infinity. You followed up, coincidentally and unexpectedly, with a question whether I was professionally familiar with the drug Scopolamine, also known as Burundanga."

"*Amigo* John, let me answer your question. *Yes*, I am very familiar with it, from personal experience and also from criminal investigations at FESCO. When you were commenting gently whether, if and when we would be making love, I hesitated to answer; I have to tell you a disturbing story and its aftermath."

"When I was a young girl eighteen years old, I had not slept with a boy. I was still a virgin; but I was not a naïve and uninformed young girl. I was well educated. My mother was very close to me; she had taught me many things about men, women, love, morality and sexual behavior, especially in these times of freedom and changing mores. Many of my girl friends slept regularly with different boyfriends; I did not. You fool around, sometimes more, sometimes less. But I was a pretty good girl. We were taught things in Psychology and Biology classes, and in Religion and Ethics. When my mother died, I lost perhaps my closest friend."

"I was then only a young 18 year old girl. I was lonely and very sad for a long time after my mother passed away. My will power had been weakened, and my general enthusiasm was quite low and depleted. I was quite depressed."

"At the end of the school year a group of our college students had been invited by one of the crowd, Rafael Uribe, scion of a powerful, wealthy and very well-known family, to a party he was giving to the graduates at his parents country house on the outskirts of Bogotá."

She paused to breathe deeply and squeezed John's hand. He was looking at her in a most supportive way, but needless to say, he felt pretty helpless since he couldn't do anything to comfort her, other than pay careful attention. He was leaning close to her and listening to her every word.

"Needless to say the house was impressive, and there were waiters and maids galore, as befits a show-off cocky young guy from such a well-to do and powerful family. There was plenty of music, food and drink: gin, whiskey, rum, beer and *aguardiente* – local brandy enjoyed by both rich and poor. Everybody seemed to be having a good time. However, there wasn't much supervision; most students were between 17 and 20 years old."

"During the party, when nobody was looking, the cynic Rafael had put a drug in my lemonade drink which he had also laced with powerful 12-year old Caldas rum. I would eventually find out that he had hit me with the infamous *Burundanga*."

"Not long after that, while everybody was dancing, drinking and jumping around, I started to lose my concentration and my thoughts became confused. This guy Rafael had turned the lights down, to make the party more 'intimate and romantic.' I was unsure on my feet; I felt increasingly woozy. He suggested that I go lie down on a bed to recover; but he didn't indicate he would be coming along."

"He took our two glasses with him and led me to one of the bedrooms very surreptitiously. I didn't even realize he had locked the door. Evidently he had done this trick before with other girls, but nobody dared to talk about it. I guess he knew that when I would recover from this episode I probably wouldn't recall a thing; or there was no way I could prove anything. After all, his father was a very rich and powerful Senator and heavy player in the political arena. Who would dare to complain, let alone accuse him and his darling son?"

"What Rafael didn't realize is that I had recovered momentarily, for a few precious seconds, enough to notice that, fortunately, I had not finished my altered drink and Rafael's glass was still on the night table. He had undressed me almost completely and I was lying quite naked in bed. He took off his clothes, imbued in part by the regular alcohol he was drinking. He cockily stood up admiring his own erection and suddenly decided to go to the bathroom to urinate before attacking me. At that instant I saw my mother's image and I said quietly a desperate prayer to the miraculous Virgen of *Chinquinquirá;* I was able to switch the two glasses before he came out of the toilet. I was laying back still in my stupor, though now I could perceive him more clearly. He took what he thought was my glass – which was really his glass *without* Burundanga; he made me drink from it and finish it. He in turn took the other glass on his night table, which was really *my* doctored Burundanga drink. He finished it in one continuous gulp. He then stood up on top of me, naked and excited, with a sadistic expression on his face. He knelt down and prepared to penetrate me with his repulsive organ like a gladiator in the Coliseum. Suddenly, as he got closer against my loin, he tumbled downwards and sideways and laid down, stretched still and immovable. I almost hoped he had died from a heart attack."

"I was starting to come back to reality when I felt a disgusting puddle of pungent liquid next to my thigh. In absolute revulsion I finished waking up almost completely and realized the beast had completed his evil sexual action; but fortunately his semen was spread next to me on the sheet and not inside me. I had been spared the whole agony. There were a few drops of blood on the bed when I finally came to. I got panicky at the thought this monster had forcefully penetrated me, a voluntary non-consensual rape; but I was alert enough to grasp that I was going through the beginning of my period, and this criminal action had not ended with the destruction of my feminine hymen." She paused and rubbed a tear from her eyes. She continued:

"I thought the bedroom door was locked. Perhaps it had been, but this creep might have opened it to go get more booze or Burundanga. I don't know. In any case, as I got hold of myself, I managed to sneak off the bed into the bathroom to splash water on my face and quickly dry myself, slide my panties up and slip my dress on. When I was sitting down on a chair putting my shoes on, the door opened. My heart stopped. I almost fainted with fear."

"But I was quickly relieved. Two of my best girl friends rushed in, saying they were so glad they finally found m. They grabbed me, all the while rushing to get me out of the room with them, saying:

'Quickly! Let's go before the *hijo de puta,* the son of a bitch wakes up!' I was still somewhat unsteady but they guided me by a side door to their car. Fortunately, we had all come to the party together. We left as quietly as possible, without making any sudden noises. Nobody saw us leave; and nobody cared."

"Only once we were in the car, did they finally have the time to ask me if I was all right, had I been hurt, should we go to the police? I gave negative answers to their questions. No one would believe us; after all, this scion was the son of the most feared Senator in the Senate, who was rumored to be involved with drugs, the paramilitary and money laundering. The scion himself was a dealer contact. My good friends took me home and stayed with me for a while having a cup of tea and making sure I was recovered enough to go to bed while they went to their own homes."

She stopped and remained silent and pensive, while John looked at her with intense tenderness.

He said: "Virginia my love, I am at a loss of words to comment on such a terrifying event. It must have been an awful experience; a horrifying occurrence. What an unforgivable degradation! That young man was a savage swine, a criminal monster. Whatever happened to him?" She interjected: "Dear John, I will tell you another time. I'm not in the mood to dwell on that now." He retorted and continued: "How fortunate that your girlfriends found you and took you home!" He paused. "Perhaps I should just stay quiet and let all this sink in. I think now we should go back to our hotel room, unless you want to stop for a moment at a café to change the mood. You must be so upset!"

She replied: "John, *mi amor*, I am sorry to have been so frank with you, my love. I didn't spare you any details because I know I can trust you. I feel you really respect me and genuinely love me. I agree with your suggestion; let's finish here. Fortunately, we have been comfortable and had such a private table. Let's pay the check and slowly go back to our hotel."

Printed on the bottom of the check was a thoughtful comment: *Gracias. Las buenas cuentas hacen los buenos amigos* – 'Thank you. Good accounts make good friends.' John commented to Virginia that the thought applies to human relationships, too. He paid the check, thanked the waiter and said good-bye to the owners.

When they got up, he hugged Virginia, kissed her gently on the lips, slid his head close to her ear and whispered: "You don't know yet how much I love you, Virginia. I care very deeply about you." She smiled tenderly at him. Her eyes were getting their sparkle back and losing the opacity they had acquired during her sad story.

They walked slowly, arm in arm, toward the peaceful Plaza Mayor. Its quiet ambience was interrupted once in a while by the sound of a guitar or a smaller string instrument called *tiple*. Occasionally one could hear a romantic vallenato or nostalgic bolero coming out into the night air through the open door and windows of a busy café. He thought he recognized the place where he had sat the day before and heard a young musician playing his guitar and singing Agustín Lara's boleros.

Tonight was a beautiful Friday evening and people were enjoying their town and their serene weekend. Virginia was calmer now and she was regaining her charming composure. She squeezed his arm and even smiled gently at him. He bent over and gave her a soft tender kiss on her lips. She opened them slightly so he could feel more fully her enticing and captivating appeal. He realized then that he was head over heels in love with Capitán Cosmos. Her sexual hypnotizing attraction was a secondary magnet derived from her appealing magnetism as an extraordinary woman.

As their lips parted, he could still feel her humid embrace. He looked into her now tranquil eyes that sparkled in the low illumination of the cobblestone square. Before he realized it he made a suggestion that he could not hold back: "Virginia, my darling friend, why don't we go back to our hotel and spend the night together in my room. You can call your grandmother Carmencita to tell her we had a lovely evening and check on her and Susan. Tell them we will have breakfast or dinner together tomorrow."

"When we are back in our hotel, I have a suggestion: If you so wish, after you have finished getting ready for bed, gently knock at my door and come into my room through the connecting door. We will go to bed to sleep together. I promise you I will not make you uncomfortable and I will not do anything other than hold you close to me. We will spend a beautiful night embracing each other tightly, loving our warmth and enjoying our company." He paused.

Virginia looked at him, gave a disarming smile, held his hand close to her bosom and said:

"My darling John Osborne, of course I will come to you as soon as I'm ready. I will go with you to bed, as you have suggested. We will spend our first night together just loving each other." She stopped; then she added: "But I will let you put your hand on my heart, so you can feel how it beats when I'm next to you. You can keep your hands on my breasts to tell me I am no longer alone." She hugged him and whispered in his ear: "And Infinity can climb on the bed also, if she wants to sleep by our feet on the cover."

****

Chapter 21

A Youthful Experience

Early in the morning, Virginia got up first, said hello to John and Infinity, and with a tender smile said: "I had a wonderful night, John; I haven't slept that well in a long, long time. You kept your promise to let me rest in your arms and I am most appreciative."

John answered: "My beautiful captain, I keep my promises. Besides, we will know through life's own signals when we are ready to cross the natural bridge between our two bodies. I'm not in a rush, as our love is not a one or two-night affair. We will have a lifetime of togetherness."

Virginia petted Infinity's soft head, She had slept most of the night without disturbing the young couple. She was stretched on the cover. Now she looked at Virginia and let out a special meow, as if agreeing to the statements she had heard.

Virginia then walked into her own connecting room. John watched her walk and admired the tempting figure under the delicate light aquamarine nightgown, which hid the body details but was transparent enough to reveal the enticing curves under it. When he had complimented her the night before as she entered the room, Virginia had commented that the stylish gown had been a birthday gift from her mother; it was a Givenchy design she had purchased in the local fashion store in Guadeloupe, when she had visited the French Island with her husband for a military conference of Caribbean nations. Virginia had made a special point to say she had not worn it before, as she was saving for a very private and meaningful occasion like the night before. That's why she had brought it with her to Villa de Leyva, hoping the night would turn out as it did, although it was almost spoiled by the unexpected story of the Burundanga episode.

When she was ready and dressed, she told John she had called her grandmother Carmencita and Susana; they would all meet in the terrace restaurant for breakfast. She had reminded them the view from there of the Plaza Mayor was impressive and unforgettable. They were delighted to be all together for breakfast.

She came into the room and smiled at him with her tempting lips and sparkling eyes, and gave him a tender kiss on his cheek.

As she was leaving, she told John not to forget to bring his assistant Infinity so she could meet the rest of the family. In the meantime, she would order his scrambled *huevos pericos* the way he had told her he loved them: fresh eggs from a country farm, prepared in a black iron skillet, with minced onions and diced tomatoes. She promised she too would prepare them that way someday to show him how much she cared for him. Then she left by her room door.

It was a delightful and friendly breakfast. The staff was very efficient and courteous, and did not interrupt their conversation.

The star of the show was Infinity, whom John introduced to the two elder ladies, who were mesmerized by her intelligence and behavior. Susana had asked if she could pet her, and John had assented, indicating only she should avoid sudden movements. Infinity was listening attentively and somewhat bored by the whole process but she understood these were professional obligations required by her owner. She was very proud of her unusual black collar, though surely she couldn't fully understand the detailed electronic software and photographic lenses that were cleverly hidden inside, and which were not obvious to Susana and Carmencita, and not even Virginia. John had every intention of explaining later to her the basic minuscule switches and controls, and the practically invisible and unnoticeable camera.

Virginia commented to Carmencita and Susana that their driver would be returning from Tunja in the afternoon, at which time they could decide if they wanted to go visit the Convent of the Holy Ecce Homo situated about 13km from Villa de Leyva. It was founded by Dominican fathers in 1620 and was notable for its magnificent chapel. They could also visit the Adobe or Terracotta House, a full-size two story house, complete with kitchen, living room, bathrooms, several bedrooms, roof terrace, stairs, electricity and running water which was designed out of clay by Octavio Mendoza, a well-known architect. It is baked in the same manner as local pottery makers produce vases, dishes and other decorative objects. It is made without any nails or steel braces and supports.

When they had finished their delightful breakfast, Carmencita said she and Susana would spend some time walking around the Plaza Mayor and visiting a couple of museums, while Virginia and Dr. Osborne – John, they corrected themselves - could do their own visiting. They would meet again in the afternoon to do some sightseeing out of town when the driver was back from Tunja. Following the traditional custom, they kissed each other good bye by hugging and touching their cheeks.

John was carrying his special laptop case with Infinity and wearing his preferred Quindío white hat. Virginia held his left hand as they walked into the

Plaza Mayor. Every time she smiled at him he had a surge of immeasurable pleasure and positive well-being. He tried to send similar waves back to her.

There were a few people milling around, but the gigantic colonial plaza was so large that they didn't crowd the open space. John told Virginia to stop for a moment as he wanted to put a black leash on Infinity to let her out of her portable cage so she could get some exercise and walk next to her master. Nobody really paid any attention to them as the few pedestrians were all busy doing their own thing and enjoying their Saturday morning. A few children were running around, playing with colorful kites and watching them as they went up in the air and made delicate turns with the wind currents. Circular loops the loops and variations brought smiles to the children and to the parents who were sharing the moment of joy. It was a popular recreational activity in town. Infinity looks at the kites with curiosity, but she didn't run after them. She stayed by her master's side. She had been trained to follow instructions at the research laboratories.

They walked slowly and leisurely toward the central decorative fountain, talking about breakfast, the weather, the happy art of kiting, the innocence of the boys and girls playing around the plaza; asking themselves, what it must have looked like back a century or two ago, when the colonial ladies and their servants walked around on their way to Mass or Vespers; or the fortunate children who could attend school came back through the plaza on their way home, perhaps like at the present time; or the cavaliers or ladies riding their beautiful horses.

When Virginia and John reached the other side of the Plaza Mayor, not far from the Parochial Church which was really their Cathedral, a small motorcycle stopped by their side. John recognized young Viviana the choir director, and the organist Gabriel. They stopped and greeted Dr. Osborne and his companion. Viviana told him that early that morning she had taken her mother to the bus station so she could go to Tunja, from where she would be coming back that same night. She had just come back from leaving an extra pair of house keys with Father Garcia, who was always happy to do that favor to Viviana's mother.

Viviana reminded Dr. Osborne about leaving Infinity with her for a couple of hours; she would be so happy taking care of her while he could wander around town with his friend and enjoy the city streets; and maybe have lunch somewhere. Dr. Osborne said he remembered his promise and he would be dropping Infinity on his way to the Mesopotamia hotel where he probably would have lunch, as he had enjoyed it so much the previous day.

Viviana said she would be home by the time he got to the hotel, which was across her house, so he could drop off Infinity. As she climbed back on the motorcycle, the flipping over revealed her thigh and it reminded him he no longer had to wonder about that image he had seen so many times before running into this girl. Viviana and Gabriel slowly puttered away, laughing as they left Dr. Osborne and Virginia looking at them. She exclaimed: "They look so happy, perhaps they are playing at young love." He smiled and assented with his head.

****

Chapter 22

A Complex Situation

Viviana and John continued walking toward the La Mesopotamia Colonial Hotel. It was originally a flour mill, now over 450 years old. They wanted to see the lovely gardens and check out the natural pool gracing the hotel grounds. It was used as a swimming pool by hotel guests. Visitors could use it too by paying a fee and changing in the wood cabin; but without getting the use of towels.

As they reached the area, John noticed Gabriel's motorcycle standing against the white wall near Viviana's house. He walked over with Virginia and knocked on the front door. Gabriel came out smiling and greeted them; Viviana appeared behind him. John told him that, as agreed, he would leave Infinity with them while he and Virginia went for lunch and a leisurely walk around that part of town. He slowly took Infinity out of her laptop compartment and checked unobtrusively that all the controls were off on the black collar. When he gave Infinity to Viviana, he didn't notice that, as she slid her hand over the black collar, she had accidentally activated the minuscule camera. Gabriel and Viviana waved good bye to Dr. Osborne and Virginia, who left quietly holding hands.

John and Virginia spent time going around the Mesopotamia gardens and the old colonial building, filled with old furniture and past mementos. They walked up to the natural pool and sat by the side of the crystal clear water. John commented that her eyes were as brilliant and reflective as the water in front of them. She gave him one of her irresistible smiles and kissed him on the lips. She also suggested that instead of eating in the Mesopotamia Hotel she would prefer to have lunch at the Boutique Hotel Calendaria Real which was around the corner. He immediately agreed as he didn't know the restaurant and her suggestion was probably a good choice. They would ask for a table on the terrace to enjoy the beautiful weather.

Once they had completed the tour of the hotel gardens, they went to the Boutique hotel and were lucky to get a table on the terrace. They had the advantage of seeing down the street toward the Plaza Mayor, but the plaza was too far to be seen and besides, they were one avenue too far west. John did notice that he could see in the distance Gabriel's motorcycle sill standing against Viviana's house wall.

Virginia and John were taking pleasure enjoying their precious moments together. They exchanged affectionate glances and listened to each other with interest as they discussed a variety of topics. They respected each other's opinions. In the meantime, they selected an appetizing lunch including *papitas criollas* – delicious small round potatoes – and refreshing fruit juice. Jon remarked there seemed to be an unending variety of tropical fruit in the country and Virginia readily agreed. Then they waited while their lunch was prepared.

While they were discussing many topics, John suddenly asked Virginia, for no specific reason at all other than genuine concern:

"If you don't mind telling me, did you ever find out what ever happened to that miserable guy who put Burundanga in your drink and almost raped you in your drugged slumber? You had already mentioned to me that one day you would tell me when you were ready."

Virginia felt silent for a while, looking at John with intense eyes, and then she proceeded to tell him the story. She took him back to the fateful evening and she started to fill in new details.

Her mother had already died. She could or would not tell her uncle Robert what had happened, perhaps taking into account the general attitude of *machismo* that still permeates her country of Colombia. She asked for private advice from a wise, intelligent and understanding priest she had known for many years through her mother and Carmencita. During confession, so he could not reveal their discussion, he tried to console her and help her. He told her that priests who are accused of abusing young boys and sometime girls were completely misguided and were doing the Devil's work. The young man who had taken advantage of her trust and confidence was in the same league. Her counselor during her confession told her to have faith in herself and almighty

God; he said God would help and sooner or later he would punish the guilty abuser. The miraculous Virgin of *Chinquinquirá* to whom she had prayed would not forget her, either.

It was perhaps only a gentle consolation, but it helped to calm her nerves, though she remained affected for a considerable length of time. She did not want to see a psychiatrist or psychologist as she did not fully trust them. She had heard 5% of psychiatrists end up sleeping with their patients. She did visit her female doctor who was also a gynecologist, without describing to her what had happened, just to get a regular physical check-up; the doctor corroborated the blood tests and confirmed everything was normal; there were no urinary tract infections or obvious sexually transmitted diseases.

Virginia paused and then resumed her story as John listened attentively. The female captain who in a short time had become his deeply beloved friend pointed out what she believed Fate had intervened to claim justice for her and thus assuage the anger of her Lord over the depravity which had befallen her.

She felt that way because several years later she had learned some secret facts through her uncle Colonel Roberto Jaramillo as the result of an investigation that FESCO had carried out on direct orders of the Senate of the Republic. FESCO had been instructed to investigate a serious criminal event which had been brought to the government's attention. Colonel Jaramillo and his Security Department had no idea there could be an indirect past connection to

Virginia, since they didn't know anything about it in the first place, nor had she in any way or shape divulged any details of her dismal occurrence. It would prove unnecessary anyway, as destiny has many tentacles, like an all-wise mythological Octopus God.

Virginia had not immediately made any correlation of the event under investigation and her own involvement, but the puzzle pieces slowly fell into place. She remembered that one day she saw a young man who reminded her of Rafael walking on one of the main streets of downtown Bogotá, accompanied by what seemed to be a black uniformed nurse or bodyguard taking care of him. He looked odd and unbalanced. He was limping heavily. He had aged ten years; he was thin and decrepit. Could he be the same arrogant young man who had abused her so savagely? At any rate, Virginia wasn't absolutely sure if the person she had seen was Rafael.

What Virginia had found out years later, when she was working for FESCO, actually took place about three months after his dastardly attack on her. The cocky scion had tried again a similar obnoxious violent trick using the drug *Scopolamine* or *Burundanga* that he had used on Virginia and probably other young women. His intended victim on this other occasion was a well-developed fourteen-year old humble country girl named *Azucena* or Lilly who was visiting a friend of hers in a *finca* owned by an important friend of Rafael's parents. The owners would not be home while Rafael and two of his friends were spending the week-end there. One of the owner's sons had invited Rafael and another friend to stay with him at the house. A couple of other fellows and their girls would probably be coming also, so they all could all have a nice barbecue and drinks without any adults around to bother them.

The girl's friend was the young daughter of the guardians who took care of the house and property. Obviously they were modest people. Rafael thought he could get away with his plan as the visiting girl was from out of town and thus not an element in Bogotá's social scene. His two friends would be going for a couple of hours to the nearest town to buy supplies and beer, maybe pick up their other girl friends, but Rafael told them he preferred to stay behind to watch a soccer game on television; although he really was intent on carrying out his diabolic plan, unbeknownst to his two friends.

The young innocent girl, Azucena, had been invited by her friend to come and spend a few days with her family to take advantage of her vacation from school in her small country town where she lived in one of the rural mountains areas beyond the *zona cafetera*. Past the coffee-growing region, further north of Medellin, drug dealers, guerrillas and even paramilitaries were very active. What Rafael did not know was that Azucena - the visiting girl - was the youngest daughter of a powerful and sanguinary drug lord known as *Cortacabezas* or Headhunter, with a reputation for merciless drug operations with considerable support from guerrilla groups.

Rafael's friend and the house owner's son had conveniently offered to drive the caretakers in Rafael's van to the small town stores to pick up their weekly supplies for the house, thus saving the couple a long trip and effort during the week. Together they would also pick up the meat for the barbecue, and perhaps a few beers and a couple of bottles of gin, whiskey and aguardiente. Rafael told the parents it was okay to go in his van, as he would stay behind to watch the house and the girls. He would look at television. Wouldn't that be very convenient?

Not long after all of them were gone, Rafael had asked the girls very politely to bring him a pitcher of lemonade and a bottle of gin from the wooden cupboard in the bar, plus a couple of glasses to celebrate with them, as he innocently put it, the girls' vacation and the end of their school term. He managed to convince the two trusting girls by being charming; plus using automatically the power of oligarchic obligation and implicit servitude by humble lowly people. He convinced Azucena and her girl friend to bring him the cool drink he had requested. The two girls didn't have much choice but to obey, as they had been taught by their parents and teachers, since after all Rafael was the son of a powerful Senator and a member a very rich family. If they didn't obey him, their parents could be in serious trouble. So they did as ordered by Rafael. The girls didn't know anything about spiced drinks nor did they see him putting the Burundanga into their glasses, which he managed to do very discreetly and evidently with great expertise. He asked them to sit with him on the couch to see the soccer game between two of the top teams in Bogotá, *Santa Fé* and *Millonarios*. They were actually flattered and they accepted.

It wasn't long before the drugged lemonade had its effect on the girls. To make sure it worked well, Rafael added a little gin to each drink, making the girls feel more grown up and mature. Nonsense. He was just making sure they were fully affected by the spiced combinations. The girls would now comply with any request. He took the guardian's daughter to her room and made sure she stretched in bed for a long sleep; when and if asked, he would tell the parents she had just conked out and was resting from the game excitement and maybe a little bit of gin; that was his fault, please excuse him. He actually thought it was too dangerous to take advantage of her spurious situation.

But that was the end of his seemingly benevolent behavior. He led Azucena into her bedroom and put her down on the bed. The innocent girls followed him meekly, not realizing what was going on, as she was already under the distressful Burundanga effects and had lost complete control of her decisions and cognitive mind. Rafael proceeded to carry out his nefarious plan. He took off all her clothes and dwelled on her young beauty, taking advantage of her sensuous breasts and the enticing nakedness of her thighs and womanly forms. He quickly undressed, so as to let his excited sexual member become a devastating weapon of fear and forceful invasions. His eyes grew bigger and threatening and his excitement became more uncontrollable. He was standing naked on the girl, who was laying under him like a docile angel. He was celebrating his erected masculinity, while Azucena was in another world, unaware of his savagery, bare and completely undressed and totally defenseless under the aggressive monster. Suddenly he knelt down panting and huffing; he forcefully penetrated the young girl's private and intimate lips, tearing apart her virginity. She screamed helplessly as he finished his horrendous attack. Rivulets of blood came out on the sheet, as she cried in fear and despair, while he fell sideways next to her and passed out.

Next thing he knew he felt his friends' hands on his shoulder, shaking him up harshly, and asking him to put on some clothes. They were obviously shocked. They helped the girl to get dressed. Then they quickly left to take Azucena to the town's local clinic to help her hemorrhage and painful condition. Fortunately the caretakers did not see what was happening. The young men told them they were taking Azucena to the clinic as she had fallen and needed assistance to prevent an infection. The humble caretakers believed them – why shouldn't they; they thought the young people were doing them a favor. Their daughter was peacefully resting on her bed, so there was nothing to worry about. Rafael had always been a very nice person. Why would they think anything else? Besides, they were simple country people and not used to the cosmopolitan degeneration that might take place in the metropolitan capital of high society and money.

Virginia was talking in a calm and incisive manner, but John could tell she was deeply affected by what she had eventually found out. She needed to explain additional circumstances to John so he would understand the entire picture, as the details until now were only part of the story. She asked if he wanted to hear the rest. He could only understand if he listened to all the details of that horrible event. It had a very serious ending that only through FESCO's investigation was eventually discovered and completed. At that time she had joined the intelligence department and had become privy to investigative operations in her uncle's criminology and security organization.

After the horrible attack to Azucena took place, there didn't seem to be any repercussions. There were quiet days of peace, as if nothing had happened. Rafael the rich young man had paid all the expenses at the clinic and given the emergency doctors and nurses an additional and substantial contribution so that no details would leak out to his parents or to Bogotá society. The three young men thought everything was back to normal. Rafael, of course, had not divulged the details of his forceful rape – as that was the truth - to his friends. They may not have approved what he had done. The caretakers were appreciative for all the help they thought they had received. The girls, obviously, were terrified to complain to anyone or say anything that would inculpate the powerful scion and his friends. So they kept silent. But a couple of young nurses had been horrified. Possibly they may have said something to her father. One of them was from the same region as Headhunter, the drug lord, and she had heard of a couple of good things he had done like building a *Casa de Ancianos* or Old People's Home. This was often done by the criminal drug dealers to show the local peasants and politicians how benevolent they really were. In other words, evil disguised as angels.

At that moment, Virginia stopped and said to John: "My dear John, I am tired of talking, let's finish our lunch here and walk toward Plaza Mayor to find another café where we can have some local pastries or *galletas,* lift up our spirits and continue my story so you know the entire tragic adventure." John completely agreed. He told her she didn't have to continue her tale if it was too upsetting. She said: "No, I want to tell you the rest of the story, John."

He paid the check; they got up and went out to stroll down the street toward the Plaza Mayor. After walking for a few minutes, they found a cozy bakery with tables outside where they decided to sit. It looked cheerful and friendly. They could see all the way toward the Plaza with the main Church of *Nuestra Señora del Rosario* – our Lady of the Rosary – towering over the colossal square. It was a good place to have their coffee and dessert and finish the violent story.

****

Chapter 23

A Celebration in Congress

After Virginia and John had ordered their coffee and local pastries, they exchanged some small talk, enjoyed the street view and commented how extraordinary it was to be sitting in the middle of a colonial city that had retained all its charm from centuries past and yet had so many conveniences for a modern traveler. They added a touch of levity by pointing out to the happy children coming back from Saturday school carrying their notebooks under their arms and looking forward to a day of no homework, no more school, and no more struggling with mathematical formulae.

While sitting there, John saw the young church organist Gabriel drive by on his motorcycle. He was probably going to rehearsal for Sunday's services. John pointed him out to Virginia, who acknowledged his signal but casually commented she thought Gabriel looked a little frazzled. Oh well, she added, maybe he had been enjoying his visit with Viviana, since they were all alone since her mother was away; but John was somewhat concerned since he had left his assistant Infinity with Viviana. They would later pick her up and check on the young choir director. Virginia told him not to worry, the girl looked like a very responsible and serious person. She then continued Rafael's saga.

She told John: "Rafael had felt pretty secure and relaxed since he thought he had gotten away with his transgression. Even his two friends had not questioned him anymore; they had accompanied him to the clinic and then they all had left in a normal way since Rafael had made the necessary financial arrangements to keep the whole affair quiet. He had also given the caretakers a generous propina for their help during his stay with his two friends at the house. He assured everyone the girl had fallen down and that was that. No reason to feel panicky. There had been no repercussions. The hospital would keep quiet; they had their contribution from a well-known Senator's scion. Nobody would dare to question anything."

"Destiny had other plans. A few days after the sickening assault on Azucena, trouble happened. It had been delayed in coming as it had taken time to prepare. As Rafael and his close friends were driving around the perimeter road of Bogota which is cut out on the oriental mountain side of the capital and which is dark and pretty solitary at night, with some unpaved egresses on the side leading nowhere, two cars were following the young men. Suddenly, by a sharp curve, one of the cars passed Rafael's automobile car and pulled right in front and stopped. Rafael's car shrieked; he started to insult the other driver calling him all kinds of names; but by then the second car had pulled close to Rafael's vehicle and he couldn't move or back up."

"Five guys with black hoods came out of the two cars, carrying machine guns, and ordered the three young men to get out, not to say a word or scream, follow them up the hill, and lie down on the grass in a spot the attackers had carefully selected beforehand. The three students were terrified. All the money in the world couldn't help them out of this situation. The hooded assailants tied their hands and feet with rope and forced the two friends to watch. The men undressed the cocky scion, took out a bottle of whiskey and forced Rafael to gulp half of it. They said it was from Azucena; and gave the rest to Rafael's other two friends. They took down their pants and left their privates hanging out in the open. The male anatomy responded automatically to this display of nudity and the men dropped some liquor on the erect penises. They gave more liquor to drink to Rafael, who was desperately trying to fight them off to no avail. They told the two friends they would be okay, as they had not been directly involved."

"When Rafael was already partly inebriated, one of the attackers told him, with a sarcastic snarl, that he had a silent message from Headhunter and his daughter Azucena: he pulled a sharp butcher's knife, which was reflected in the pale moonlight, and amidst terrible screams and the absolute fear in the faces of the victim and of the two witnesses, they castrated the young scion. They left him lying on the grass in a pool of blood, where eventually, early next morning some policemen found him and his two petrified friends. As the attackers had left the horrific scene of the crime, they had kicked the two friends in the testicles for good measure, to remind them of their indirect participation in the whole ordeal with Headhunter's property: his young innocent daughter Azucena. Rafael's car was off the road. It had been set on fire and was burnt beyond recognition. It would take two days for the hospital to identify the victims, and several days to restore them to relative mental equilibrium, except for Rafael who had been affected for life."

"While the above episode had taken place, and before any public details had been discovered or divulged, *el Congreso de la Republica de Colombia,* the august and noble Congress of the Republic of Colombia was celebrating a historic vote to negotiate peace with the Guerrillas and Paramilitary. It was also the birthday of one of the most powerful and feared senators, Rafael's father. Congress was in full quorum for an important electoral procedure. It had stopped its deliberations to honor the Senator and present him with birthday tributes. Among them, at the last minute, an elegant note had urgently been delivered to the powerful congressman by a page boy, with a box covered by a tri-color ribbon celebrating the national yellow, blue and red colors of Colombia. The stylish envelope with the note indicated that the birthday gift box should be opened right away, while Congress was in session, as it was important for the vote at hand. The Senator asked his colleagues to wait for a minute and excused himself for the interruption. In front of all his colleagues, without any further ado, he opened the birthday package which had been inspected by security for explosives and cleared. He took out a black plastic bag out of the box and asked his secretary to open it with her scissors."

"As she opened it and passed the contents to the Senator, his face turned pale white and then completely ashen. All color had drained out. His hands trembled and shook. The secretary fainted on a desk, almost vomiting on it."

"The Senator had taken out a beautiful silver plate, normally used for the best social graces. On it was a sliced penis and bloodied scrotum. A small note inside the package said that scrotal sac was a gift from the father of an innocent girl, to the Senator's father of the scion who had taken advantage of her, raped her and left her bleeding in the hospital. That muscular sac from the powerful, rich and oligarchic scion would no longer protect the Senator's son's testicles, blood vessels and spermatic cord. It was a bitter revenge sweetly completed on a stylish silver plate normally given in high society's circles on special occasions."

"The Senators were awestruck; absolutely shocked. Male and female members were scandalized and terrified. A loud cry went up in the august chamber. In the midst of the uproar, the Congress was immediately adjourned. Its voting session was postponed until next day. It was *definitely* not a subject for high society conversation at that night's social gatherings."

Virginia explained to John that the details of the whole incident in the country house, its gory reprisal and the Congress spectacle were not fully known until the perpetrators of such a savage revenge were accidentally arrested a couple of years later and eventually confessed their crime to an intelligence unit headed by Colonel Roberto Jaramillo. They were locked up for life; they were still behind steel bars. But their leader, the bloodthirsty criminal drug dealer Headhunter was not detained by Medellin authorities until a couple more years had elapsed and the judicial authorities in the Supreme Court in Bogotá had been able to establish a full-proof case against him. By then, Virginia had joined FESCO and was aware of all the details of the investigation. However, no one ever found out what her own ordeal had been at the hands of Rafael, the eunuch to be, except for her grandmother Carmencita.

Virginia now sat completely silent for a while. John could see how stressed she was, though outwardly she seemed very much in control and greatly relieved to have been able to share her deep experiences with the man she was now so much in love.

****

 *Chapter 24*

Infinity's Moment

While still sitting at the café sipping their coffee and munching on their desserts, John noticed the assistant church sacristan walking back from the hill area where Viviana's house was located. He seemed in a hurry, limping toward the church. Perhaps he was late to clean the pews and prepare the building inside for Saturday's Vespers and Sunday's Masses. He pointed him out to Virginia, who wondered why he was walking with such an apparent rush despite his limping affliction. She took a break to call Carmencita at the hotel, suggesting that, since John and she were still busy, Carmen and Susan should go visit the Adobe House that afternoon. They would enjoy the unusual clay house. Later in the evening, they would all get together for dinner, maybe at the Hotel Restaurant Mama Santa; and tomorrow on Sunday morning they could go together to visit the Ecce Homo Monastery. They all agreed on the plans; that would allow John and Virginia extra time to be together alone. That would be perfect for all of them. Carmen confirmed their driver had returned from Tunja and was available to take them to the unusual house.

John and Virginia decided to leave the bakery and take a walk around the colonial streets to enjoy the colorful local arts and crafts. They paid their check and thanked the servers. John carefully put the laptop case around his shoulder.

As they got up to exit the terrace, John saw Father Garcia coming up the street rather hurriedly. Padre Garcia waved at John and asked him and Virginia to join him while he continued on his way. He apologized for being in a hurry when John invited him to join him and Virginia for a coffee. Padre Garcia said he was doing an errand that had him somewhat worried. Perhaps John and Virginia could accompany him in case he needed some assistance. They gladly agreed to escort him, since they had no other fixed plans now that Carmencita and her cousin Susana were going to tour the Clay House by themselves.

John asked Padre Garcia if he and Virginia could help him with a problem. The friendly priest seemed somewhat distraught. He told them that Gabriel the organist had come into church for the usual Saturday music rehearsal, but he seemed nervous, distracted and almost catatonic. That was very peculiar, as Father Garcia had known the young boy for a long time and he was always punctual and respectful. He didn't say much of anything, almost grunting. He seemed scared.

As Viviana had not appeared for leading the choir rehearsal, Father Garcia had asked his assistant sacristan to go to her house and remind her of the usual choir practice. He was rather surprised that she hadn't shown up, as she too was very punctual and reliable. Her mother had gone to Tunja that morning with an early bus, and as usual, had left the house keys with him for any emergency. He didn't give the keys to the assistant, as he thought the latter would give the message to the girl. But the boy had knocked on the door. He didn't get any reply. He said to Father Garcia that he had heard a meow, as if there were a cat in the house, which surprised and scared him. So he had gone back to church and told Father Garcia, who became noticeably concerned. That's why he was glad he ran into John and Virginia to accompany him to see what was the reason for the delay.

John was able to explain immediately to Father Garcia that the peculiar meow the boy had heard was his cat, acknowledging the knocking on the door. He had left Infinity with Viviana, since she had insisted she would take good care of her, just as she had done very well the day before. Besides, she had told him that she was actually planning to become a veterinarian.

So, earlier in the day, John had left Infinity and Gabriel alone with Viviana. Father was not concerned about the young couple having been left unaccompanied, as he knew their character, and they were close friends. Besides, there is always confession; but he wasn't in the mood to joke about those things. He was actually very anxious there had been no answer to the door knocks. So he was bringing the front door key; and was relieved he was not alone.

After a short walk up the slightly hilly street, they reached Viviana's house across the Hotel Mesopotamia. Everything seemed normal in the neighborhood and in front of the house. Father Garcia knocked on the door; there was no answer. Nobody heard any noise. He knocked again. They all heard a cat's meow. Dr. Osborne knew his assistant was well; at least she was alive. Father proceeded to open the door with the spare key Viviana's mother had given him. John made sure the cat would see him immediately; she was well trained and would not sneak out. She would wait for her master.

Padre Garcia went in first, followed by Virginia and John. Padre Garcia blurted out: "Viviana, are you home? Where are you *niña*? Girl, are you all right?" Virginia looked around in the living room and the bedrooms and didn't see anyone. Infinity was still by John's feet. She looked up and meowed insistently to her master. Dr. John Osborne recognized the urgency in her cognitive call from research experiments at the laboratory. He said: "Infinity, search! Go! Proceed!" He added: "Where is Viviana?" Infinity turned around and strutted off at once.

All three people followed her instinctively. She led them to a rustic kitchen which had a small eating table in the center. Padre Garcia let out a quick shocked cry of surprise. Virginia also expressed anxiety as she exclaimed: "There she is, Padre!" Viviana was lying down on the floor, behind the table. Strange enough, her head was resting on a pillow. There were no signs of violence. The girl had a blanket covering her limp body. The only outward sign of any unusual occurrence was the partial sight of her thigh, just as John had seen it previously during those few times when that same vision had surged in his mind at the most peculiar moments. He realized it must have been some sort of unexplainable premonition. Other than that, nothing indicated any violent assault or suspicious activities.

Virginia quickly realized the girl seemed to be all right; there didn't seem to be any trauma involved. Strangely, she appeared to be quite comfortable. Virginia asked herself: what was Viviana doing, lying with a pillow under her head to protect her and a small blanket to cover her body in a modest way? Father Garcia was at a loss of words and asked for God's guidance, saying: "Poor Viviana, what happened? *Dios mío!* My Lord, did Gabriel the organist do anything to her?' He remembered the young boy had been in an obvious catatonic condition when he had returned to the church for music rehearsal; but evidently there was something else peculiar here.

Father Garcia had always considered Gabriel to be a young honest student, who respected people, his neighbors, the Church and his parish leader, Father Garcia. He was always polite, and truly very fond of Viviana. What had happened? What had he done? Was he guilty of any unsavory play toward Viviana since her mother was not in town? Father Garcia couldn't believe it.

At that time, Dr. Osborne explained to Father Garcia that his friend Virginia was a well-regarded and experienced professional security officer in

FESCO, where she was known as Capitán Virginia Cosmos. He suggested to Father Garcia to let Virginia make a preliminary inspection of Viviana and the kitchen, before getting overly nervous and creating a scandal, as the girl seemed outwardly fine and unhurt. Maybe there had been no foul play, the young fellow hadn't done anything unacceptable and he wasn't guilty of molesting or mistreating Viviana. Father quickly agreed to the positive choice.

After the initial moments of surprise and shock, Virginia found a wet cloth, and wiped Viviana's face and neck. She just seemed asleep as if she had fainted. But how come she was lying down in such a natural pose? How did that happen? John remembered he had left both young people and Infinity in good condition before he and Virginia went to lunch. He had seen Gabriel later driving his motorcycle alone to the church at the Plaza. Virginia noticed he was frazzled, as she put it. Father had seen the boy and he seemed somewhat catatonic. What was the reason?

As they sat there checking Viviana to make sure she was all right, Infinity went up to her and touched her cheek with her paw, licked her eyelid and meowed into her ear, as if making a continuous call for attention. In her cognitive tests she always expected a reaction from her master. Otherwise she would not be able to operate positively and successfully.

Virginia looked at John. He went to Infinity and instructed her to continue by pressing her collar. After a couple of minutes, Viviana finally moved her head slightly, put her arm around Infinity, clutched her warmly and said in a soft voice: "Oh, sweet Infinity, my friend, *mi gato de Villa de Leyva!*" After she said 'Infinity, my friend, my cat of Villa de Leyva, she opened her eyes wide and was absolutely scared and stunned to see three adults standing by her side. "Father Garcia, what is wrong? What is going on? Dr. Osborne, I didn't hurt your precious cat. Father, am I going to die?" He was still trying to recover from the whole episode. Viviana's recovery was such a relief that he could barely answer: "No, my young child, *niña,* you're not going to die, you just passed out. You're going to be all right, thank God; and Infinity." And he smiled at her, rather cheerfully, holding her hand and petting Infinity's back.

John too was trying to slowly recover from his initial fright. He realized Viviana did not seem to be hurt in any way. At that moment he heard a familiar sound alarm coming from his laptop. He turned his head around, wondering what had triggered that signal. It only worked when he was carrying out tests with Infinity and the electronic software was in operation with the black collar on Infinity's neck. He recalled he had purposely turned off all the signaling and transmitting buttons on the collar when he left Infinity with Viviana.

However, unbeknownst to him, when earlier in the day he had given his assistant Infinity to Viviana to be taken care of, she had accidentally activated the power buttons on the black collar as the cat slid in her arms.

When Dr. Osborne heard the alarm beep, he realized immediately that the collar had probably been secretly transmitting information and pictures to his laptop computer. Nobody knew that other than Dr. Osborne. Now he was in a quandary: Was this the right moment to divulge to Virginia the secret of his laptop and black collar cognitive research? No one knew this research secret on which he had worked for so long. He looked at Virginia and she looked at him, with a puzzled look in her eyes. What was he thinking about? What was the alarm sound she too had heard? John looked back at her. He told Father Garcia to please wait a minute by Viviana's side. She seemed to be safe and unhurt. He wanted to discuss a professional issue with Virginia. Father assented, of course. He was so relieved anyway by the positive outcome of what could have been a disaster. What would Viviana's mother have said if she had walked in on them with her daughter prostrated on the ground and everybody standing around her?

John signaled Virginia to join him in the living room where he was anxious to test his laptop, but he wanted her to be present. She followed him, questioning what was happening. He asked her to sit next to him on the couch. He explained to her, asking her to keep his information covert as he needed to reveal to her the secret details of the black collar and the minuscule operating software that allowed him to transmit orders to Infinity and receive video information on her activities. He suggested that perhaps they could find out what had happened to Viviana. He didn't want to reveal the source of his research. But if the plan worked, and the video showed data that could clear the young organist Gabriel, she could certainly tell Father Garcia, as a professional security expert, without divulging the secret process. He would take her word for it.

He connected the laptop to the black collar. The electronic system was intact and in a few minutes he was able to recover the video that unwittingly Infinity had been transmitting. Some of it was unusable since the micro camera had not been positioned in any specific position.

John suggested to Virginia that she go back to Viviana and Padre Garcia while he checked the video. They could help the girl refresh herself and perhaps get her ready to go to choir rehearsal later, if she was behaving normally. Virginia agreed, as it was very wise to assist Viviana to get back to her usual self, unless John found something very suspicious in the filmed information.

Dr. Osborne remained looking at the strange video. The miniature system had never been developed to film situations like the present one, especially since it was not directed to specific visual targets or people. Some of the images were not clear enough or in the proper frame; but after a while they got sharper and perceptively understandable. Infinity had probably stopped moving and was then just watching Gabriel and Infinity.

To John's relief, none of the visual intelligence portrayed any unacceptable sexual situations between Gabriel and Viviana. They actually spent most of the time playing cards, watching soccer or soap operas on television, or talking about music and the choir arrangements. However, one section caught John's attention. He went to get Virginia so she could see it too, before discussing it with Padre Garcia.

While Virginia had gone back to check on the girl, she had served Padre Garcia and Viviana a plate of hot soup with bread and cheese. Then the girl had gone to her bedroom with Virginia, washed her face and slowly gotten dressed. She appeared to be in fine condition; perhaps still only a little dizzy and unsure on her feet, but certainly pretty well recovered from whatever had happened.

John wanted Virginia to see a specific part of the video. He had studied it carefully, and wanted Virginia to share it with him. It showed Gabriel and Viviana sitting in the kitchen having some cake and fruit juice, which her mother had left for the young people. The mother knew Gabriel very well, since he had been a little boy, and she was happy that Viviana had him as a friend. He seemed to be respectful and not out to take advantage of her daughter Viviana. Oftentimes, the two youngsters would be left alone while the mother went to market or church or visit neighbors. No one ever questioned the relationship or its moral implications. They were simply good friends without excessive petting or other sexuality involved, certainly no more than other normal, nice, growing young teenagers. Villa de Leyva was a town where people knew each other and not subject to all the perversions available in the big cosmopolitan cities. Besides, smart parents and even Father Garcia realized that young people had to go through a natural period of development and evolution of their normal relationships.

John showed Virginia what seemed to be the explanation of what had happened to Viviana and Gabriel at noontime, while John and Virginia were having lunch and discussing the intense events that had transpired with Rafael's assault in the lonely hilly perimeter road of Bogotá, and the chaotic session in the Senate of the Republic.

John didn't actually want Virginia to show the following sequence to Father Garcia, but he asked her to explain it to him in an acceptable manner. It seemed undisputable that the two young people were not doing anything wrong. Basically, they were eating the light lunch Viviana's mother had left for them to enjoy while she was in Tunja.

What appears to have happened is that, for whatever reason it seemed necessary, Viviana had needed to get a cup or a pitcher from the top shelf of the cupboard. She had climbed on the chair to stand on the counter, in order to reach that shelf of the cabinet. The video showed Gabriel was helping to hold her, when Viviana's thigh sensuously slipped out from under the dress; the image captured Gabriel's surprised look. He couldn't hold back and resist the temptation to put his hand up under her skirt against the thigh, very close to the personal area of her panties that was considered anathema or a mortal sin if you were a decent guy.

Viviana had reacted to the unexpected touch with such a startling shock that she lost control of herself and passed out. Fortunately she did not crash down on the floor like a dead weight. The video showed she actually slid slowly between Gabriel's arms. He was able to hold her and help her just slump on the floor. He was terrified and became catatonic. But his genuine sentiments for Viviana, for whom he always had latent love feelings, made him bring a soft pillow to protect her head. She didn't appear to be hurt. He put a blanket to respectfully cover her appealing body and the skirt in disarray.

The video showed Gabriel was so nervous, and became so distressed and uncontrolled – frazzled, like Virginia had said when she saw him from the café terrace – that he automatically headed toward the church for rehearsal, where he probably ran into Father Garcia. Deep in his heart he most likely knew he had not done anything wrong or harmed his friend Viviana, but he panicked and felt he had committed a grievous sin; but he couldn't say anything to the priest, as he was too anxious; maybe at the next confession, since anyway his admission would remain secret and undisclosable.

Virginia saw the covert video and agreed with John to tell Father Garcia what had happened in the kitchen, without explaining too much in detail about the tape, and leaving out the part of the accidental thigh caress. Father might sooner or later find out at confession, which anyway would force him to retain the indiscretion under sacramental secret.

Viviana and Virginia came out of her bedroom and looked placidly at Padre Garcia and John. The young girl had recovered her composure and her cheeks and eyes had regained their normal expression. She greeted everybody saying: "Thank you so much for helping me through this moment of uncertainty and panic. Fortunately nothing bad has happened and I haven't broken any bones." Of course, Virginia and John knew exactly what had triggered the loss of equilibrium, but it was unnecessary to bring it up.

The main condition was that Viviana had just fainted and Infinity and Father Garcia had helped to resolve the situation – with Virginia and John's assistance. They got ready to go back to rehearsal and left the house. Father Garcia locked the door with the emergency key and Infinity was pleased to be carried by Viviana close to her chest. This time she did not utter a sound or a meow. Viviana walked next to Virginia. John was talking intensely with Padre Garcia. There was a deep sense of relief amongst all of them. At the church, Father Garcia greeted all the choir students as if everything was normal; he said 'sorry they were a little late,' went over to Gabriel whose face color had disappeared, waved at him with a sign of 'peace be with you, son, everything is in order.' He added: "By the way, today I'll be hearing confessions before the six o'clock Mass, would you be interested?" The boy looked up at him and simply said: "Oh yes, Padre Garcia, that's an excellent idea. It will keep us all in peace."

Virginia and John gave a friendly embrace to

Viviana before they left. The young girl thanked them again with an angelical smile. She gave Infinity back to John, who put her back in her laptop cage. Viviana whispered 'good bye' to Infinity; a soft meow quietly came out of the laptop case as Infinity looked at Viviana.

When they turned around, Padre Garcia gave them an appreciative farewell hug. They waved to Gabriel who was sitting by the old organ. He seemed greatly relieved. He managed to wave back and give a faint smile. John said to Virginia: "He is a very lucky young man."

They sat in the last pew of the church to listen to the music for about ten minutes. Virginia finally squeezed his hand and said: "Let's go, my dear Dr. Osborne." She kissed him gently on the lips as they got up to leave. When they reached the door, John and Virginia couldn't help looking back. Viviana waved to them, smiling happily and touching her lips with her palm; Father Garcia also waved to them, making the sign of the cross. He flashed them a grateful smile.

****

Chapter 25

A Family Dinner

The loving couple went back to the Plaza Mayor Hotel to rest for a while in the lobby while waiting for Carmencita and Susana to come back from their tour to the Adobe House. Virginia and John were certain they had enjoyed that visit as the house is most unusual, having been designed and built by an architect using clay as his main material. They talked to each other about the touchy situation with Viviana and Gabriel. They were so glad it had turned out all right and nobody had been hurt.

Virginia thought that Viviana was not completely aware of what had happened in her kitchen, and John agreed with her it was better not to dwell on the details, especially as everything was normal now. Father Garcia would speak to Gabriel to discuss a few items that needed explanation and paternal guidance; probably one of the most effective ways would be through the sacrament of reconciliation or confession, so that the boy would be able to talk freely and recover his sense of self respect. Padre Garcia would firmly but unequivocally tell Gabriel that he should not have left the girl alone; in that serious situation he should have advised the Father right away, as it could have become a very grave incident requiring medical assistance. Fortunately it turned out that additional help was not warranted. John expressed the thought that the English might have used the verb *swoon* to express Viviana's fainting sensation, meaning a condition of being overwhelmed by a sudden and shocking state of ecstasy or rapture. Viviana might have had a moment of unexpected sensual emotional feelings.

Virginia and John also talked for a few peaceful moments about his research with Infinity, at which time he showed her the special training video taken at the Botero Museum, when Infinity had climbed on the large black marble hand sculpture in the entrance hall as a demonstration of her cognitive expertise.

Virginia and John went up to their rooms to change for dinner. They would be joining Carmencita and Susana for the private family social occasion. John would leave Infinity in the room, organized for the evening since she wasn't going to join them for dinner at the Mama Restaurant. She had had enough excitement for that day. And so had they.

They met in the hotel lobby, kissed and hugged each other in the usual Colombian way, a reflection of the cultural warmth of its people, and left arm in arm toward Mama Restaurant where they were given a nice corner table which allowed for privacy and coziness. They ordered a plate of appetizers for the group and their individual dinners.

John offered a bottle of champagne to celebrate the eminent occasion. The owner said the only bottle of champagne he had available was a vintage bottle of Champagne Taittinger, at a special price, which his father had acquired several years previously from the local representative of the illustrious French brand. In fact, he recalled they had purchased it from the company owned by a Swiss gentleman who had a well-known import and food organization. That was fine with John: it was a special gathering with Virginia's close relatives. And in his heart he knew it was even more meaningful. He twinkled at her.

They talked about the day's activities, without discussing Viviana's incident. Virginia's grandmother and Susana had enjoyed their visit to the unusual clay house. They had stopped for lunch in Sumarchán at a local restaurant where they were served very appetizing fare, especially local sausages. The chauffeur ate at the same place, but at a different table; he had met somebody he knew in the army.

About half way through dinner, discussing their various activities of the day, Susana happened to mention the name of Carmencita's husband and Virginia's grandfather, Comandante General Francisco Jaramillo Pinzón. They talked briefly about him and the events of that fateful day, when he had fallen and fatally injured his head.

At that moment John remembered that once before he had asked Virginia if they ever had found the evil brain who was the criminal instigator who had planned the attack on her father, Brigadier General Rogelio Jaramillo Cosmos. He was very conscious now that the General was Virginia's father and Carmencita's son. He was also thinking of Jean-Pierre, Virginia's fiancé. He knew also that Colonel Roberto Jaramillo was Virginia's uncle, since he was her father's brother. Virginia had said she would eventually tell him what had happened to her father and Jean-Pierre.

Carmencita hesitated for a moment; Susana asked Virginia if it would upset her to talk about it. Obviously, they had information that was personally sensitive, and perhaps Virginia would be distressed talking about it. But Virginia was perfectly at ease with John now. She trusted his reactions and genuine interest. Carmencita and Susana didn't know Virginia and John had already discussed many other disturbing and bloody events. Virginia felt no compunction discussing this very personal drama with him. In fact, she remembered she had told him once that she would let him know what happened. She just didn't like to dwell on that painful subject, preferring to forget about it if at all possible.

Virginia commented in a slow and deliberate manner about the developments that had taken place over several months and even years concerning the terrible truck attack that had resulted in the death of her father and fiancé – as well as the driver of the automobile. It had led to other domino effects that resulted in extremely effective and sensitive developments that continued long after the truck event. In fact, she was already working at FESCO when a kind of unexpected closure resulted. Her uncle Roberto had been directly involved.

"After the truck ambush, the two perpetrators had escaped in a motorcycle, leaving the truck blocking the road for several hours while it was finally removed by the police with help from the army. They had turned back going toward Bucaramanga, as traffic was at a standstill. They had been able to speed away down the mountain road in their motorcycle. They were eventually caught when they were driving in the valley by the river. The perpetrators did not put any resistance, as they were not habitual criminals. They were doing the entire assault as a means of obtaining fast cash for drugs and aguardiente. They were hoping to impress a couple of *puticas* – young prostitutes – in their street area."

"Evidently, they did not fully realize the enormity of their crime. They were under the effects of some hallucinogen. The police and army units that were successful in arresting the culprits kept them detained without further ado, until the judicial systems of Boyacá, Santander and Cundinamarca could combine their official prosecutorial efforts to sentence the two felons to twenty-five years in prison. They had not been able to divulge who had given the specific orders to kill Brigadier General Rogelio Jaramillo Cosmos, my father; they kept insisting they didn't know themselves, as they were just being used as peons in the murder scheme. They didn't even know who was Brigadier General Jaramillo, nor anything about him."

Before telling her story, Virginia had asked Carmencita if she was all right listening to the account about her son's murder. Carmencita said that it actually made her feel better to hear again some of the details of the judicial process. She believed in the honorable - even if painful - application of the laws and constitutional procedures set up by the government and protected by her husband and sons. She did not accept corruption in politics, economics or any phase of her country's operations.

Virginia continued speaking, while John listened most attentively. They kept eating calmly but pensively, even as she kept giving more details. John couldn't foresee the end of the story; it was so powerful.

She elaborated: "While in prison, the young perpetrators of the infamous crime were occasionally involved in conversations with other inmates, especially at meal time and during recesses when they were allowed to exercise, play soccer or even cards. They would exchange stories and rumors. Thus it happened that by hearing commentaries made by the prisoners, a story eventually reached the warden's ears. He passed it on to FESCO's headquarters. Ultimately, it reached Colonel Jaramillo's office. It has been an unpredicted strike of luck."

"It seemed that the local Bucaramanga coordinator of the ambush was a small drug dealer known as *Mico* or monkey, who answered directly to orders from a bigger dealer somewhere in the mountainous regions outside Medellin. FESCO learned, in due time, that the nickname of that powerful drug trader was something like *Headcutter* or *Headhunter*. He had provided all the financing and purchasing means necessary to acquire a heavy duty truck and setup the whole ambush operation through the local drug dealer, *Mico*, who got paid a mighty sum for successfully carrying out the murdering enterprise. Because he had succeeded in getting rid of Brigadier General Jaramillo, the dealer whose nickname was subsequently confirmed via the grapevine to be *Cortacabezas,* had given a performance bonus to the intermediary *narcotraficante*."

"Unfortunately for him, but auspiciously for the authorities, this small time drug dealer had made the mistake of boasting one day about his actions, when he was pretty inebriated at a local bar surrounded by a bunch of *puticas*. Those young prostitutes were paid off handsomely for their sexual services as long as they kept quiet. One did not; she paid the price as they found her a few days later with her neck slit and her breasts cut-off."

"Eventually, FESCO's ultra secret service had been able to round up this local gang. They all ended in the same prison compound behind bars, where the two Jaramillo executioners were serving their time. However, the petty but still dangerous dealer maintained a certain amount of control over the peons, as he called them, and occasionally was still able to give them cash for providing miscellaneous services and passing on orders to their poor uneducated friends outside. None of these gang members had a decent family structure nor did they care about life or suffering."

"Several years had passed since Brigadier General Rogelio Jaramillo had been assassinated. By then, I had joined FESCO and ended up serving in my uncle's unit. It was led by my father's brother, Colonel Roberto Jaramillo. To protect my involvement in FESCO, I was known as Captain Virginia Cosmos. The name Jaramillo was never used.

By sheer chance, I was assigned to research the scandal that in the past had reached the Senate of the Republic. The gross crime had not yet been solved nor its perpetrators detained and incarcerated."

"One of the local gang members arrested after the Jaramillo ambush, and later when the Senate scandal had left politicians and members of society perplexed and shocked, had boasted one day how he would have loved to play with *Cortacabezas's* daughter – the same one that had been attacked by Rafael, the rich boy and Senator's scion., He had heard, vulgarly, that she was rather sensuous - pardon me, Carmencita and Susana - had tempting breasts, was pretty good looking and ready to be picked like a ripe country fruit. That was his *big mistake*."

"Her father, the sanguinary drug lord Cortacabezas, also heard about the guy's comments. The unlucky young fellow would pay a final high price with his life: He was found stuffed in the trunk of a taxi cab, mercilessly stabbed multiple times. But it was the enlightening clue FESCO had been waiting for, to make a direct link to Cortacabezas."

"Those comments eventually reached FESCO's offices and my own ears. Until then, it had been impossible to link any activities or threats to Cortacabezas, who for all intents and purposes had clearly been the brain behind General Jaramillo's truck ambush. Now, circumstantial evidence proved he also was the ultimate planner and executioner of the ambush in Bogotá's parameter road, of the Senator's son Rafael and his friends. Somebody would have to pay a high price for its gruesome consequences."

"One of the young prison inmates had a black background which was rather similar to the first two gang youngsters arrested when they were trying to escape on their motorcycle. They had grown up together in the same dangerous streets. They had been gang members. Except that now that young inmate was working, unbeknown to other detainees, for the 'other side:' proficiently and 'loyally' for the Colombian Government. His initial long prison time had been reduced in exchange for cooperating with the Police and Army, by giving information and other details that he would learn within the prisoner compound."

"As a result of all these intelligence and judicial activities, eventually Cortacabezas had been arrested and prosecuted. He was put behind bars to serve a long sentence, while the government sought to have him extradited to the United States. But he still had plenty of money and assets to use for his diabolic trade, even from inside jail. He could silently direct drug operations and personal vendettas, and even occasionally secure guns for his criminal associates."

Virginia apologized for talking so long, but said she would soon complete the long story, as it was almost finished and she wanted John to know.

She related more details: "One fateful time, when my uncle Colonel Jaramillo and I were at the prison investigating criminal leads, we were specifically questioning the elusive Cortacabezas. He was sitting in a room at a table across from us, with a despicable attitude and a grimacing smile. Suddenly, he found out that the FESCO officer in front of him was the brother of *the* Brigadier General Rogelio Jaramillo Cosmos who he had ordered to be brutally ambushed and assassinated. Cortacabezas became violently enraged and uncontrolled; he lounged forward toward my uncle Roberto after reaching for a small pistol he had concealed on his person. It was relatively easy for him in prison to get a gun surreptitiously, as guards could always be bribed to let the bad guys with money operate within the penal complex."

She continued her narrative. She described how, as Cortacabezas took out his pistol aiming it at Colonel Jaramillo, there was an instantaneous gun shot from behind the colonel. She explained how she had used her own pistol to blow out the hand of Cortacabezas as he pointed out his pistol to the Colonel's head. She had seen Cortacabezas from the corner of her eye; she had turned around automatically, and before anyone could react otherwise, she had taken out her pistol, and applied her training with the English M5-MI6 group, to calmly fire at the attacker's hand as he was ready to shoot Colonel Jaramillo. A second shot had followed immediately to the groin area: Colonel Jaramillo had also reacted instantaneously to the vicious attack..

The aggressor had been stopped at the last second. He remained alive for a few days, thus permitting further questioning while at the prison hospital. He died within three days. Virginia felt no guilt or remorse. She was not too fond of macho criminals; machismo was one of her deep phobias. Without any doubt, she had saved her uncle's life and he would never forget it.

She slowed down, looked at Carmencita and John, smiled gently and concluded: "Thus, Providence applied justice to the man who had assassinated my father and fiancé, and who had perpetrated an inhumane violent act of excision, even if somehow it could be justified as coming from a desperate father. But his daughter was not his little girl princess – she was just one more *asset* in his properties. Crime and love don't really go hand in hand."

She sighed and sat quietly for a few moments, while the rest of the group absorbed the painful narrative.

****

Chapter 26

Love above Plaza Mayor

Although it had been a deep emotional story, the small group was sitting together enjoying the resolution of the overwhelming events, and was grateful to God for having protected Captain Cosmos and Colonel Jaramillo during the gun attack. The death of Cortacabezas was not missed by anyone, except his daughter, even though he really treated her as another piece of personal property. He had created a world of terror among his followers. Actually, many of the people operating in his network were relieved when they found he had perished trying to shoot FESCO officers. Additional information eventually came out from other prisoners, who now could talk without fear of being cut up, blown up, shot or executed.

The four people finished their champagne and dessert, which they topped off with the traditional *tinto*. Dr. John Osborne asked Carmencita and Susana if the next day they were planning to attend Mass with Father Garcia and then visit to the Ecce Homo monastery. Pensive after Virginia's narrative, he inquired if he could join them on their return trip to Bogotá. Would there be enough room for him? That way he wouldn't have to call Pedro who would be happy to have some free time on Sunday to spend with his mother and girl friend. They said 'yes' right away. Virginia said he could sit in front next to the driver and his machine gun. Susana suggested she sit in front so that John could sit in back next to Virginia. That seemed a better choice.

John explained, looking at Carmencita and glancing at Virginia, that he had decided to shorten his vacation trip to Villa de Leyva, so that he could return as soon as possible to Zurich. He had to settle business matters at the Research Center in order to come back to Bogotá without delay. He said he had a very important project to finish when he returned to Bogotá. He looked at Virginia who didn't say anything, but she looked at him and rapidly moved her eyelids to signify: 'Yes, hurry back.' Carmencita and Susana smiled too. They were probably thinking the same thing: The couple wanted to be united without further delay.

They walked back leisurely to the hotel, enjoying the lights around the Plaza Mayor and the local people milling around. There didn't seem to be many foreign tourists, unless they were still eating in the restaurants around the square. You could hear music coming out of some eateries. People weren't rushing anywhere. They were content sitting, talking, and eating. They were living peacefully; they couldn't all be in love. Or could they?

At the hotel, Carmencita and Susana said good night and went to their room. They all gave each other the customary hugs, and confirmed they would get together in the early morning for breakfast. followed by Mass at the Plaza Mayor Church. Father Garcia would be happy to see them sitting among the crowd; and Viviana would be pleased to let them see how she directed the town's children's choir. Additionally, on Sunday, a few of the old parishioners joined the group to reinforce the chorus. It sounded even better.

Virginia and John were finally alone. They smiled at the thought. John found her very calm even after the serious events she had described. He made a comment; she answered that it was a relief for her to have divulged that terrible past, like she had done on the previous night. Now she felt at peace knowing that John was also aware of all those tragedies.

They walked upstairs to get to their connecting rooms. However, before going in, they decided to go to the rooftop terrace to take a last look at the extraordinary view of Plaza Mayor and the mountain crests to the east, which were peacefully reflected under a timid moonlight.

They stood there feeling warm and intimate in the evening magical surroundings. John was behind Virginia. He put his arms around her, and gently kissed her all along her neck, from the shoulder to the tempting ear lobe, and whispered: "I love you, my dear Virginia." She turned around and placed her moist lips against his; and then replied: "I love you too, John." And she hugged him tenderly.

John breathed in her femininity and was hypnotized by her subtle scent. "How long will you love me?" she asked. He answered: "I promise to love you forever, until death do us part." Without being facetious, she looked at him straight into his dreamy eyes. She whispered: "How do I know this is not just an excuse to get me in bed?" And she smiled peevishly at him.

John held her in his arms without saying anything. Then, slowly and emphatically looked straight into her captivating eyes, which were shining brightly in the mystic evening light, and gravely asked her: "*Captain Virginia Cosmos, my beloved Virginia Jaramillo, will you marry me?*"

Virginia remained silent for a few moments. She was looking at John and studying his convincing features and body language. Finally, her face distended and lit up; she touched his lips and replied: "Yes, John, *I will*. I will marry you forever." They kissed tenderly, mixing their hearts and souls. They had just sealed their fates with the tip of their tongues.

She put his hands on her inviting breasts and said: "John, let's go to bed to celebrate; and give the news to Infinity. I know she will be delighted."

John answered: "I can hardly wait, my love. Besides, Infinity really is now the Cat of Villa de Leyva." They embraced warmly and blissfully and walked downstairs hand in hand.

Their hearts and souls were in turmoil, and their bodies were in romantic commotion at the thought they soon would be linked in a loving and perhaps sexual embrace. Virginia hugged John and gave him one of her hypnotizing looks and irrepressible smiles. John could not resist her. He kissed her moist lips as soon as they had closed the door to their room.

The sound of the bells of the central church echoed through the peaceful sandstone plaza and reached the lovers in their slumber, as if to cover their deep feelings with a tender mantle of invisible and eternal love. Then it was quiet. You could hear the peaceful breathing of the two bodies.

For a few brief moments, suffused rays of moonlight entered through the partly open curtain, and gently bathed the interlocked couple. Soothingly, the soft rays continued to one of the corners of the couch, where the light reflection rested on a peaceful and deeply satisfied Infinity Von Braun, her long and subtle feline body stretched out full length on her blanket, perhaps aware that now she was the official Queen of Villa de Leyva.

INDEX

Chapter	Title	Page
1	The Arrival	7
2	Meandering in Colonial Downtown	25
3	The Old Convent	38
4	A Sensory Botero Interlude	52
5	Cognition Conference	61
6	A Didactic Luncheon at Casa Vieja	76
7	Cats and Dogs	91
8	A New Moon, a Million Stars	103
9	An Evening of Anticipation	112
10	Full Moon Hypnosis	134
11	A Momentous Day	153
12	Full Moon over the City	169
13	Tête-à-Tête in Casa San Isidro	189
14	Boyacá's Bridge of Freedom	206
15	Music at Colonial Cathedral	216
16	Funeral of Mother Angelica	228
17	The Choir Resonance	239
18	A Surprise Call	250
19	Reunion in Villa de Leyva	259
20	Burundanga Cumbia	265
21	A Youthful Experience	283
22	A Complex Situation	290
23	A Celebration in Congress	301
24	Infinity's Moment	307
25	A Family Dinner	321
26	Love above Plaza Mayor	332
	Index	337

Printed in the United States of America

www.ingramcontent.com/pod-product-compliance
Lightning Source LLC
Chambersburg PA
CBHW071314150426
43191CB00007B/622